The
Unnatural Scene

The Unnatural Scene

a study in Shakespearean
tragedy

Michael Long

Methuen & Co Ltd

First published 1976
by Methuen & Co Ltd
11 New Fetter Lane, London EC4P 4EE

© 1976 Michael Long

Typeset in Great Britain by
Preface Ltd
Salisbury, Wilts
and printed in Great Britain by
Butler and Tanner Ltd, London and Frome

ISBN hardbound 0 416 82130 8
ISBN paperback 0 416 82140 5

Distributed in the U.S.A. by
HARPER & ROW PUBLISHERS, INC.
BARNES & NOBLE IMPORT DIVISION

For
LAURETTE
and for
FRANK MILES and JOHN RATHMELL
who taught me with great kindness.

Contents

Acknowledgements

My thanks are due to Mr Timothy Cribb, Prof. John Cagnon, Dr John Rathmell and Prof. Raymond Williams who read all or a large part of my typescript; and to those at Methuen and Co, particularly Miss Janice Price, who were very helpful and encouraging. A special thanks is due to Dr Robert Hodge who often read untidy drafts at an early stage and was of inestimable help with his characteristic mixture of generosity and severity in judgment. My students at Churchill College, Cambridge, from 1970–4 included some fine Shakespeareans who, if they read this book, will remember our work together from which I hope they learnt as much as I did. Finally my wife whose superior sense of the theatre has, I hope, had some effect on these thoughts from the study; and who has always been ready to give endless, sustaining support.

Author's note

The edition of Shakespeare's works which I quote and cite throughout this book is 'The Alexander Edition', first published by Collins in 1951. I have used it as the best easily available, single-volume text. Inevitably it contains versions of some passages with which I would disagree, including passages which are quoted in my text. But no alteration which I would like to make to such passages is substantial enough to have an effect on the critical argument. I have therefore not altered Alexander's text at any point.

From this the poem springs: that welive in a place
That is not our own and, much more, not ourselves
And hard it is in spite of blazoned days.

We are the mimics. Clouds are pedagogues
The air is not a mirror but bare board,
Coulisse bright-dark, tragic chiaroscuro

And comic color of the rose, in which
Abysmal instruments make sounds like pips
Of the sweeping meanings that we add to them.

(Wallace Stevens: *Notes Toward a Supreme Fiction*)

I would be ignorant as the dawn
That merely stood, rocking the glittering coach
Above the cloudy shoulders of the horses;
I would be — for no knowledge is worth a straw —
Ignorant and wanton as the dawn.

(W. B. Yeats: *The Dawn*)

Behold, the heavens do ope,
The gods look down, and this unnatural scene
They laugh at.

(*Coriolanus* V.iii.)

I

Social order
and the kinetic world

... one must still have chaos in oneself to be able to
give birth to a dancing star ...[1]

Nietzsche: *Thus Spoke Zarathustra*

1. Festive-comic release

When the Lords of Navarre vow, with 'statutes', 'oaths' and 'strict
observances', to shut themselves off from life and wage their war
against 'the huge army of the world's desires', we sit back and
wait for the 'brave conquerers' to be humbled and defeated. And
when Duke Theseus talks severely to Hermia of parental will and
'the law of Athens' we look forward to the play's showing how
the course of love will make these sanctities, and the cool
measure of the voice that speaks them, look less stable and less
admirable than the speaker imagines. *Love's Labour's Lost* and
A Midsummer Night's Dream are festive comedies *par excellence*,
plays in which the whole structure of Shakespearean festive
comedy is completely and adroitly exhibited, and we know as
they start that the prides and certainties of civil men will be put
in their place by the vigorous, tumbling, irresponsible world of
holiday, mirth and love. The unpredictable and the uncontrol-
lable in life will thus be happily acknowledged and the audience
will leave, we hope, with an enhanced capacity for the acceptance
of 'nature' to take with them into the workaday world.

The festive-comic structure, in Shakespeare's hands, offers an
ideal form in which to express what is, fundamentally, a happily
accommodated attitude to the status of human cultures and

individual wills in a world which they do not entirely control. Each of the comic plays built within terms of this structure makes a complex dramatic statement about what men achieve and how they order their institutional and cognitive world. The statutes of Navarre and the laws of Athens symbolize the entire social fabric — of institutions, laws, mores, norms and values — in terms of which a group of men has socialized itself, come to its agreed definitions of reality and shaped its experience of the world. And what is offered by the happy intelligence of this saturnalian art is a view of such a social fabric which has a beautiful poise about it and a peculiarly resolved kind of ambiguity.

This poise is one which eschews, on the one hand, the easy derision of an anarchist and, on the other, the equally easy confidence of those for whom a particular set of social meanings seem to exhaust all possible human meanings. And the ambiguity consists not in any inert detachment, or in what we ordinarily mean by hesitation, but in a capacity for tolerant, sympathetic and indeed enthusiastic engagement with many of the most volatile energies of life. Knowing the ability of such energies to topsy-turvy the workaday world, it knows also the power of a civilized mind to work out its own terms for their acceptance. It is a view which comes from a superbly capacious kind of accommodation, making plays in which the wayward vitality of the non-socialized world is something which men, without fear, may take into themselves as nourishment. The plays thus celebrate the *adaptability* of culture and of cultured men, the capacity of human structures to bend and not break under pressure from nature.

Stated thus baldly and simply this 'model' might seem schematic, and likely to promote reductive versions of the plays. But this is belied both by the excellence of the modern criticism which has worked on the plays in these terms — notably that of C. L. Barber[2] — and by the success of modern productions of the plays staged in this way. What we have here is not a pattern which has been imposed on the individual dramatic life of the plays but one which, having served succinctly in their creation, can serve equally succinctly in their recreation in the mind or on the stage.

We have begun here to understand a basic feature of Shakespeare's thinking and to get close to some fundamental elements in his vision.

No such thing could be said about modern interpretations of the tragedies. We may argue and disagree about the basic structure and vision of Shakespearean comedy — we have terms in which such things as structure and vision can be discussed. But with the tragedies we can hardly begin. The offered definitions of the structure of Shakespearean tragedy with which I am acquainted are either selective (they help with this play but not with that) or schematically reductive — when brought into close contact with the actual literature they begin to violate what is patently there in the text. Some twentieth-century critics have felt the need for 'structure-oriented' terms: they have talked of image-structures as against character-centred criticism. But the critics who developed and used these terms were talking of smaller-scale structures than are needed to grasp the whole range of the plays. And they were also, in my view, exhibiting the very foolish notion that attention to characterization is a Victorian folly.

The reasons for this failure are not clear to me, for I do think it is possible to attempt to get near to the thought-model which underlies Shakespearean tragedy as well. It is not a matter of providing some reductively theoretical short-cut to 'Shakespeare's tragic universe', but of working down through the individual texts to some sense of the perceptive and organizational habits of the mind which made them. I did not start my study of the plays with this in mind. I simply wanted to understand certain plays which seemed very difficult to me, and some, like *Hamlet* and *Measure for Measure*, which have seemed difficult to most people. But as I studied the plays separately three things began to come more and more imperatively clear: that the plays illuminated each other more than I had expected; that they connected with the world of the festive comedies more closely than I had thought; and that the social-psychological analysis of human cultures made in many of them was of formidable detail and coherence. I mean by this third point that it came to seem very important to me that these plays present not just individuals moving in a 'universe' or 'world' but men seen in social situations of highly specific kinds, social milieux which receive the highest degree of social-psychological documentation. Criticism has spent a good deal of its time talking about the ethos of Rome in *Coriolanus*; but it has tended to spend far less time on the equally important and detailed social ethos given in the Venice of *Othello*, the Vienna of *Measure for Measure* and the Elsinore of *Hamlet*. Yet it seems to me that each of these societies has as big a role to play as Rome, and the social-psychological imagination which has gone into their dramatic realization is just as sure and just as vital to the whole tragic movement. And in each case, as we look at this specific social setting, we aid our comprehension of an individual character who has caused a great deal of trouble for criticism — Othello, Duke Vincentio, and Hamlet.

So the quality of Shakespeare's social psychology was one of the things which came out of my separate studies of the plays, and which began to make me turn my attention towards the larger, general problem of their entire vision. And it did so even more when I thought of it in relation to the idea of festive comedy which I have just summarized. For if we look back to the festive-comic model for a moment we shall notice something important about its basic meaning which leads straight to the tragedies. When I said that these plays celebrate the adaptability of human cultures I should also have said that there is, of course, nothing 'easy' about the processes involved. The plays' celebrations of this adaptability never feel fatuous, partly because of the confident power of Shakespeare's evocation of nature as containing potencies which are so clearly beneficial to men, and partly because he is a sedulous and sometimes savage ironist about the validity of what the model conventionally says. If the model says all's well that ends well the play built upon the model will often suggest dark countervailing forces. Jack often hath not Jill, or at least hath not until he has got rid of some of his silliness and vanity. And even when he hath, it is often after a fight of some considerable intensity like that between the pairs of lovers in *A Midsummer Night's Dream*. The green world outside human societies is not only rich pasture. It also exposes the psychic adventurer to

> the opportunity of night
> And the ill counsel of a desert place   [*MND* II. i. 217–18]

where his happy imaginings may turn into terrors. The joke which goes too far, the dream which becomes nightmare, the wit which stings, the passion which hurts and the mockery which is 'not generous, not gentle, not humble'[3] — all are factors which keep the poise of these plays so immaculate, so far from complacency, by acknowledging that the forces released by the festive world are great enough to cause real trouble.

This 'dangerous' aspect of festive comedy has been well noted by Barber, discussing its social origins:

> When we write about holiday license as custom, our detached position is apt to result in a misleading impression that no tensions or chances are involved. For those participating, however, license is not simply a phase in a complacent evolution to foreknown conclusions: it means, at some level, disruption . . . The instability of an interregnum is built into the dynamics of misrule: the game at once appropriates and annihilates the mana of authority. In the process, the fear which normally maintains inhibition is temporarily overcome, and the revellers become wanton, swept along on the freed energy normally occupied in holding themselves in check.
>
> [*op. cit.*, pp. 37–8]

The unstable, disruptive, 'wanton' aspects of festive release, and the difficult tension of its relationship with fear and inhibition, are never far from Shakespeare's concerns even in the lightest and gayest of these plays. The ease with which the experience of the high-energy world of the unsocialized can slip from exhilaration to terror, from creativity to destructiveness, is always a part of his meaning of 'nature'. The moment where, as Barber says

> the perceived structure of the outer world breaks down, where the body and its environment interpenetrate in unaccustomed ways, so that the seeming separateness and stability of identity is lost   [*ibid.*, p. 135]

may be a part of the enriching metamorphosis of festive-comic
release. But it is not hard to see that such a moment could also
hold terror, bewilderment and destruction. It may only be a short
step from holiday to chaos, or from uninhibitedness to madness.
And it is easy to see that the powers of the natural world which,
in the comedies, cause a sense of breathlessness and wonder at
their beautiful celerity

> (the lightning in the collied night
> That, in a spleen, unfolds both heaven and earth,
> And ere a man hath power to say 'Behold!'
> The jaws of darkness do devour it up)   [*MND* I. i. 145—8]

are not entirely different from

> the most terrible and nimble stroke
> Of quick cross lightning,   [*KL* IV. vii. 34—5]

which flashes above the naked head of King Lear and, as psychic
experience, leaves him 'cut to th' brains'.

The point is not that in the comedies we have a beneficent
nature and in the tragedies a destructive one. There is winter in
the festive-comic universe; and in the universe of the tragedies we
have

> All blest secrets,
> All you unpublish'd virtues of the earth,   [*KL* IV. iv. 15—16]

which are able to be

> aidant and remediate
> In the good man's distress.   [*KL* IV. iv. 17—18]

It is the same nature, the same non-human world of the
uncontrollably kinetic, capable either of destruction or creativity.
The real point is that this world of nature's kinesis is
powerfully perceived and continuously present as 'other' in the
language in which Shakespearean drama goes about its investi-
gations of the human world. We have here a mind which sets this
natural world over against the structured and institutionalized
world of human culture in a rich variety of ways; a mind,
indeed, for whose vision this opposition is fundamental. It is

therefore a mind which sees any human culture as necessarily entailing delimitation and encapsulation, since no one structure can successfully institutionalize all the potential and actual energies of the natural world. The structure of a human culture is seen as built upon the raw chaos of the contradictory and the unpredictable — a vulnerable thing.

The festive comedies, as I say, celebrate the capacity of men and cultures to negotiate the difficult balances and ambiguities involved in their psychic life when it is seen in these terms. They celebrate the adaptability of the civilized mind as it goes out to confront regions of dangerous volatility and then returns to the social world nourished by the experience. They celebrate the capacity of social man to come to terms with the awkward inversions and ribaldries of the holiday world which set his structures in disarray; so that the effect of the plays is one of comic exhilaration as we experience the success with which difficult energies can be absorbed by men who must return to the workaday world. The image of the house surrounded by fields or woods is the central one — a house which can open its doors and allow free movement back and forth between the society indoors and the wild world without.

But that image, of the house in fields, is there in the pattern of the tragedies too, and there with the same meaning. It is there in *King Lear* and *Macbeth*; and it is there also in *Hamlet*, where Elsinore rears its walls against the sea, in *Antony and Cleopatra*, where the Roman Empire is surrounded by the sea and by the slime of the Nile, and in *Measure for Measure*, where the false Duke pretends to return from the open fields bringing wisdom and release to the gates of the city but where, because it is pretence, he brings instead a painfully grotesque parody of festive, social reintegration. But here we have houses which do not open their doors, except to cast out the errant to their fate. They keep their doors firmly shut and their bulwarks impregnable, fearful of volatility and therefore preventative of release. What we see in the tragedies is the fatal inadaptability of cultures and the fatal inadaptability of minds trained in and adjusted to a given set of civilized mores. The tragedies are repeatedly concerned with the workaday world's hostility to the world of the kinetic — with the

ways, in other words, in which the demands of socialization make
men blind or inflexible, shutting off their consciousnesses from
forces which are within and around them, closing their minds in
hostility and fear until, at the worst, they are, as Hamlet puts it,
'bounded in a nutshell'. And they are concerned as well with
what happens when the nutshell cracks so that minds which are
invaded and inundated by energies which disrupt and knowledge
which bewilders sink below the level of their society's 'normality'
to find a volatile, kinetic world of the destructive and the absurd
to which accommodation is nearly impossible. This is the journey
from culture into trauma, the tragic counterpart of the journey
from Law into release.

This tragic vision, then, is fully integral with the vision of
Shakespearean comedy – as might be suggested by the way in
which Shakespeare can modulate from one to the other in the
'problem plays'; or, in plays like *Macbeth* and *The Winter's Tale*,
from the way in which he can re-introduce shaping elements from
the pattern of release into the tragic world. The main difference
touches again on that question of social-psychology. For the
festive comedies handle the business of human social attachment
in a largely symbolic way – it is a matter, quite simply, of *Law*.
But the tragedies move very much further in the direction of
realism, and that realism is both psychological and social. The
plays in which specific cultures are presented in the greatest
detail – *Othello, Coriolanus, Measure for Measure, Hamlet,
Troilus and Cressida* – seem to me to constitute an intricate and
detailed body of thought about the nature of human socialization
and the mechanisms whereby specific human groups achieve and
maintain their coherence. The plays contain a finely realized
understanding, basic to their tragic vision, of social distance- and
stratification-systems, of ethnocentrism, of fanaticism and hero-
worship, and of the power-structures in which puritanism and
philistinism are engendered. While the festive-comic plays give us
Law which, looked at from the perspective of holiday, seems a
somewhat arbitrary and wooden construct, the tragedies investi-
gate the nature of that Law very closely. They look closely at
how men attach themselves to a social structure and shape their
identities thereby, and at how this attachment creates habits of

perception, behaviour and evaluation which are radically de-limiting. The comedies teem with ambiguities and metamorphoses which are let into the flexible and recipient minds of civilized men; the tragedies present us again and again with minds in fear of ambiguity, in fear of flux, chance and change, minds which close and grow brittle round a set of social values, minds for which the volatilities of unstructured experience hold terror, not release.

That, in brief, is what this book is about. It aims to trace the ways in which a group of different but inter-connected plays explores the attachment of human beings to their cultures; and the trauma which attends them when their culturally structured worlds and selves break down to let in the powers of the bewildering, chaotic and dangerous 'other' world of raw kinesis. I find this to be the thought-model which lies beneath and unifies the group of plays which runs through from the 'problem plays' to the great tragedies. Within the group we have had a play of the grotesque like *Troilus and Cressida*, where the world of culture and the world of kinesis are held against each other in deadlock, where all is 'bias and thwart', 'tortive and errant', as life-giving powers twist and strain in semi-paralysis. Also within it, and at the opposite end of the tonal scale, are plays like *Macbeth* and *Antony and Cleopatra* where the forces of the 'other' world making for vitality and release are eventually as unstoppable as they are in the comedies. And there is also *King Lear*, which twentieth-century criticism has been right to see as the heart of the matter, where the complex relationship between traumatic destruction and creative release is most fully explored in a great metaphysical play about social man and the wild world.

The habits of thought which underlie this vision, both in its festive-comic and in its tragic manfestations, bear witness to a mind with an extraordinarily developed sense of this wild or 'other' world and its role in human affairs. We get that sense from the immense energy which such a mind sees in the non-human world of nature – in the Shakespearean poetry of thunder and lightning, storm, sea and flood, and animal life which is swift and wild. We get it also in the way this mind perceives such energies *within* the natural animal, man – in the poetry of love, both passionate and bawdy, the poetry of dreams, of imaginings both wonderful and horrifying, the poetry of Queen Mab. And thirdly we get it in that characteristic Shakespearean poetry which catches the presence of such energies as they move 'wantonly' through the language of people who may or may not be aware of the manifold resonances of what they say — the poetry of pun, paradox, ambiguity and multiple tone. These three characteristics are related to each other, and all are related to this central vision of the human world and the 'other' world which that human world can only very partially control. A poet with a vision like this looks at the human world in a very 'conditional' way. He looks at it with an 'under-view' which knows that its laws and its most esteemed values are limited, fragile, vulnerable, half-achieved and half-understood. And he embodies that under-view in his great tragic plays.

2. Schopenhauer and Nietzsche

In a way, that may be all the introduction that I need before moving to discussion of the individual plays. But I have talked of Shakespeare's 'under-view' of the human world and begun to suggest that this is the perspective that criticism of the tragedies will need; and I have also talked of social-psychology. Both these considerations lead me to the great German tragic theorists of the nineteenth century. For it was here that something of that same under-view was recovered and recreated, and here also, in the two great predecessors of Freud, that we may find a psychology of social life equal to the task of understanding Shakespearean tragedy. It was in *The Birth of Tragedy*, and in the work of Schopenhauer which preceded and gave rise to it, that a way of thinking about tragedy and social-psychology which this book seeks to exploit was first created. It is therefore worth going back to that source, to clarify my basic viewpoint and to do justice to the two writers who still seem to me most capable of leading us back to the vision of Shakespearean tragedy. We get thereby a second perspective, to complement and aid that which festive comedy provides.

The necessary under-view, the traumatic critique of culture, was, as I said, *recovered* by these German metaphysicians. This under-view and traumatic perspective, which I see as the very *idée maitresse* of Shakespearean tragedy, has by no means always been appreciated by critics and audiences. It is not an accident that the era of neo-classicism, which had singularly little use for the idea of a natural power which is beyond human control and which requires the difficult and chastening acknowledgment of civilized men, should have exhibited so total a failure with tragedy. The neo-classic idea of Shakespearean tragedy gets nowhere near to the nature of the plays because, fundamentally, it derives from a way of looking at the world which can only confront Shakespeare's vision of the kinetic 'other' world with incomprehension or fear. That small group of literate gentlemen, who lived in cities in north-west Europe but were attached so firmly to their own cultures as to think of themselves as constituting The World, failed with Shakespearean tragedy in ways which are significant and representative.

Tate's alteration of the ending of *King Lear*, for the benefit of those who had what was to be Dr Johnson's difficulty with the original text, is only the most famous example of a culture's innocence of any need to contemplate, and inwardly accommodate, those forces in life which are volatile beyond all human control. The complaint against Shakespeare's neglect of poetic justice, made by Johnson as much as by lesser figures, derives from a mentality which cannot bear to allow that the morally ordered human world does not command one's absolute and unambiguous loyalty, and hence that an idealized and sentimental celebration of it (which is what poetic justice is) might not promote one's unqualified gratification. And the equally representative view of how tragedy, which is about things which are painful, can nevertheless give pleasure, is just as much a part of this same radical incomprehension. The neo-classic answer to this dilemma, as given by Hume for example,[4] also derives from a mentality which has no way of allowing that the contemplation of the uncontrollably destructive in life might be something in which a civilized mind would *willingly* engage. Hume therefore must reduce the impact of tragedy, modulate its passion into sentiment and its despair into elegy, and claim it as the function of 'art' thus to present what is difficult in life in a form suited to the undisturbed entertainment of civilized men.

The failure is catastrophic. There is an entire dimension missing from the moral thought of both Johnson and Hume. The sceptic and the religious moralist, though otherwise entirely hostile to one another, are here joined as eighteenth-century men by what, in sum, amounts to a shared conviction – the conviction that the relationship of the ordered to the wild is that the former supervenes upon the latter in a way which is unambiguously gratifying. In the end it is always that conviction, so opposed to the Shakespearean under-view, which makes it impossible for a neo-classic mind to get very far with the tragic vision of this gothic or barbarian poet.

I rehearse this well-known case simply to insist that the nature of the failure is representative and salutary, and to make it clear that a recovery from it was necessary. The failure is representative in that any unambiguous attachment to, or normative belief in, the idea of social order or cultural achievement is liable to prove fatal to an understanding of tragedy. It was the work of the moral psychology of Schopenhauer and Nietzsche, each feeling that he had the epistemology of Kant behind him in the effort, to break up that complacent and myopic attachment. And each of them placed the idea of tragedy at the point of social complacency's most extreme breakdown, where no system of moral evaluation with any right to claim an adherent can do justice to what happens and what is felt when the 'other' world does its worst with human attempts to make institutions out of it.

Nietzsche, as is well known, was to become a stern critic of his own early work *The Birth of Tragedy*, and one of the main points of his self-criticism was that he felt it owed too much to the erring Schopenhauer. In the preface to the second edition of 1886 he regretted his dependence on Schopenhauer's doctrine of tragic 'resignation' and wished that he had not had to 'obscure and spoil Dionysiac hints with formulas borrowed from Schopenhauer'.[5] And in *Ecce Homo* he spoke of the 'cadaverous perfume of Schopenhauer' and said that 'their tragedies prove that the Greeks were *not* pessimists: Schopenhauer was wrong'.[6]

Ultimately there is a sense in which Nietzsche is quite right to make these points — a sense in which Schopenhauer's idea of tragedy is weak in just these ways and a sense in which Nietzsche's work, even in the early book on tragedy, is best understood not in its continuity with Schopenhauer's but in contradistinction to it. But the relationship is not that simple, and it is certainly not a matter of polar opposites. It was one of Nietzsche's greatest intellectual and imaginative gifts to be able to depend on other writers in a very creative way — to appropriate what he wanted, to use it as his own property in such a way as to transcend it, and then to leave it behind with a critical dismissal often devastating in its accuracy and power. That is roughly the nature of his unfolding relationship with Wagner, and it is also the nature of his relationship with Schopenhauer's theory of tragedy. The severity of his later criticism of Schopenhauer is really an index of how deeply he had been indebted to the man whose vigour and freedom of imagination he held to be second only to that of Montaigne.[7] To get the whole tradition in better perspective we must go back to Schopenhauer as its source.

Schopenhauer does not really have a fully-fledged 'theory of tragedy'. What he does have is a few brief pages in *The World as Will and Representation*[8] which, taken in the context of the work as a whole, are of fine suggestive power. The work begins in epistemology, with Schopenhauer upholding what he takes to be Kant's greatest philosophical achievement — his recognition of the mind's interpretive and mediating quality and hence of the unknowability of the *Ding an sich*. He also criticizes Kant for abandoning this view and filling in the awkward *lacuna* between mind and thing with the doctrine of *noumena*. He himself wishes strictly to maintain that knowledge of the outside world is necessarily and absolutely a refraction of the perceiving mind; so that each man's 'world' is nothing but a representation, image or idea (*Vorstellung*) in his own mind.

But he also held that another kind of perception of the world existed — an inner knowledge that we have of ourselves as 'rooted in the world', as part of it, as agents in its dynamic rather than erring spectators of its unknowableness. This was the world of will (*die Wille*), and Schopenhauer saw it as a world of blind, unconscious, kinetic powers in which the mind lives not as perceiver but, willy-nilly, as agent in a vast tumult of energy which joins it to all other minds and all other things.

I doubt whether all this is of much use to modern epistemology; but his main concerns are not epistemological, and the *Vorstellung/Wille* dualism bears its richest fruit, for all the lack of definition and consistency in Schopenhauer's terms, in the field in which his greatest significance as a thinker lies — moral psychology. The idea of the world as *Vorstellung* is at its best in giving him a sense of the mind's capacity to deceive itself by abstraction and conceptualization. We deceive ourselves by taking our 'representations' as 'real' when they are not; and we further deceive ourselves into misinterpretation of the world by codifying these representations in concepts and abstractions which are ineptly stubborn and rigid. And the other term in the dualism, the idea of the world of *die Wille*, is at its most useful in giving him a contrasting sense of the world's flux and turmoil of energy to which those unbending constructs of the mind can do no adequate justice. And that is why Schopenhauer is such a great instigator of useful thought about the moral-psychological vision to be found in the tragedies of Shakespeare.

Working with this moral-psychological dualism Schopenhauer is able to say very important things about the dynamics of mental life, seen as a tragic or tragi-comic drama. He is unusually perceptive and original on the distorting qualities of language as its moves from the perceptive to the conceptual, upwards in what he called the 'edifice of reflection'; on the unusually perceptive (and hence anti-distorting) quality of the language of great literature; on the unalterableness of human character, engaged too vitally in the world of will to be altered by the edicts of mere consciousness; on the egoism which arises from experiencing one's own self with the immediacy of will while seeing others as mere objects in one's represented world; on humour, created by the incongruous appearance of a phenomenon in the wrong conceptual bracket which the mind's simplifying logic has made for it; on *ennui*, arising when the satisfaction of one of the will's demands gives way to new demands which the consciousness

could not foresee, or as a product of the will-driven mind's
inability to live in a stasis of tranquillity; and on madness, seen as
a lethe in which the mind takes refuge when the will's perpetual
disruption of its consciousness has become unendurable. On all
these subjects Schopenhauer is the precursor of Nietzsche and
Freud, setting in motion many of the moral-psychological terms
with which this tradition has recovered for the modern world that
dimension of moral thought which we need to understand
tragedy.

His own ideas about tragedy derive from this dualism and its
workings as he surveys it all with the volatile and caustic
merriment of his pessimism. He often called the conflict involved
in *Wille* and *Vorstellung* a tragi-comedy, looking with an arrogant
and amused under-view at what the unseen workings of the
world's will did to men's representations of it, in a manner which
Nietzsche was right to call 'cheerful'[9] because its derision is so
much more sane, liberating and vigorous than it is dispiriting. He
saw the world as one where 'the will performs the great
tragi-comedy at its own expense' and where

> no one has the remotest idea why the whole tragi-comedy
> exists, for it has no spectators, and the actors undergo endless
> worry and trouble with little and merely negative enjoyment.
> [*WWR* II. p. 357]

Thus,

> our life must contain all the woes of tragedy, and yet we
> cannot even assert the dignity of tragic characters, but, in the
> broad detail of life, are inevitably the foolish characters of a
> comedy.   [*ibid.*, I. p. 322]

And when we have got over the manifest absurdity of enter-
taining any optimism about our powers to succeed in life, then

> at last human life offers no other material than that for
> tragedies and comedies.   [*ibid.*, II. p. 581]

There was for Schopenhauer therefore nothing 'unusual' about
tragedy; and nothing was nearer to it than its apparent opposite,
comedy. Both these things take his model near to that of
Shakespearean tragedy, which is of the kind which Schopenhauer

praised most highly:

> it shows us the greatest misfortune not as an exception . . . but
> as something that arises easily and spontaneously out of the
> actions and characters of men, as something almost essential to
> them, and in this way it is brought terribly near to us.
>
> [*ibid*., I. p. 254]

What he called 'the mishaps of every hour' which provided the
material for comedy were close cousins of 'the unfortunate
mistakes of the whole life' which were the basis of tragedy. Both
are produced by the consciousness's inability to control or even
understand the world which it so limitedly captures in its
concepts, for

> every individual, every human apparition and its course of life,
> is only one more short dream of the endless spirit of nature, of
> the persistent will to live.   [*ibid*., I. p. 322]

The dream, the apparition, the 'houses of cards' which we build
in defiance or ignorance of nature's dynamics, are always ready to
be destroyed by 'the great drama of the objectification of the will
to live'. For

> knowing is a secondary function . . . The *heart* alone is
> untiring, because its beating and the circulation of the blood
> are . . . the original expression of the will. [*ibid*., II. p. 240]

There is, as I said, no 'theory of tragedy' here. But there is an
idea of tragedy which sees it as central to the dynamics of mental
and psychological life ('here is to be found a significant hint as to
the nature of the world and of existence') and comprehensible
only to a mind which is liberated from attachment to its own
'representations' and fully apprised of a high-energy world of
on-going destructive power before which, at any moment, the
mind may be rendered powerless.

But 'destructive' is the key word here. Schopenhauer was
temperamentally incapable of allowing that this world of the
will's dynamics might be anything other than a force which made a
destructive mockery of the human world which offered to

understand or control it. He therefore has two possible reactions to its dealings with the human world. One is the famous 'resignation' for which Nietzsche was to criticize him and the other is his laughter, his derision. He can never get the *joy* which he knew was there in comedy (consisting in 'an invitation to the continued affirmation of the will') to have anything to do with the way he expresses himself on the subject of tragedy. Here his compartmentalizations become preventative. The 'great tragi-comedy' will promote his derisive laughter; the greatest tragedy will call forth his resignation:

> we feel ourselves urged to turn our will away from life, to give up willing and loving life . . . we become convinced more clearly than ever that life is a bad dream from which we have to awake . . . the dawning of the knowledge that the world and life can afford no true satisfaction, and are therefore not worth our attachment to them. It is this that the tragic spirit consists; accordingly it leads to resignation;
>
> [*ibid.*, II. p. 433]

but neither can have anything to do with the joyfulness, the release, the affirmation which comedy gives when it too records the dealings of *die Wille* with the *Vorstellungen* men set up in ignorance of its powers. With Schopenhauer the beginnings are there — in a metaphysic which sees tragedy as the most quint-essential manifestation of the psychological dynamics of social life. And the beginning is there also in the notions of resignation and caustic laughter — both of which are still useful in pointing to vital tones in Shakespeare's tragic world.

Nietzsche takes over the tragic dualism of Schopenhauer's metaphysic. His Apollo is a descendant of Schopenhauer's *die Vorstellung*, his Dionysos a descendant of *die Wille*. His terms follow so closely because Nietzsche is in fundamental agreement with the comprehensiveness of the tragic critique of culture that Schopenhauer made. But now the dualism is very much more complicated: we really have to note five terms in Nietzsche's model, not two. Three of them derive from *Vorstellung*, two from *Wille*. The psychological drama of culture and nature to be found in *The Birth of Tragedy* is thus more subtle than

Schopenhauer's, and Nietzsche's idea of its quintessence, in tragedy, even more suggestive.

The first of the three terms derived from the idea of *Vorstellung* is that upon which Nietzsche vents his greatest scorn — the spirit of Socratic man, who trusts the conceptualizations of his mind with idiot confidence. The familiar phrases in which Nietzsche characterizes this spirit make clear the dependence of the idea upon Schopenhauer and the complete hostility to the idea of tragedy which Nietzsche sees in such a spirit. The civilization of Socratic man is a 'pretentious lie' set up by 'benighted souls' who are 'strong in the sense of their own sanity'. It is a 'bourgeois mediocrity', committed to what is 'sensible' and to 'trivial ignoble cheer', and its 'dubious enlightenment' has a 'corrosive influence upon instinctual life'. Its 'optimistic dialectics' assume that the universe is knowable, even that nature can be *conquered* and *corrected*. Thus 'the whip of its syllogisms'; thus its attempt to 'staunch the eternal wound of being'. It is a matter of 'drastic secularization' with no sense of the limitations of its logic, bent upon capturing the world in its 'Alexandrian net', reducing it to an 'Alexandrian Utopia'. It believes in 'moral norms', 'moral order' and 'poetic justice' — a barren matter of

> forces of nature put in the service of a higher form of egotism. It believes that the world can be corrected through knowledge and that life should be guided by science.
>
> [*B. Trag.*, p. 108]

I think that those phrases do brief and approximate justice to the range of things which the idea covers; and it seems to me a feat of magnificent, imaginative generalization on Nietzsche's part to perceive and fix some of the very long-distance connexions upon which the idea depends. It is a powerful and suggestive picture of man civilized, cultured or educated in the most delimiting of senses, of civilized man who conceives of his culture as a powerful and comprehensive artifice built to protect him from a nature which is now defined as inferior and felt to require no acknowledgment from him. The knowledge of culture's partiality which tragedy contains, and the sense of relativity with which it looks upon the idea of social and mental order, is something which can be looked upon by this spirit only with incomprehension or fear.

The second term in Nietzsche's model describes a less perverse, less hardened, less irreversible form of cultural attachment — that of the Doric. It is a matter of

> a perpetual military encampment of the Apollonian forces . . . defiantly austere . . . in a continual state of resistance against the titanic forces of nature. [*ibid.*, p. 35]

It is the idea of order again, but not, as with the Socratic spirit, bent wilfully upon self-assurance; rather it is moved defensively in that direction by lack of contact with the 'other' world of nature which might redeem it from ossification. Here the music of Apollo becomes 'etiolated', it becomes 'thin, monotonous harp music'. It has to do with the death of religion as myth becomes 'systematized, under the severe, rational eyes of an orthodox dogmatism' — again something short of the 'drastic secularization' of the Socratic spirit, but with a tendency in that direction, a tendency which, without the redemption of Dionysos, will 'freeze all form into Egyptian rigidity'. It is what happens when the spirit of Apollo becomes 'pathological . . . imposing itself on us as crass reality'.

Again I think that Nietzsche's bold and rangy imagination has run together many disparate things in creating this second form of 'over-attachment' to the idea of man-made order. The element of fear and defence is vital to it — carried as it is in that image of the military encampment; but it is different from the tyranny and despotism of Socratic logic. The idea of the Doric involves a decline from flexibility, vitality and grace seen as deriving from diminished contact with the nature which the mind orders.

It is logical now to break this sequence, postpone discussion of the third and fourth terms, and look at that which occupies the fifth place.[10] It is the second of the terms into which Nietzsche has broken down *die Wille*, and it is at the opposite end of his scale from the Socratic. The fifth term is barbarian Dionysos, by whom

> all the savage urges of the mind were unleashed . . . until they
> reached that paroxysm of lust and cruelty which has always
> struck me as the 'witches' cauldron' *par excellence*.
>
> [*ibid*., pp. 25–6]

It is a matter of 'feverish excesses', 'brutal and grotesque', a
'terrible witches' brew concocted of lust and cruelty' which the
gods of order can only reject as 'licence'. Apollo can only confront it with Doric rejection, because it cannot redeem but only
destroy. It has to do with extremes of violence

> when the infliction of pain was experienced as joy while a
> sense of supreme triumph elicited cries of anguish from the
> heart. [*ibid*., p. 27]

It embodies those elements of the titanic and the barbaric with
which no culture can enter into reconciliation.

There is not a lot on this subject in Nietzsche's book, but it
has its place and it is important to note it. Nietzsche's recognition, relatively understressed though it is, of that which is
purely and unalterably destructive in the Dionysiac, does much to
rescue him from the charges of bloodthirsty brutality to which he
has often been subject. And it is also useful to note this idea of a
savagely uncreative Dionysos because it has an interesting correlative in one Shakespearean play which Nietzsche's terminology
can help to interpret. The play is *Macbeth*, where that same image
of the witches' cauldron is used to embody some very similar ideas
about those utterly destructive elements in the 'other' world
which lies outside human structuration and control.

The two remaining terms are those between which the highest
art (which for Nietzsche as for Schopenhauer was tragedy) creates
its immaculate balance. It is between these two terms that the
'constant conflicts and periodic acts of reconciliation' take place.
The first (number three in the sequence of five) is the dream
Apollo; and the second (number four) is the Greek Dionysos.

The idea of the dream Apollo is an idea of order which, knowing its partiality, aware of its status as 'illusion', stands for those
aspects of culture which involve 'discreet limitation', 'freedom from
all extravagant urges', 'sapient tranquillity'. It is a matter of taking

proper delight in the *principium individuationis*, with a certain levity or sublime calm quite unlike the fanatical attachment felt by a Socratic mind to the validity of its particular *Vorstellung*. It is the spirit of the god

> whose looks and gestures radiate the full delight, wisdom, and beauty of 'illusion'. [*ibid*., p. 22]

It deals in 'a strict consequence of lines and contours', out of a sublime pleasure to be found therein rather than in any fear of nature or in egotistical self-assertion. One of its highest products is Homeric 'naivete', which is neither primitive nor paradisal but

> the ripest fruit of Apollonian culture — which must always triumph first over titans, kill monsters, and overcome the sombre contemplation of reality, the intense susceptibility to suffering, by means of illusions strenuously and zestfully entertained. [*ibid*., p. 31]

Nietzsche does not have Schopenhauer's unrelieved scorn for this illusion — so long as it stays behind the lines which indicate its limits as 'dream' — and he thus feels no need to stop at the Schopenhauerian impasse of 'sombre contemplation of reality'. He moves *through* that to the 'temperate beauty' of Apollo, temperate because, while it embodies a commitment to the idea of order, it is far removed in its delicacy and restraint from that 'restless bid for universal power and glory' which characterizes the impulse to order when it gives itself over to the crassness of fear and egotism.

The fourth term, with which this Apollonian dream must constantly have dealings lest it lose its lightness and become gross in its attachment to the idea of order and power, is Greek Dionysos. Here we have those parts of *die Wille* which, though still of formidable and frightening power, are not purely destructive. It is like 'physical intoxication'. It shatters the *principium individuationis* to forge collective bonds. Under its hegemony

> earth offers its gifts voluntarily . . . the slave emerges as a freeman; all the rigid, hostile walls which either necessity or despotism has erected between men are shattered.
> [*ibid*., p. 23]

It is a creative breakdown from which, for all its terror and power to destroy, civilized man can be redeemed. The act of redemption brings the famous 'metaphysical solace', which has its connexions with Schopenhauerian resignation but in which a 'joy' is created, stronger than 'a Buddhistic denial of the will'. As we undergo the dissolution brought about by this Dionysos we look into the abyss and begin to feel 'nausea'. But tragedy assists us with this, the central concern of all Nietzsche's writing — not to recoil from that nausea in fear but to undergo it, to pass through it, to be nourished by the powers of Dionysos, and to emerge from it by the agency of the light Apollo. Dionysos — with his 'hunger for existence', his 'immense lust for life', 'the extravagant fecundity of the world will' — has done his work. A new Apollonian transfiguration recreates us whole, in one of those 'acts of reconciliation' which the opposing principles make together.

There is a good deal in this which is vague. The vision of the book was created, as Nietzsche later said, 'from precocious, purely personal insights, all but incommunicable', and it was 'terribly diffuse and full of unpalatable ferment'.[11] The book, for example, does not make it clear what this final act of reconciliation consists in; and Nietzsche is far too temperamentally committed to the idea of Dionysos to give the Apollo who rescues one from him any very real substance in this particular act. Thus the return to Apollo, though it is demanded by the model with which Nietzsche works, is hardly stressed. But, nevertheless, the work gets its stature as the greatest imaginative attempt yet made to encompass the whole idea of tragedy in a coherent psychology of social life from Nietzsche's formidable speculative and generalizing powers. And taken together with the allied tragic metaphysic of Schopenhauer it begins to offer something of a theoretical recreation of the Shakespearean model, a chart of its basic contours.

The terms in which these two allied metaphysics operate, then, offer a set of archetypes for a tragic psychology of social life seen in its dramatic engagement with nature. As such they repeatedly seem to 'summarize' or boldly outline the essential movement of a Shakespearean play and to help to keep before us the underlying structures and patterns within terms of which the details of

Shakespeare's unequalled dramatic variety are created and marshalled. One *can* use such terms reductively, as substitute for that detail and variety; but there is no essential reason why one should, and certainly there is nothing in either of the two metaphysicians to prompt this kind of use of them. Their terms are offered at a level of very general and archetypal significance; and employed with this in mind they can often take us surprisingly close to the specifics of an individual play. Basically what they offer is a way of thinking about the dynamics of social and personal life which parallels that of Shakespeare in two ways — firstly in the simultaneity with which what is personal and what is social are perceived, and secondly in the continuous reference of social action to its participation in an energetic and manifold drama played out between the capacities of the human mind and the energies of the natural world. They thus help us to 'recover' the Shakespearean under-view.

3. *The civility of Marcus Brutus*

We have, then, two ways of approaching the basic thought-model which shapes and contains Shakespeare's tragic vision. We may move in the direction of realism from the symbolic Law/Nature conflict of the festive comedies; or we may move in the direction of social variety and specific detail from the archetypal tragic theories of Nietzsche and Schopenhauer. The two converge on the vision of the plays of the great tragic period, upon which it i now time to embark. And at the entrance to that period ther stands the tragic story of a single man, Brutus in *Julius Caesar*.

The play in which the tragedy of Brutus is to be found neither so great nor so coherent a work as the others which I sh analyse. It is, I think, essentially exploratory and tentative, shifts in focus and tone being an index of the extreme cau with which Shakespeare handles the issues involved in play. It does not present Rome, and the social psycholog Rome, with the same comprehensiveness and coherence as *(lanus* and *Antony and Cleopatra*. And its hesitation abo value of Caesarism does not suggest to me any delibera resolved ambivalence — rather a decision to beg the quest

to bide time. It lacks a dramatically functioning network of structuring images, which suggests that the thought from which it derives does not involve the coherence of vision and depth-analysis to which such imagery in Shakespeare normally bears witness. Unlike *Troilus and Cressida* and *Measure for Measure* it is a real 'problem play', dichotomous and contradictory in itself where they are only problematic in that they present critics with tones and analyses which they find hard to stomach.

But the tragedy of Brutus which lies within the play is coherent enough; coherent enough indeed to suggest, as we contemplate it, aspects of the whole Shakespearean vision to which it is an introduction. It overwhelms the play in which it is set, for it is on the figure of Brutus that Shakespeare's mature tragic imagination settled, and it is in him that we can first examine what that imagination produces as it contemplates the limiting qualities of human cultures and codes.

Brutus is an extremely civilized man. If we think in terms of moral probity, scruple, courage, selflessness, good-humour in the face of adversity, honesty, incorruptibility, tenderness and kindness, courtesy and politeness — if we think in terms of these criteria, which must stand high on any ethical scale, then Brutus comes out as an extremely virtuous man. And the virtuousness, having everything to do with what it is to be civilized and socialized, consists in a readiness to use the powers of his mind to calculate maximum benefit for others and thereby to make morally responsible judgements. And what this virtuous, civilized, quiet-voiced, sober, intelligent and painstaking man achieves is utter desolation. He murders his friend; he brings about mob-violence and civil war leading eventually to the disenchanted suicides of himself and another friend; and he shatters his domestic peace (which is finely registered in the play) to such a degree that his erstwhile tranquil and devoted wife runs distracted and kills herself in a particularly hideous fashion, by swallowing hot coals. Nemesis was never a more dismally ironic force. No other Shakespearean tragic protagonist is quite so unimpeachable as Brutus; but none is the creator of any more complete futility and desolation. One can almost hear Schopenhauer's acidic recognition of the kind of tale it is.

A bleak, tragic irony, then, about one way of being 'civilized' or 'virtuous'; and a tragic irony which will take us well into the whole vision of the tragic plays. As we describe Brutus as 'civilized', 'cultivated', 'intelligent' or 'scrupulous' we do so in a way which makes us aware of the radical limitations, as well as qualities, to which those words point. The words of praise begin to suggest debilitating circumscriptions, having principally to do with a loss of responsive and perceptive powers. When we say that Brutus brings his intelligence to bear on problems of moral judgment we begin to realize that we are saying that that is *all* that he brings. He does not bring to bear an entire and experiencing 'self' or 'sensibility' so much as an intricate, ratiocinative instrument working within the necessarily selective and hence reductive terms of his particular codes. He works with Nietzsche's Socratic assumption that the universe is knowable and, being known, corrigible; and with that kind of language which Schopenhauer would call 'conceptual' as opposed to 'perceptive', too high up in the 'edifice of reflection' to do anything except grossly distort. And he frames his moral thinking within terms of the best ethical systems that he has learnt — principally stoicism — and thus lives a moral life which is representative in an exemplary way of the inherited, shared and acknowledged wisdom gathered within those systems.

The result is that he experiences himself and others in a peculiarly debilitated way. The debilitation stems from over-codification, and that in its turn from his being so civilized, so utterly a social being. His opening confession in the play (though he of course does not realize what a major confession of human weakness it is) registers this debilitation very strongly:

> I am not gamesome: I do lack some part of that quick spirit
> that is in Antony. [*JC* I. ii. 28—9]

What Brutus appears to have said, and doubtless thinks he has said, is that he is not such a wassailer as Antony; but in the light of what I have said about kinesis and festive release the simple word 'gamesome' takes on a bigger, and sadder, aspect. It begins to suggest an isolation from kinds of generative, organic power without which life is sterile — something which goes far towards explaining that lifeless indifference which gradually enshrouds the oddly passive figure of Brutus as his tragedy progresses.

This sense of an isolation from the generative powers of the kinetic recurs in many ways throughout the play. It is arguable that Cassius, who knows him well, is permitting himself an irony of some shrewdness when, after Brutus has listened politely to his complaints against Caesar and promised to consider the matter in good time, he confesses himself

> glad that my weak words
> Have struck but thus much show of fire from Brutus,
>
> [I. ii. 176—7]

for there is something terribly and poignantly accurate about the ironic possibilities of the word 'show'. Certainly, insofar as it suggests the absence of any real inflammabilities in the personality of Brutus it touches a key theme of the play; and one which, for example, will be in our minds again when we see how, at the murder itself, Brutus is lacking in that kind of deep and spontaneous emotional conviction which 'fire' suggests. When he bids his fellow-conspirators to

> let our hearts, as subtle masters do,
> Stir up their servants to an act of rage,
> And after seem to chide 'em   [II. i. 175—7]

he is talking as a man in whom the immediate instigation of the emotive is absent and who therefore must have recourse to a false and substitute version of it, induced into action, to give him the necessary generative prompting.

The 'clinical', 'abstract' and over-codified qualities of Brutus' sensibility, then, are functions of his alienation from the generative and instigatory powers of the kinetic. He is not 'gamesome'; and that, in the context of Shakespeare's tragic metaphysic, is quite enough to make all his virtues and all his civilized scruples balefully inadequate. As we follow the dismal course of his life it is this distance from basic energies which comes through again and again. Indeed it is a distance which we see him sedulous to preserve, as he quite deliberately buries his innermost psychic movements so that their energies go continuously untapped and their

promptings continuously ignored. Thus his attitude to the 'phantasma' or 'hideous dream' which comes 'between the acting of a
dreadful thing/And the first motion' is simply that it must be
ridden out like a storm. It is a temporary disorder of entirely
negative significance, an 'insurrection' – like the 'figures' and
'fantasies/Which busy care draws in the brains of men'. They are
all the insignificant figments of wayward imagination which
occasionally disrupt the measured calm of the civilized mind and
which Brutus tends to attribute to simple physical causes, like
'tiredness' or (with Caesar's ghost) 'the weakness of mine eyes'.
The inner energies of the psyche are for him what they were for
Theseus – airy nothings of interest only to poets who, for some
reason, are curiously given to rolling their eyes in a fine frenzy.
Brutus (who, one remembers, thinks that poets are 'jigging fools')
can never contemplate the possibility that the play of such energies is in any way essential to the business of being human. When
they present themselves troublesomely in his mind so that 'poor
Brutus (is) with himself at war', his reaction is to close himself
about them and withhold them from expression or communication. In this condition the mind is only an interim and untidy
version of its civilized self, something which cannot be of interest
even to his friends. These 'passions of some difference' breed
'conceptions only proper to myself'.

One might say, with an eye to Nietzsche's terms, that the
military encampment of Apollo in his mind is ruinously complete, its order-idea become 'pathological . . . imposing itself on
us as crass reality'. Or alternatively, looking back to the festive-
comic model in its handling of such things, one might say that he
lacks Holofernes' 'good gift' whereby the apprehensions of an
extravagant spirit are begot, nourished and delivered in an alive
and breeding mind.[12] Just as we come from *Love's Labour's
Lost* with an idea of the healthy mind as a chaos of swarming fertility whose offspring hunger for deliverance, and with a sense that
there is something inalienably mirthful in this process of unimpeded creativity, so we come from the humourless Brutus with a
sense of this creativity held down and suppressed by a man who is
determined to be calm, resolute and contained. The most powerful and terrible image of this is that in which he counsels Cassius

to bottle up the anger he feels in the quarrel scene at Sardis — to force its energies back within 'though it do split you'. This fearsome readiness to hold in the energies of the psyche under damaging pressure, in the name of an idea of what constitutes the 'civilized', is the basis of Brutus' attitude to the kinetic. And it is also the key to his tragic sterility.

This stance — fatally impervious to the kinetic, and so successful in resisting its intrusions into his calm social bearing that, as Plutarch had said, he was able to

> frame and fashion his countenance and looks that no man could discern he had anything to trouble his mind —[13]

is enough to be the cause of the desolation, sterility and *ennui* which is Brutus' life. All his 'even virtue', 'untired spirits' and 'formal constancy'; all that Roman courage which 'will not falter' and which will urge others to 'be not affrighted'; all the 'kind love, good thoughts, and reverence' of a spirit 'full of good regards' and 'armed so strong in honesty' — all these come to their dismal parody of a fruition in his ending 'sick of many griefs' as a natural consequence of his being a *merely* civilized man in a Shakespearean universe. It is the same lack which makes him so fatally ignorant of what fluid human contact is — the ignorance which makes him 'stubborn' and 'strange' in friendship, and which makes him pathetically confident that he will win the friendship of Antony by appealing rationally and calmly to a bundle of mere *values*.

The result, as I have said, is sterility and *ennui*; but there is something particularly baleful in this *ennui* of the civilized mind and something especially painful in the way in which we see him experience it. We can appreciate this if we compare him for a moment, as he has been usefully compared before, with Macbeth; for Macbeth is also driven back to a condition of torpor and resigned defeat which stems from his having cut himself off from the nourishing and life-giving powers of the world. But Macbeth is man enough, or animal enough, to know what he has lost, to know the pleasures of the creatural world which are now denied him, and to be ready to fight like a bear to retain life. But there is something far more destitute than this in Brutus, for he is so civilized, so trained in readiness to accept the curtailment and, if necessary, the elimination of creatural life in the name of a social cause ('when it shall please my country to need my death') that he cannot even recognize, let alone protest against, the abysmal dwindling of life in himself when it comes.

Thus, when he has permitted himself the momentary confession that he is sick of many griefs, he immediately gathers himself again, on being reminded of his 'philosophy', into that determination which is represented by the claim that 'no man bears sorrow better'. From here on he will 'endure with patience' and without protest. But this, which for him represents a noble forbearance in the face of the world's trials, is felt by us as a painful exhibition of moral irrelevance almost to the point of the outrageous. He buries all creatural protest against the news of his wife's death, fortified by reliance on his stoic exercises of meditation, just as, when he faces death himself, 'he meditates' himself into the required mood of indifference. His version of Macbeth's 'tomorrow and tomorrow and tomorrow' is characteristically without complaint. His expectations of fulfilment have been drastically reduced by his moral cogitations:

> That we shall die, we know; 'tis but the time,
> And drawing days out, that men stand upon;
>
> [III. i. 100—1]

so that now, as the days begin to draw out, he is ready to be satisfied with the bleak comforts of his knowledge — 'it sufficeth that the day will end', 'I know my hour will come'. Trained in a civilized ethic which is hostile to so many aspects of Shakespearean kinesis — to the imagination, to creatural need, to instinctive quickness of sympathy — he is ready simply to bow his head before adversity and accept with meekness the destruction of himself by forces which he has disabled himself from understanding or even apprehending. His decline is eventually into an unimpassioned and unprotesting grief which simply inundates his being and reduces him to silence:

> Now is that noble vessel full of grief,
> That it runs over even at his eyes.   [V. v. 13—14]

The last twist of the knife is given at the end of the play. It is bitterly appropriate that the members of his society who survive him should deem it fit to exalt his nobility and see to it that his funeral be 'ordered honourably', for the way in which they laud and revere his memory — in Roman-civic terms of honour, nobility, honesty, sense of the common good, virtue, order and purity of motive — grates on our ears with tragic irony as it is announced by Antony and Octavius. The things which serve in the Roman mind to redeem him from being a mere conspirator are for us the very things which made his life so bleak. As will later be the case with other tragedies in which a civic code proves itself so inadequate to life, nobody has learned anything. A society will go on unchanged. With Shakespeare one cannot be so sure as one can with Milton that there will be a new acquist of true experience from a great tragic event. He never under-estimates the imperviousness of social man to the experience of tragedy, and the difficulty which social man will have in accommodating himself to the traumatic critique of his values and attachments which tragedy makes.

Plutarch said of Brutus that,

> having framed his manners of life by the rules of virtue and study of philosophy, and having employed his wit, which was gentle and constant, in attempting of great things, methinks he was rightly made and framed unto virtue. [p. 102]

The words which North used in his translation — 'framed', 'rules', 'employed his wit', 'constant' — must have provided the mind which had created the kinetic world of the festive comedies with food for ironic thought; and what came out of that thought is the dismal tragedy of the dramatic protagonist's life. The under-view of Brutus' civilized values which results is more than the trad-itional Christian critique of the Stoic as lacking 'love'. The criticism is total, not local. It is not a matter of one missing feature, but of something lacking in the entire grain of the man. What Brutus lacks is something far greater, far more energetic, but also far more commonplace than what is ordinarily meant by Christians when they talk of 'love'. It is nature's volatility, every-thing that is touched on by that single word 'gamesome', everything that the festive comedies have made of 'nature' — quickness, passion, impulse, wit, equivocation, laughter, forgetfulness, irresponsibility. It is the Mercutio-element that is lacking: it is Brutus' tragedy that he would have thought Queen Mab was the passing affliction of a care-worn mind.

Nearer to the essence of Shakespeare's view of this civilized Stoic is that of Schopenhauer:

> the Stoic sage as represented by this ethical system, could never obtain life or inner poetical truth, but remains a wooden, stiff lay-figure with whom one can do nothing. He himself does not know where to go with his wisdom, and his perfect peace, contentment, and blessedness directly contradict the nature of mankind.   [*op. cit.*, p. 91]

Though the Christian critique of Stoicism must have contributed considerably to Shakespeare's sense of Brutus' tragic shortcomings, his final viewpoint is different. Schopenhauer is nearer to it, because he, with his remarkably energetic conception of the kinetic world of *die Wille*, thinks within terms of some of the same polarities as does Shakespeare.

4. Tragedy and compassion

The tone of Shakespeare's portrayal of Brutus' tragedy is unwaveringly compassionate. At the risk of being banal, I would insist that one is never allowed not to *feel sorry for him* — but then would quickly add that sympathetic sorrowing is keenly felt as *pain* and not as any lofty perusal of what may be idly compassionated from a secure position of moral superiority. It involves a peculiarly active sympathy then; and also a peculiarly fine and acute one, since it is not opposed to, but in alliance with, the maximum of intelligent and analytic understanding. Also, it is important to note that we have here a pain and a compassion which are buoyant, life-giving; one cannot be simply 'dispirited' by a full response to Brutus, for all the unrelieved bleakness which overwhelms his life. The reason for this is not of course as Hume thought — that 'art' has 'mollified' and 'softened' what in life is unpalatable. Rather it is because a vital intelligence has illuminated it, which is stimulating in itself; and even more because that intelligence, rooted as it is in a sure and generous awareness of those possibilities for life which in Brutus go thwarted, allows us to experience a kind of *willing release* from certain temptations which a limited idea of what it is to be civilized could otherwise hold for the spectator.

That peculiarly Shakespearean compassion, which associates so perfectly with what is also painful and clear-sightedly analytic, points to a way of understanding and receiving Shakespearean tragedy with which Nietzsche and Schopenhauer, with whom I have stayed thus far, cannot be of help. Schopenhauer, as I said, offers either *resignation* or *derision* as his chief responses to those feeble attempts of the human mind to capture and subdue the kinetic world in its concepts which he finds quintessentially represented in tragic drama. Nietzsche offers either the *metaphysical solace*, which is more affirmative than resignation, or, more affirmative still, the *joy* with which the traumatic journey is completed, having traversed the menace of 'nausea' and emerged fructified by the powers of Dionysos. All four terms will be of help with the experience of Shakespearean tragedy; but none of them, it will be noticed, includes the vital element of compassion.

I do not want to abandon what Schopenhauer means by resignation, which is not quite so negative and defeated a response as it may seem, having as it does a great deal in common with what Christians have meant by the term 'acceptance'. It represents a cessation of protest which comes from fullness not emptiness, something quite different from the passive surrender of the Stoic and consisting in a high, and still live, awareness of the mind's limitations as it confronts a vastly powerful universe. And I would not want to lose sight of the idea of derision either; for the crisp and caustic merriment at the expense of human pretensions which calls forth Schopenhauer's most disbelieving laughter is a vital element in the tough and exuberant mind of Shakespeare as well. It runs counter to most ideas of compassion; but that is only a comment upon what compassion may too idly be made to mean — something inert which must find this kind of

laughter 'problematic' as it is given full play in the hilarity of
Troilus and Cressida and the bitter parody of *Measure for
Measure*. The kind of compassionate spirit which finds the
abrasiveness of such plays to be 'a problem' must also fail to
notice that this same strong, liberating and quite unsoured
derision is one of the great powers of mind developed by Hamlet
and King Lear in trauma, requiring from us an acknowledgment
of its vigour rather than a prim, moralistic commentary on its
shortcomings.

So both of Schopenhauer's terms will be useful; and so also
will Nietzsche's. For his idea of the Dionysiac joy in tragedy
records what I have called that 'willing release' from the temptations of the merely civilized — from the temptation, perpetually
offered by the exigencies of social life, to the belief that Brutus-
like delimitations are right and inevitable, that his life is life itself,
and that what lies outside it is an unendurable chaos against
which the sane and socialized mind must simply preserve its
protections. The vision of Shakespearean tragedy has this sense in
full, resting as it does upon his generous confidence in life's
capacities for amplitude and fulfilment which is always the basis of
his presentation of tragic failure and tragic difficulty. And the
idea of the metaphysical solace is part of an idea of the *release*
which lies at the heart of tragedy about which Nietzsche speaks
so cogently. It is this which makes him talk of a 'strong pessimism', the paradox of which is generated by tragic experience in
which the nausea which is our first reaction to terror and destruction is turned into 'imaginings with which it is possible to
live'.[14] There is a sublime optimism in Nietzsche's vision of
tragedy, corresponding to something similarly blithe in the mind
of Shakespeare. For they both know that the debilitation which
comes from unknowingly living an unfulfilled life, and the bad
faith that comes from choosing to live thus for reasons of safety
or convenience, are not only opposed by a difficult or destructive
chaos. They both know that they are also opposed by immense
vitalities to which a mind can have access, undestroyed.

But there is still the absent sense of compassion, still a sense in
which both Nietzsche and Schopenhauer withhold themselves

from the characters of tragedy and, fearful of extending them the full Shakespearean compassion, use them as an exemplary opportunity for the recreation of their own affirmative minds. One thing from Nietzsche can take us into the reason why. He regards the debilitated and over-ordered mind of socialized man as having been cowed by 'necessity or despotism',[15] but feels no obligation to distinguish between the two. Had he been able to make this distinction the compassion of Shakespearean tragedy would have been more within his grasp; for it seems to me just to the degree that we can see this debilitating urge to order as *necessary* rather than merely despotic that we shall know how to extend compassion. Schopenhauer's derision or Nietzsche's joyous release would be enough on their own if civilized man's urge to order, both in his mind and in his created laws and institutions, were merely a matter of the despotic. But the element of the necessary in this urge is fully seen and acknowledged by Shakespearean tragedy; and it is this which makes his vision bigger than theirs, which makes his social-psychological portraiture both more precise and more humane, and which means that his work requires the element of compassion as a continuous presence in our response to every part of it.

Shakespearean tragedy knows that we must structure our experience, that it is psychically impossible to live without doing so, that the fullest destructuring that the mind can achieve is in madness, and that it is not just the petty despotism of the timid which makes social man look upon that possibility with Lear's prayer 'let me not be mad'.[16] It knows that it is necessary to social man that his 'frame of nature' should hold to 'the fix'd place', because

> The tyranny of the open night's too rough
> For nature to endure.   [*KL* III. iv. 2—3]

It is certainly too rough for one comfortably to demand from one's theatre seat that anyone who fears it shall be called a despot.

And Shakespearean tragedy also knows that social life necessarily entails Law, and hence emotional attachment to what Law embodies, and hence the blindness and lack of relativity which such attachment breeds. It knows, in other words, as the festive comedies knew, that Law is Law and that holiday is holiday, and that institutionalized and permanently maintained uninhibited-ness is an idealist's fiction. It therefore knows that, in society as in mind, the order which debilitates, and perhaps debilitates tragically, is not without its causes, and is therefore in some sense *necessary*. To Nietzsche this was not so. In *Schopenhauer as Educator* he wrote:

> It is so provincial to commit oneself to views which a hundred miles further on are no longer binding. East and West are chalk marks which someone draws before our eyes to tease our timidity,   [p. 4]

but the superior social psychology, and hence the superior com-passion, of Shakespearean tragedy makes it clear that those confi-dent words 'provincial' and 'timidity' will not quite explain the delimitations involved in such commitments.

At the risk of shackling myself with too hasty a formulaic generalization before discussion of the plays has begun, I would say that Shakespearean tragedy sees the delimiting structuration of social and mental life as being *absolutely necessary and yet necessarily reductive*. But for the mind of social man to live out the difficult tensions implied by this is extremely difficult. To do so requires a flexibility, an openness, a consciousness of ambi-guity and relativity to which however the very necessity of social and mental ordering is compellingly opposed. The exigencies of social and personal life, compassionately and intelligently seen by Shakespeare, drive civilized men to fear flux as an under-mining, unstable and unsafe incursion into their named and institutionalized worlds. It is a necessary function of the dynam-ics of social life to encourage this tendency towards over-rigidity, over-attachment or normativeness, so that any man's own part-icular structure tends to take on the significance for him of an absolute. And what is not contained within it is then called (socially) disorder and (psychologically) madness.

We are still far short of the despotic — though the plays will of course deal with social order imposed and sanctified with the wilful absoluteness of the despotic in both *Coriolanus* and

Measure for Measure. But we can see, if we look in this way, as I think Shakespearean tragedy demands, that it will call for an extremely delicate balance of response. The balance will, on the one hand, involve those kinds of response which tend to celebrate tragedy's freeing us from the restrictions of other men's blindnesses — as does Schopenhauer's derision and Nietzsche's joyous release. But on the other it will involve compassion, which is sympathetic recognition of that blindness as necessary, normal, the reaction of imperfect beings to difficult pressure, needing their order and needing their commitments, whatever may lie a hundred miles further on.

It is the supreme achievement of Shakespearean tragedy to keep up this delicate tonal balance in all its immaculateness, making the experience of his tragedies a kind of training in keenness of feeling, refinement of emotional response. The derision is there, for his exuberance is as strong as that; so also is the sense of joyous release. But, at the same time, there is that continuous compassion which knows that those who cannot escape from their entanglement in the Law and ethos of a particular culture are not, any more than Theseus was, to be understood merely as despots acting from some unprompted wilfulness.

The Moor of Venice

> *Othello:* A horned man's a monster and a beast.
> *Iago:* There's many a beast then in a populous city,
> And many a civil monster.   [IV. i. 62—4]

1. The noble hero

The heroes of the two plays with which I shall begin, *Othello* and
Coriolanus, have a great deal in common. Shakespeare looks at
the warrior-hero, with his magnificence and his sense of patrician
caste, with a distinctive kind of social-psychological interest. He is
interested in the mind of the man himself, and in the role he
plays for others, for whose ideals he is an eloquent symbol.

Each of the two great warrior-heroes of the tragedies embraces
a high idealism. Othello is sumptuously Petrarchan and courteous
in love, chivalric in bearing, magnificent in war; Marcius is also
magnificent in war, and terrifyingly absolute in his commitment
to the political ideal of patrician Rome. Each combines vast
pride with a curious humility — a humility before the ideal which
he serves. And that humility, with its naive absoluteness, links
with the child-like if not childish, qualities of them both. Each,
in the pursuit of this ideal, conceives of himself as eschewing all
baseness and venality, to rise 'aloft' and 'above' in fine language
and grand gesture. This enables him to feel his elevation above
the ruck of common men, with their common desires and con-
temptible mediocrity. It is part of an aggressive egotism which
they share, giving them a relish for the most absolute of all
possible commitments wherein their mettle will be tested to the

utmost and they will be seen to survive with bearing and *élan*. But each experiences, as he encounters the difficult complexities of social life, a complete collapse of the personality. And each is reduced to total bewilderment by the experience — Othello 'perplex'd in the extreme', Marcius utterly unable to understand either his rejection by the patricians of Rome or his repudiation, with the unbearable taunt of 'boy', by his ally Aufidius. The two plays, together with the savage comedy of *Troilus and Cressida*, constitute Shakespeare's most mature thinking about the twin heroisms of war and love.

The idea of Othello suffering a 'collapse of the personality' as his magnificent egotism encounters problems with which it is unfit to deal takes one of course, to what has been a centre of much critical controversy about the play in the twentieth century — the essay of Dr Leavis.[1] Othello, said Leavis, is brought face to face with tests of moral strength 'outside his experience' in which his military ethic of magnificence, pride and bravery will not equip him as a married man facing marriage problems. Under stress from Iago's manipulation, therefore, the moral unsatis-factoriness of his idea of love is exposed and

Othello's inner timbers begin to part at once, the stuff of which he is made begins at once to deteriorate and show itself unfit.   [p. 144]

A similar case, which can be considered simultaneously, has been made by A. P. Rossiter.[2] He builds upon Leavis' central points about Othello's weaknesses and gives a psychological commentary on their origins and nature. Thus we have his jealousy, which is 'a sign of weakness in love, not of strength', his 'sense of inferior-ity', the 'total dependence of his self-esteem on being loved', his 'monomania'.

Both Leavis and Rossiter have a certain sense of triumphant diagnosis in their readings, which makes me want to alter the tone and balance of some of the things they say; but beyond that I don't think it is possible seriously to deny the force of their readings; and I certainly think that any attempt to return to the Coleridgean—Bradleyan sentimentality of the 'noble hero' is un-likely to bear much fruit. Leavis' moral case and Rossiter's psychological one cannot be reversed; but what they require is extension. For both the moral and the psychological terminologies are lacking in something which bulks very large in Shakespeare's play — a social dimension. While both critics successfully dispose of the romantic idea of the noble hero, both still retain the romantic tradition's idea of the hero's dramatic isolation; and for this the play gives no warrant. As with so many of the plays I shall discuss below, the central figure is set in a context of social action and interpersonal dynamics which has been created and analysed with great detail. Shakespeare's psychology is always social psychology, and this play is no exception. It is not just about 'the Moor', but about the 'the Moor *of Venice*'; and it is to Venice that we must turn if the full tragedy of the collapse of the heroic personality is to be properly understood.

2. *Venetian vulnerability*

As soon as we look not only at Othello but also at Venice we notice that it is not only the hero who undergoes a dramatic collapse of the personality. He is paralleled in this by three native members of the Venetian nobility, in whom we witness other very important instances of collapse before experience with which they are unable to deal. The three are Brabantio, Desdemona and Cassio,[3] and Shakespeare weaves together the lives of all three of them in a way which makes it clear that this propensity for collapse, this vulnerability and incapacity, is a wide and shared cultural weakness.

The collapse of Brabantio opens the play, and the early scenes in which he is at the centre of the drama are full of vital documentation about the culture of Venice. He is noble, a gentleman, fully aware of 'My spirit and my place', knowing that he carries authority with him in almost all the great houses of the city, and knowing that his is a powerful voice in directing the state and its law. He is eloquently at ease in Venetian polite society, as we see in his skilful exchange of rival maxims with the Duke. He knows how to expect and receive what Roderigo calls 'reverence', must be addressed with 'all civility' and is himself elegantly deferential in his address to the Duke, with his 'Good, your grace, pardon

me' and 'Humbly I thank your grace'. His Venetian sense of
continence gives him little relish for the rowdyisms of the night
which open the play, when those who are 'full of supper and
distempering draughts' disturb the peace of his household. He
expects 'obedience' from his daughter, having brought her up in
elegance and propriety as

> A maiden never bold,
> Of spirit so still and quiet that her motion
> Blush'd at herself.   [I. iii. 94—6]

This descendant of the *senex* of the comedies is an ordinary
Elizabethan gentleman who would agree with the orthodox
Tudor writers on personal conduct and political order that
Courtesy is of the essence of civilization, and that offences done
to the mores of such a culture are tantamount to turning civic
rule over to 'bond-slaves and pagans'.

The play begins with such a person. But it begins with such a
person transformed, during the space of nineteen lines spoken by
no more powerful a persuader than Roderigo, into a vengeful
rabble-rouser:

> Strike on the tinder, ho!
> Give me a taper; call up all my people.
> This accident is not unlike my dream.
> Belief of it oppresses me already.   [I. i. 141—4]

At the end of Roderigo's carefully freighted appeal to the gentle-
manly values of 'duty, beauty, wit and fortunes', set against a
challenge from outside the gentleman's world — 'an extravagant
and wheeling stranger/Of here and everywhere' — Brabantio is
inundated by the apparent realization of his worst fantasies and
fears ('not unlike my dream') and by that familiar concomitant of
fear, a panic readiness to believe anything that he is told.

The collapse is ugly and total, and it very clearly prefigures
what we will get in Othello himself. A few lines below it turns
into that insidious mixture of loathing and self-pity which will
characterize the fallen Othello:

> Who would be a father?

O treason of the blood!
Fathers, from hence trust not your daughters' minds,

[I. i. 165; 170—1]

and when his daughter stands up to him before the senate his angry bewilderment turns into an ugly hatred of the most intrinsic bonds of love and affection:

I had rather to adopt a child than get it.   [I. iii. 191]

It is as Othello's hatred will be. The daughter is now a mere loathsome object — 'it' — and the act of generation is regarded with venemous contempt — 'get'.

So the play begins with the first of these collapses and in doing so it opens up the figure of the *senex* to profound social-psychological scrutiny. It is no passing anger; nor is it a mere conventional or symbolic device for getting a play about youth's rebellion into motion. We are witnessing the disintegration of Brabantio's culture. It is the first presentation of that Courtesy-culture on which the play will spend a great deal of its time, and we see the values of that culture buckle and collapse frighteningly as Brabantio is brought face to face with an experience with which his culture does not equip him to deal. We watch a culture reach the limits of its capacity and then snap. And we see its exquisitely civilized language give way to a language of terror, loathing and abuse.

The collapse, as I say, is total. Brabantio does not recover from it. At the end of the play we hear from Gratiano that the shock has killed him, though by then we are disinclined to accept Gratiano's Venetian explanation of it in terms of what sounds like the laudable phenomenon of 'pure grief'. Brabantio has simply been incapable of admitting into his world of Courtesy-consciousness the experience of his daughter's being married to a black man; or indeed of his daughter's being married to anyone to whom she took, away from her father and regardless of his values and desires, an independent love and loyalty.

At the other end of the play is the collapse of Desdemona; and again what Desdemona is, and what she is for Venice, has been dramatically established in full detail. It has been mainly registered in her own behaviour towards Othello, where her husband is her 'lord' to whom she does passive and quiet obedience; in Othello's descriptions of her as the ideal woman of this gentleman's world, with her idealized beauty and her skills in such matters as singing, dancing, needlework and 'high and plenteous wit and invention'; and in the florid Petrarchanisms and flourishes of Courtesy with which Cassio attends her:

> let her have your knees.
> Hail to thee, lady! and the grace of heaven,
> Before, behind thee, and on every hand,
> Enwheel thee round!   [II. i. 84—7]

She is the female apotheosis of the Venetian Courtesy-world; and her fate as such is handled so that we experience, with intense pain, the demands that this makes of her and the limitations in her consciousness that it creates.

Our reaction to her passive obedience to the role is never more painful than when Othello strikes her in public and is then able to call her back like a tame animal:

> *Oth.* Mistress!
> *Des.* My Lord?   [IV. i. 246—7]

By this time the ritual obligations of her role are coming through to us as atrocious — as they began perhaps to seem in the first Act when we remembered that it was a woman's life that was so elegantly *played for* in the scene in the senate. And her inability to step outside the role-demands, even to see any need to step outside them, comes through as intensely painful. She is fatally ill-equipped by her role in this culture to deal with the brutalized and *dis*courteous husband that Othello becomes.

And so, before the savagery of his accusations, she collapses and cannot resist. In the scene which follows that in which he strikes her, she greets him with 'My lord, what is your will?' and 'What is your pleasure?', and he replies with his torrents of abuse. From here to the end she is inert, passive and unresisting. Between one of his outbursts of violence

> (a cistern for foul toads
> To knot and gender in)   [IV. ii. 62—3]

and the next

> (ay; as summer flies are in the shambles,
> That quicken even with blowing)   [IV. ii. 67—8]

she can insert only the pathetic and fragile pleas of her role-language:

> I hope my noble lord esteems me honest.   [IV. ii. 66]

And eighty lines after her entrance to this scene she is collapsed into resignation, preparing herself to be laid out on his bed like a sacrifice, in the 'shroud' of her wedding-sheets. The fragility to which her culture has bred her has been made apparent:

> I cannot say 'whore';
> It does abhor me now I speak the word,   [IV. ii. 162—3]

and her consequent unfitness to cope with Othello's hatred and sexual violence is fully understandable in these terms.

We must, I think, feel some irritation with Desdemona in these last scenes; and indeed pained irritation is a strong component in our feelings at many points in the play as we watch the members of this culture in their awful failures of understanding and response. Rossiter is surely right, if slightly over-aggressive, to find her a 'pathetic, girlish, nearly-blank sheet'; and as she responds so inertly to Othello's savagery and bullying, some part of an audience's response must be a pained irritation which is amazed to see her react so feebly to her husband's violence. But we can only accommodate this feeling, in our experience of the whole play, if we remember her disabling Venetian background. This is the daughter of Brabantio:

> A maiden never bold,
> Of spirit so still and quiet that her motion
> Blush'd at herself.   [I. iii. 94—6]

She is a woman, in other words, civilized almost out of existence by the requirements of Courtesy-culture; a woman in whom the kinesis (of 'motion') has been rendered 'still and quiet'.

In her, as in all the other characters of this Courtesy-culture, the toughness, the strong energy, the buoyancy of mind which goes with a certain coarseness to make the non-Courtesy characters like Emilia and Iago so resilient, has been sedulously removed. She lacks everything that is registered in her description of Iago's deflationary wit and bawdy talk — 'old fond paradoxes to make fools laugh in the alehouse'. And this means that something is missing for which Shakespeare has a very much higher regard than does Desdemona. Its absence, expunged by Courtesy, makes her effete, fragile and passive. In Cassio's world of courtly-Petrarchan adoration she is a goddess, perfect, chaste and divine. In the real world, where the alehouse-element exists whether Venice will have it or no, she is equipped only to be a victim, the unresisting and non-comprehending human sacrifice who sings the sad and beautiful willow-song.

The third instance of traumatic collapse of the personality touches rather immediately on this matter of the alehouse-element. If we have it in mind, something which might keep us reminded of the entire Falstaff-element in man, then there is a tragi-comic significance in Cassio's inability to hold his drink. His chaste purity of manner, capable though it is of reaching to a kind of 'daily beauty' which can make Iago feel ugly, is nonetheless made to appear in all its fragility by Shakespeare's drawing attention to his delicate stomach. It is a tragi-comic equivalent of the collapses of Othello, Desdemona and Brabantio, the point perhaps where our derision must fuse with our compassion to experience Venice for what it is. Two glasses of wine and a couple of soldiers' songs and all those elegant flourishes of word and gesture fall about his ears: it is as important a tragi-comic comment on Venice's idea of man and nature as is the drunkenness of Lepidus on Rome's. Alcohol and other drugs figure largely in the play in presenting the Venetian world-view; and the serious point of the scene might be said to be that the Venetian idea of man would have more chance of success if we lived in a world where alcohol did not exist, and indeed where the stomach and the brain had no merely physical (hence both base and limited) existence at all. Cassio indeed seems to espouse some such wish — 'I could well wish courtesy would invent some other custom of entertainment' — but all the Courtesy in the world will not expunge the physical necessities of animal matter.

The interesting and appalling thing is that this culture cannot contain so ordinary a manifestation of man's physicality. Cassio's reaction to the crime of drunkenness is very intense:

> O god, that men should put an enemy in their mouths to steal away their brains! That we should with joy, pleasance, revel and applause, transform ourselves into beasts!

> It hath pleas'd the devil drunkenness to give place to the devil wrath. One unperfectness shows me another, to make me frankly despise myself.

> Every inordinate cup is unblest, and the ingredience is a devil.
> [II. iii. 280–3; 286–7; 297]

The Venetian mind dare contemplate no Shakespearean holiday. The fragile Venetian man that Cassio has aspired to be can only see the animal and ungodly in man, the Falstaff-element that drinks and revels, as an unmitigated disaster. When it looks upon this side of life, the high religiose language of perfection and Courtesy-divinity can only turn with distaste into its opposite — the language of beast and devil. Again it is the traumatic breakdown of a culture. Cassio has couched his entire being in terms of the Venetian ideal, and has no tolerance or capacity for ambiguity with which to accommodate what lies outside its range. Thus, when the whole structure breaks down under the influence of alcohol and he sees other things in himself, he is reduced to a comic-ridiculous version of that same self-pity/self-hate complex that we get from Brabantio and Othello — 'to make me frankly despise myself'.

For Iago, outside the culture of Courtesy, such an intense reaction is absurd. Alcohol, after all, is 'a good familiar creature'; but in saying so he knows, as so often, that he is stating the kind of truth which Venetians cannot bear. He knows perfectly well that his own accommodation to those aspects of men which make drunkenness a normal and quite unterrifying thing ('Come, you are too severe a moraller', 'You, or any man living, may be drunk at some time') is quite impossible for a Venetian gentleman. For Cassio, with his whole being couched in terms of Courtesy-culture, the acknowledgment of drunkenness would entail complete loss of self-meaning. His Venetian definition of himself as a man has gone; and what is left is not 'man' at all: 'I have lost the immortal part of myself, and what remains is bestial'. The immortal part, we hear, is his 'reputation'; and when we hear that, the scene has brought to completion its tragi-comic under-view of the Venetian value-system. To see the immortal part of a man as consisting in his reputation is to evince the most extreme form of attachment to a social structure of values, which in Shakespeare's universe, as in Schopenhauer's or Nietzsche's, means the most extreme folly and the most extreme vulnerability. It directly prefigures the outrageous irrelevance of Othello's cry when he fears that his wife is unfaithful: 'Othello's occupation's gone'.

3. The Venetian view of nature

There is, then, a Venetian view of man and a Venetian view of nature, embodied in a coherent value-system which the play shows to be tragically vulnerable in the actual world. The general outlines of this view of man and nature can be most quickly seen by noticing how the upper-class inhabitants of the city use certain key words. When Venetians refer to 'nature' they really mean what is natural according to the gentle customs of their class – a nature which does not include goats and monkeys and foul toads, raging motions, carnal stings and unbitted lusts, blood, poisonous minerals and mines of sulphur within a man's 'in-wards', the 'uncleanly apprehensions' which, as once again Iago knows very well, 'in sessions sit/With meditations lawful' in every man's mind. This 'nature' is felt to 'err from itself' when it touches what is unpleasant, 'grossly to rebel' against itself when it drives maidens never bold to 'the sooty bosom of such a thing as thou'. Such happenings can only be the product of drugs which, like alcohol, are not part of 'nature' – no more than are hot hands and fitchews and other aspects of the phenomenal world which are suggestive of dangerous sexual potency. Such things have no part of what Brabantio confidently calls 'rules of nature'. The words which Venetians use for phenomena such as these, which crowd the language of the play, tend to be the words that Cassio used for drunkenness – 'devil' and 'beast'.

Male members of the Venetian upper classes may have a little experience of this devil-beast nature, provided they keep it safely in the officially-allowed district of prostitution — for Cassio labours under no fear that feasting with a fitchew will harm at any rate his immortal part. And all of them will permit themselves a certain wonder and enchantment when a glimpse of the wild-world of

> antres vast and deserts idle,
> Rough quarries, rocks, and hills whose heads touch heaven
> [I. iii. 140—1]

is provided, mollified by romance, by the stories of one who is paid to keep them from it. But beyond this their attitude is one of distaste and disbelief. Its presence in men can never get any acknowledgment in their language. Their civilization is protected from the enchafed flood; and Montano's question:

> What ribs of oak, when mountains melt on them,
> Can hold the mortise?   [II. i. 8—9]

is one whose ironic implications for the ribs and mortises of their own social structure is seen by nobody.

Their culture, then, is a thin skin of elegance, formal deference and careful continence stretched over a world of raging motion and energy from which they wish to keep their distance. The imagery of this unacknowledged world abounds in the play, making a terrible wanton revel in their language largely without their knowing it. The skin is glassy and inhuman, like Othello's idea of perfection as 'entire and perfect chrysolite'; and under it, insistently pushing up to the surface to demand their unwilling and horrified recognition, is the 'under-nature' of the foul toads. One image which runs throughout the play is worth isolating because it presents this model with great clarity. It is the image of a hideous birth, whose conception takes place in Act One and delivery in Act Five.

At first it is remote and small in 'the womb of time', then 'engender'd' in the brain of Iago:

> Hell and night
> Must bring this monstrous birth to the world's light.
> [I. iii. 397—8]

Thereafter we hear of its foetal formation — 'tis here, but 'tis confused' — and later Othello senses its quickening and growth in the womb of Iago's brain:

> As if there were some monster in his thought
> Too hideous to be shown,
>
> As if thou then hadst shut up in thy brain
> Some horrible conceit.   [III. iii. 111–12; 118–19]

Iago pretends to wish that 'grosser issues' will not come to light, but Emilia and Desdemona now sense its growth as 'some un-hatch'd practice', some 'conception' now felt to be in the brain of Othello. Emilia fears

> a monster
> Begot upon itself, born on itself,   [III. iv. 162–3]

and Iago's talk of 'many a civil monster' suggests its unwelcome capacity to exist within the whole collective consciousness of Venice. Othello fears the suppression of 'villainous secrets'; but then, with the vaginal ragings of 'a cistern for foul toads/To knot and gender in' and 'the gate of hell', the thing begins to be born in him. Desdemona's 'Alas, what does this gentleman conceive?' is her bewildered response to its coming, and then his eyes roll and his frame is shaken and we get 'the strong conception/That I do groan withal'. When the 'monstrous act' comes it is delivered as the tragic loading of their marriage-bed, to which Venice's end-less capacity for blindness has its ready and dreadfully predictable reaction:

> The object poisons sight;
> Let it be hid.   [V. ii. 367–8]

This frightening image gathers into itself much of the play's most important movement and thrust. That part of nature's kinetic energy which cannot be let into Venice to create greater resilience and vitality pushes its way up from beneath in a grotesque form. It shatters the fragile world of Courtesy, where 'motion/Blush'd at herself' and spirits were 'still and quiet'.

That is the essence of Venice's view of nature, and that is what the existence of Shakespeare's nature does to it. That is the Venetian *Vorstellung* of the world, and the havoc made of it by the tumult of *die Wille*. As we move to this play from the comedies we are made to look at the social psychology of the *senex* who resists nature, and then at the social psychology of those who resist the *senex*. What we see is that that resistance is minimal, for the resisters have no more capacity than the *senex* himself to appropriate the powers of nature to their service. Desdemona makes the classic anti-*senex* speech about the duties and rights of the new generation which she and her husband begin. But neither she nor her husband, nor anyone else in Venice, has the remotest idea of the generative energies involved in this process of renewal. They reject the *senex*, but carry on in themselves the self-same ignorance of, and resistance to, the kinetic world. There is thus no birth of spring leading to summer and harvest. The first breath of cold from Iago kills this all-too-tender plant, and instead of rebirth we get that monster which he has engendered.

4. *Suit, distance and stratification*

That is the model; though to leave it there would still be to state it too generally. In fact it is made to work in the play in great and specific detail, supporting a wealth of social-psychological documentation. It is to that detail that we must turn, to see its presence in social behaviour and manners as much as in language. The play makes its critical examination of the behaviour-patterns centred upon such key words as 'duty', 'honour', 'service', 'courteous' and 'humble' in an active presentation of Venice's social praxis. In this praxis, the elaborate codes of Courtesy provide the means whereby their society maintains its class-stratification. In its terms are embodied subtle and penetrating mechanisms for maintaining social 'distance', and this structural distance is introjected into the consciousness of individuals with the same damaging results as is the idea of nature.

Almost everyone in the play is busy making suit to somebody

else. Iago, at the start, tells us that

> Three great ones of the city,
> In personal suit to make me his lieutenant,
> Off-capp'd to him   [I. i. 8—10]

and, disappointed in this lobby, he bewails 'the curse of service' where 'preferment goes by letter and affection'. He tells us also of the 'duteous and knee-crooking knave' and the 'forms and visages of duty'. He has an axe to grind of course, but subsequent events do not prove him to be an unreliable observer. The whole of his first conversation with Othello swarms with similar references. Iago talks of Brabantio's power to sue and pressurize in politics, his 'might to enforce' the law to please himself. Othello, in his turn, will rely on 'services, which I have done the signiory' to get his counter-suit heard in high places, and can press his claims in competition with Brabantio, as one descended from 'men of royal seige'. Nature's resistance to the *senex*, and with it the young life of a marriage, is fast disappearing beneath mechanisms of decorous social insinuation in which Desdemona is a mere 'issue'. We see this, with growing distaste, as political in-fighting; but to the characters of the Courtesy-world it is proper and elegantly civilized social behaviour, embodying their agreed system of deferences.

Gradually, as the play builds up, this making of suit, this capping, crooking and lobbying, assumes claustrophobic proportions. Before the senate, Othello sees it as a game of eloquence, scarcely more 'personal' than the wit-game of maxims played at the end of the scene between Brabantio and the Duke. He is supremely confident of his own loquacious capacities for success, freighting his appeal with those flattering, self-flattering and caressive reminders to the Duke about 'the trust, the office I do hold of you'. That this is about a marriage is almost outrageous; and it will seem even more so when he tells of his wooing of Desdemona in exactly the same language. Words like 'pliant' and 'beguile' carry into courtship these same suing tones; and the elegant and courteous Cassio has been employed to assist his suit, as one well versed in the art of political lobby. The often-quoted lines about the insubstantial foundations of their marriage:

> She lov'd me for the dangers I had pass'd;
> And I lov'd her that she did pity them,   [I. iii. 167–8]

are part of a general wrongness of tone which runs through all the language in which their love and marriage exists. And at bottom it is the Venetian distance-system which has got into their personal language and ways of seeing each other as a frail substitute for more intrinsic bonds.

Many Renaissance writers, particularly satirists, devoted their critical attention to this courtly and elaborate game of suit and service, and many had the same view of it as the scornful Iago. Ben Jonson, for example, bent all his capacities for anger and vituperation against men who made themselves mere 'instruments' or 'engines' in the game of suit. But none got so far inside such a culture as does Shakespeare in *Othello*. None saw, as he did, that it is not just lying and flattering suits to unworthy persons which do the human damage, but the business of suing itself, even in noble causes. For here we see the habits of suit woven into every part of the social fabric and working deep into the consciousness of all a society's members. Its effect is to tie interpersonal bonds with very slender threads, reducing social intercourse, even within intimate relationships like marriage and friendship, to a very fragile network incapable of carrying much tension or weight. No primary, face-to-face relationships between people can ever come into being. All are made secondary, to be carried by intermediaries and suits and tokens – like the fatal handkerchief. A thin network of deferential balances, a world of mere 'political' words, does service as a society's entire mode of communication, and the deepest impulses of human emotion are censored from the life of the group, unable as they are to enter into the 'civil conversation' of Courtesy and the discreet habit of suit.

It is thus that the play comes to its crisis, precipitated first by a love-token and then by a suit – with Desdemona as Cassio's intermediary and 'solicitor' to her husband. It is a terrible picture of human inadequacy and helplessness. A fatal distance is set between man and wife by this etiolated social code, from which, even in their most personal engagements, they cannot free themselves. Their relationship is secondary and role-centred; and in the catastrophe of it she is still pressing blindly on with Cassio's wretched suit, unaware that any other mode of human communication exists and unable to recognize the language of another mode which Iago has induced in her 'lord'.

This is the context in which we can understand the collapse of Othello's heroic personality, the destruction of his marriage, and the tragedy of the *Moor of Venice*. For a good deal about Othello is entirely consistent with Venice as a whole, a good deal of his being is humanly representative of these norms and codes. He has made his love and life in Venetian terms. His love-language is etiolated and devitalized — in the direction of idealism and sublimation — in the way that the language of Courtesy is. He has seen his wife as an object to be sued for, a prize to be won. He can court after her, apotheosize her as a goddess, possess her as an index of his social elevation, worship her ecstatically as a Courtesy-religious symbol of perfection. The only thing he cannot do is talk to her as an individual woman.

His love, then, is Courtesy-love, and it is the same with other features of his character. The pride that he takes in his own glamour and spectacular excellence is not only a personal thing: it is also the narcissism of this exquisite culture. His claim to possession of a 'perfect soul' is a Venetian claim; and his insistence on his wife's social status — which must see her attended 'As befits her breeding' — sees him entering into this culture's terminology with an *élan* which is not just personal. His idea of women is Venetian — 'delicate creatures' of chastity, grace and elegant accomplishment; and that 'over-eloquent' quality of his joy on arrival in Cyprus is purest Venice, as is his repeated insistence that love has no connexion with appetite and baseness. His sense of continence, which will bid the celebrant 'not to outsport discretion', and of the values which endorse it ('for Christian shame'), are orthodox; and so is his idea of what is becoming in youth, as he praises Montano for his 'gravity and stillness'. He shares the Venetian idea of nature, which errs from itself when it runs towards unpleasantness, and of the 'under-nature' which he also finds devilish and beastly. The outbursts of violence and obscenity are, on the Venetian model, the only manifestations that this under-nature can take in a mind which has eschewed recognition of it and named it foul.

But then there is another factor, another aspect of his participation in Venetian culture, which, in him, heightens ordinary vulnerability to even greater intensity. Again more of Shakespeare's beautifully clear-sighted understanding of the psychological dynamics of social life has gone into creating it. Othello is vulnerable even above the Venetian norm, and pitiful even above that norm, because of his special relationship with the core-culture. Othello is not native to this culture; and its modes have been learned and are practised by him with something of the outsider's difficulty. He is vulnerable and pathetic as ordinary Venetians are; but then vulnerable and pathetic again, over and above that, in the manner of an *assimilado*. The dramatic presence of his blackness in this whitest of all possible worlds has its meaning principally here. Added to the normal Venetian fear of the 'under-nature', and of the social rejection which must befall those who slip into it, there are also in Othello the *assimilado*'s classic fears. He fears that he has not sufficiently mastered this culture's ways — the 'soft parts of conversation/That chamberers have'; and Iago, another outsider, can see very well how the fear of failure and rejection will play even more terribly and tormentingly upon Othello than it did on Cassio:

> riches fineless is as poor as winter
> To him that ever fears he shall be poor. [III. iii. 177—8]

The *assimilado*'s slight over-playing of the required role is finely registered in his hyper-sensitivity about his own dignity and achievements, his over-spectacular parade of the power to eschew baseness, and the gestural grandiloquence of his *coups de théâtre*. The 'admired ego' and the self-pity, which Leavis and Rossiter bring out, have their social location here — in a man who can afford even fewer falls into baseness than the native Venetian, and who consequently must act the codes with abnormally wondrous and abnormally conspicuous perfection. A great deal of the pain and pathos of watching him derives from the fact that this is

more than merely an extravagant ego. It has to do with
Nietzsche's 'necessity', not his 'despotism'. It is an ego which *has
to be* like this in order to live in Venice; and its fall is the tragedy
of *The Moor* of Venice.

That is how the Othello whom Leavis and Rossiter describe in
purely personal terms is set down by Shakespeare in the Venetian
world. It is important to see him in this context for a variety of
reasons. It gives one a sense of the play's wholeness and breadth
of vision and alters the tone of how we respond to Othello and
the quality of our compassion for him. It also prevents that sense
of dissatisfaction with which both Leavis and Rossiter close their
accounts of the play. I will come back to Leavis' dissatisfaction in
a moment; Rossiter's is as follows:

> I find that the peculiarly distressing effect of *Othello* — what
> Bradley calls its 'painful' quality — turns on this feeling of a
> hollowness at the centre, by the time the end is reached. There
> is a mixedness of feelings, an instability of apparently accepted
> values, an absence of stable ground underfoot in all the evalua-
> tions of sex and so of those of 'love', which makes me dislike
> the play's *Stimmung* as much as I admire its artistic contriv-
> ance. I think it is because, on love (its ostensible theme), it
> leaves me as much just nowhere as *Measure for Measure* does.
> [p. 206]

Leaving *Measure for Measure* aside, this is a great pity; for
what has happened here is that the complex and detailed Shakespearean picture of Venetian culture has been taken at the grossly
reduced level of mere *Stimmung*, as a kind of generalized 'tone'
or 'ethos' of the play. And then, a further reduction, that
Stimmung has been felt simply to impart itself to the reader as
belonging to Shakespeare rather than to his created society, so
that the play rather than the place in the play, has been felt to
have this 'hollowness' and this 'absence of stable ground under-
foot'. But of course the 'hollowness' does not just impart itself to
the reader as a generalized tone which cannot be analysed or
considered. It is part of what the play most lucidly analyses and
understands. The hollowness of these people and their culture is
what the play is about, and it is about it in a sure and resolved

manner, determinedly sympathetic (hence 'painful') but determinedly analytic as well. Venetians are 'left nowhere' by what happens, for again nobody in the play acquires any true experience from the great event; but the audience, which has no reason to miss the clarity, tact and detail of Shakespeare's presentation of this culture's etiolated mores, will have no need to come away with Rossiter's sense of confusion. Rather, I think, they will come from the play with a sense of the beautifully achieved clarity of Shakespeare's vision. It is a clarity created by that exactitude and justness of analysis which Shakespeare's mind paradoxically achieves even at the moment of its greatest intensity of sympathetic engagement. It has everything to do with his powers as social-psychologist, the simultaneity with which he perceives a personal psychology as a part of the exigencies of social life.

5. *Another outsider and another marriage*

Leavis' disappointment also stems from this absence of a social dimension to his thought about the play. His objection is to Iago, whom he finds a 'clumsy' device for the exposure of Othello's weaknesses. But, as I said, Leavis has not really completed his critique of the romantic reading of the play, for he has still conceived of the romantic hero in dramatic isolation. Put Othello back into Venice, where Shakespeare has so clearly put him, and the Iago who also lives there will begin to look very different. Iago's reaction to the culture of Venice is as interesting as Othello's, and as finely observed. The social documentation of his life in Venice is remarkably full, and it also engages our full critical sympathy with his being.

The Iago who lives in Venice, as a full dramatic character in his own right and not just a clumsy instrument for the exposure of the isolated hero, is a man of many qualities, attractive in a whole number of ways. His relish of activity, his deflationary insights into Courtesy-culture, his courage, his doggedness, his fighting quickness of wit — all the things that make him a better soldier than Cassio and so easily able to outwit the 'wealthy curled darlings' of his world — all these are on his side, and they get, as

Rossiter saw, their regard from the play. He is in many ways cleverer than the nobility around him, certainly more deeply rooted in life's essential energies. His accommodation to the base and low gives him a vitality and a stability which they so poignantly lack, and the *sang froid* of his knowledge of the physical world ('the wine she drinks is made of grapes' etc.) is both admirable and relieving. He may be the Blatant Beast of slander in the verbal paradise of Courtesy; but Shakespeare's view of that conflict of values is not as simple-minded as Spenser's.[4]

All this is there, and Iago knows it is there. But the stratification of Venetian society and its elaborate distance-system exclude him from any complete social membership. He is, as more than one critic has noted, 'a good NCO but definitely not Officer Material'. As the characters of the Courtesy-world persistently dub him 'honest', the word comes more and more to feel like a term of essentially dismissive praise — the kind of quality that servants are expected to have. He can run lowly errands for the exquisite élite, fetching Desdemona from the sagittary and being 'set on' as Othello's spy. But beyond this, whatever his abilities, he cannot go. Again there is no reason to miss this fully documented social rejection, and certainly no reason to mystify him with notions about the Elizabethan Vice.[5] It is from this palpable social rejection, experienced by him (with much justification) as the rejection of strength by weakness, that Iago's frustration and then hatred derive.

Coleridge must have lived in more fortunate times than ours if he could find this malignity 'motiveless'. For anyone who has heard the voice of the 'poor white man', or who knows what Jew-baiting and nigger-baiting are, Iago must represent a masterly social portrait. He has everthing that Sartre describes as the social psychology of the anti-Semite[6] — a man so degraded in self-image by social rejection that it becomes an imperative for his ego to find somebody who is beneath even him, like the Jew (or the Moor), onto whom he can project the unbearable view which society has of himself. And if we know how this kind of race-hate so often takes the form of fantasies of sex-hate, then we shall understand still further what Iago is. In Iago, another outsider to the world of courtesy, we see a mind in the grip of just such a vortex, where frustration develops into a need to project, fantasize, blacken and destroy. He saves thereby his own self-esteem. Or, as Shakespeare made him put it, he 'plumes up his will'.

That is the other outsider, whose fate counterpoints that of Othello; and there is, just as importantly, another marriage, and another married woman, counterpointing Desdemona. It is an index of Shakespeare's clarity of mind on matters of love, sex and marriage in this play that Emilia needs only twenty-odd lines at the end of Act Four (talking saucily to Desdemona about infidelity) and about forty lines in the last scene to bring his investigation of his themes to an adroit conclusion, and the play to its self-completeness. She fills up all the 'lack' and 'hollowness' with tones that nobody else speaks in the entire play. We assent to her words and deeds without qualification. Her courage ('I care not for your sword') and her direct talking (''twill out, 'twill out . .') come from roots that go deeper into life than those of any other character. She still has all the robustness which Courtesy has bred out of the others; and in contrast to their collapses she comes back unswerving at the worst assaults of both Iago and Othello. And she knows, as Desdemona didn't, what wifely loyalty is and what it isn't;

> 'Tis proper I obey him, but not now.
> Perchance, Iago, I will ne'er go home,   [V. ii. 199–200]

stepping outside her socially defined role when deeper promptings stir.

There is no cause to be condescending about her performance in these last scenes, noting the low-life qualities of the good-hearted servant etc. *Her* life and *her* marriage are also at stake in the catastrophe of the play; and, not for the first time in the play, we are reminded of the painful remnants of her love for her husband and the anxious desire she has to hold him to her:

> I know thou didst not; thou'rt not such a villian,
> Speak, for my heart is full.   [V. ii. 177–8]

All the more moving then is her unhesitating strength when the truth is seen, and all the more terrible the comment that it makes on the passive inability of all the others to do anything but buckle into self-pity before traumatic shock:

> You told a lie — an odious, damned lie.
> Upon my soul, a lie — a wicked lie.   [v. ii. 183—4]

It is as simple as that; but it represents human capacities far beyond the range of anyone bred in the mores of Venice. Emilia seems to me to be nothing less than the most complete person in the play, in whom all that is lacking in the others wells up with inescapable rightness to command our complete assent. She is the one person who gets anywhere near to what Shakespeare, as opposed to the Venetian senate, may have meant by 'all in all sufficient'.

3

The hero of Rome

Coriolanus is about power: about State, or *the* State;
... If you cannot be excited about what happens to
the Roman State (a branch or *exemplum* of what
happens in *States*), then you cannot feel the play. For
it is a kind of excitement very different from that
generated by 'What happens to George?'
A. P. Rossiter: *Angel With Horns* [*ed. cit.*, pp. 235, 240]

O mother, mother!
What have you done? Behold, the heavens do ope,
The gods look down, and this unnatural scene
They laugh at.   [V.iii. 182—5]

1. Shakespeare's Rome

Rossiter is right. Rome, the place and the ideal, is at the centre of
attention in this play. And if one of its citizens, the hero, bulks
large in the scene it is not just as an individual ('George') that he
does so, but as a Roman phenomenon. All the crises of his
character are crises of Rome and Romanness; all the tensions and
conflicts of his society are lived out in his being. Of all Shakespeare's 'plays about cultures' this is perhaps the most tightly
woven. Every individual life in it is part of the process of Rome's
life. Nowhere is the simultaneity of Shakespeare's social and
psychological thought more convincingly demonstrated. With no
play would it be more fatal for a critic to try to understand a
character while taking his eyes off the social situation in which he

acts and is formed. That is true of the hero above all, for it is in the very nature of Rome to create and use such a hero.

So we must begin with Rome, and stick to it; and that may be helped by considering what Shakespeare makes of Rome in the group of three plays which he made out of Plutarch. Rome for Shakespeare is always a dehumanized or 'denatured' society. Its codes and languages are remote from basic kinds of affection — from those senses which are carried on such words as 'bond' and 'kin' in the world of *King Lear*. The demands of its public life are hostile to familial and sexual life: nowhere in any of these Romes can a family be created and survive, or a friendship, or sexual love. Its mob is fickle, rootless, violent and untrustworthy; its aristocracy is vain, power-crazed and pretentiously rhetorical. Both have unlovely ambitions and ugly manners.

Romans tend to live by codes — militant and beglamouring codes of caste in *Coriolanus*, codes of order, rank and efficiency in *Antony and Cleopatra*, codes of Stoic fortitude in the Brutus of *Julius Caesar*. The rigidity of these codes puts stops upon their emotional vitality and encapsulates their beings in littleness, stubbornness and gracelessness. A strong part of our eventual response to them is that they are absurd — we shall need Schopenhauer's capacities for comic disbelief and derision. But they are also menacing. Rome is a 'man's world' which beglamours a narrow idea of manhood with the name of strength and is totally ignorant of all those rich and powerful tones which Shakespeare, in dozens of his plays, early and late, creates out of the world of women. And Rome is mightily pleased with itself, its heroes repeatedly apostrophizing themselves with the formality of the third person, and naming the deeds of the city and its great ones with magniloquent orotundities of phrase.

In *Julius Caesar*, as I said, Shakespeare was very careful and hesitant about such a Rome. This characteristic over-view of Romanness was not yet fully developed; but in *Antony and Cleopatra* and *Coriolanus* he creates it with massive coherence and solidity. The two later Romes have a great deal in common, though the *tone* in which each is presented is unique and individual. In *Antony and Cleopatra*, as we shall see, the sense of Rome as derisory, absurd, ludicrously inflated in its littleness, is very strong. In *Coriolanus* it is also absurd, but there is not much room for feeling that because its menace is so real and pressing. Here it has a hideousness which is felt, very close, as ugly and butchering, and it is near to the centre of our response to be appalled. The physical violence and moral brutality of Roman life are brought too close for very much laughter at its absurdity; and while some kind of laughter (savage and sardonic) has its role to play in what we will eventually feel about Rome when all is done, nevertheless, when the play is in motion, other feelings are overwhelmingly more important. It is brought so close, as not in *Antony and Cleopatra*: the potching and the mammocking, the ravishing and avenging, the scotching, notching and broiling of Rome and its wars and the thunder-like percussion of its hero's, sounds play upon our senses with awful immediacy. But it is the greatness (and perhaps the difficulty) of the play that, even as our senses are so forcibly assaulted by what is terrible, there is also a sustained lucidity there, requiring us to think, analyse and probe into Rome as Shakespeare has done, listening to the horrible percussion with an ear for the structure of the music. That structure, when we get it, is very subtle indeed, and extremely coherent.

Rome, then, is the case *par excellence* of culture as anti-nature, culture as Law reared in all its stubborn determination against the potencies of the kinetic world. The 'perpetual military encampment' of the idea of order is complete. If the model for cultures in the tragedies is of walls reared against nature in myopic defiance, then Rome rears them more formidably then anywhere else. Its dominant tone is the one which Eliot picked up for his *Coriolan* poem:

> Stone, bronze, stone, steel, stone, oakleaves, horses' heels
> Over the paving,

and while Marcius may talk of a 'world elsewhere' as he is cast out of Rome's gates, we never see it and neither does he. The other cities, Corioli and Antium, are merely rival replicas of the Roman model; and nowhere in the mind and language of Rome's inhabitants is there any sense of the existence of a 'world elsewhere'. The completeness with which Rome drives itself into the mind of its population is irresistible.

It is the patrician concept of life that dominates. It is not 'Shakespeare's idea of nature' which produces the imagery of eagles, ospreys and tigers,[2] but Roman patricianism, projecting onto the animal world its social fantasies about the magnificent beauty of those who rule by power and terror. And their idea of the gods, as given by Volumnia, is a similarly crude projection of their own sense of power and hierarchy; the gods relate to the aristocracy as the aristocracy does to the plebs, or the Capitol to the meanest house in Rome. The Shakespearean kinetic qualities of appetite and accommodated humour can appear only in the unappealing form of Menenius' banterings — a weary and jaded version of that which, in the clowns of the comedies, once carried a high charge of life. In the mouth of this conniving old *roué*, who conceives of himself as a great statesman and repository of worldly wisdom, it is no more vigorous than it is in his nearest Shakespearean relative, Pandarus. Corn is just something to be locked away in warehouses, too much of its nourishment being held to produce the sloth and superfluity which is the Romans' contemptuous idea of peace. And the highest form of emotional volatility and fulfilment to which a Roman mind can reach is in blood and slaughter, the heady excitement of which generates a peculiarly unpleasant rapturousness which, as we shall see, is full of transferred eroticism.

The play explores the dynamics of such a society with fine detail, and traces the modes of its painful combat with all the possibilities of life. We are concerned with a barbaric caste-system, a warrior-aristocracy whose natural apotheosis is Marcius and whose value-system is adhered to with unquestioning attachment by all the members of the class which principally generates it. When they prevaricate with these values they do so only for reasons of expediency: it is not a prevarication which entails any actual questioning. The whole system is also in large part introjected by the members and representatives of other classes, like the Tribunes, so that the quality of their resistance is poisoned at the root. To get into this system we must first look at its fundamental basis — which is a concerted attack upon instinctual life. And then we must look at two special cases of its operations — in Volumnia and Menenius. We will then be able to see what the hero is, and what functions his being has in the praxis of Roman life.

2. *Transferred eroticism*

Cominius is something of a Roman 'norm'. Among the aristocrats he is a moderate or a mediocrity according to your views; and he provides us with the most complete picture of what is involved in Rome's hostility to the kinetic life of the instincts and in Rome's hero-worship. It is the transfer of eroticism into fanaticism and violence, and we get a good deal of its detail in his famous speech in praise of Marcius' defeat of the Corioles:

> I shall lack voice; the deeds of Coriolanus
> Should not be uttered feebly. It is held
> That valour is the chiefest virtue and
> Most dignifies the haver. If it be,
> The man I speak of cannot in the world
> Be singly counterpois'd. At sixteen years,
> When Tarquin made a head for Rome, he fought
> Beyond the mark of others; our then Dictator,
> Whom with all praise I point at, saw him fight,
> When with his Amazonian chin he drove
> The bristled lips before him; he bestrid
> An o'erpress'd Roman and i' th' consul's view
> Slew three opposers; Tarquin's self he met,
> And struck him on his knee. In that day's feats,
> When he might act the woman in the scene,
> He prov'd best man i' th' field, and for his meed
> Was brow-bound with the oak. His pupil age
> Man-ent'red thus, he waxed like a sea,
> And in the brunt of seventeen battles since
> He lurch'd all swords of the garland. For this last,
> Before and in Corioli, let me say
> I cannot speak him home. He stopp'd the fliers,
> And by his rare example made the coward
> Turn terror into sport; as weeds before
> A vessel under sail, so men obey'd
> And fell below his stem. His sword, death's stamp,

Where it did mark, it took; from face to foot
He was a thing of blood, whose every motion
Was tim'd with dying cries. Alone he ent'red
The mortal gate of th' city, which he painted
With shunless destiny; aidless came off,
And with a sudden re-enforcement struck
Corioli like a planet. Now all's his.
When by and by the din of war 'gan pierce
His ready sense, then straight his doubled spirit
Re-quick'ned what in flesh was fatigate,
And to the battle came he; where he did
Run reeking o'er the lives of men, as if
'Twere a perpetual spoil; and till we call'd
Both field and city ours he never stood
To ease his breast with panting.   [II. ii. 80–120]

Menenius is delighted — 'Worthy man' — and we have a full
picture of the authentic hero before us, the man they have made,
the Rome-idea embodied at its most perfect.

It is a superb piece of dramatic poetry in the living metaphor
of which the Rome-idea is both presented and analysed in depth.
It has received a great deal of critical comment, particularly with
regard to those images which cut down such Roman concepts as
'valour', 'noble' and 'worthy' by insistence on the mechanical
hardness which they entail. This is usually felt to be there in the
'thing of blood', and in the image of the die for coining or medal-
striking in 'death's stamp' and 'struck'. Such images closely reson-
ate with others in the play, such as that in which Marcius is said
to move 'like an engine'.

But the more I consider this speech the less I am convinced
that that sort of analysis will get to its core. The sense of
mechanization is there, but it is not the crucial issue. Things
which are not mechanical, but only too alive, seem to me more
important, both in its metaphoric life and in its basic rhythms.
The chin, brows, spirit, flesh and breast of a man are there, his
muscular movement, the smell and sight of blood on him; and
there is the movement of swinging, lurching, gasping and rousing,

the movement of bodily convulsions; and there is also the blood-tingling and exhilarating identification with the scene which Cominius gradually induces both in himself and in his audience. I think it is principally the swarming sexuality of the speech which carries these kinds of energy, and carries them in a horribly perverse way.

The early part of the speech, as Cominius overcomes his opening disclaimer and begins to warm to his task, alerts us to such expectations with the imagery of Marcius' 'Amazonian chin', the Volsci's 'bristled lips' and the reflection that Marcius might have been forgiven had he chosen to 'act the woman'. These images take their place in the picture of Marcius at puberty, still beardless but about to be 'Man-ent'red' by proving himself spectacularly in performance. In that context the Amazon is particularly odd and disturbing, for a boy is becoming a man by being like women who in their turn are unfeminine; and the oddity of that lingers in the mind to alert one to suggestions of similar wrongnesses of tone as the speech progresses. As it does, such suggestions become very powerful indeed.

The mention of Tarquin, a rapist, in a sentence containing 'made a head' and 'mark' activates the latent pun on virginity-taking in the first phrase and the Elizabethan slang meaning of 'mark' as vagina.[3] Gradually the fight with Tarquin becomes shadowed with the suggestion that it is a combat in virility. Marcius' standing astride the 'o'erpress'd Roman' activates further bawdy — both 'press' here and 'strike' below being Elizabethan slang words for copulation. In such a context 'Man-ent'red' and 'waxed like a sea' become shadowed by further suggestions of sexuality in penetration and orgasm. Such words as 'brunt', 'brow-bound' and 'lurch'd' are suitably calloused and ugly, and the commonplace pun on 'swords' completes this part of the speech with a further stress on warfare as an aggressive combat in predatory sex.

It is Shakespeare's 'wanton' language of pun and ambiguity beginning to revel within a speaker's formal mode, unbeknown to him. Up to this point the wantonness is mild, the connotive auras of the words which can encompass a sexual meaning being only

fleetingly on view. But as Cominius gets into his stride, and the
celebration of Marcius becomes more ecstatic, they become horrifying. To turn terror into sport is to make warfare into woman-
izing; and the image of men falling beneath Marcius' 'stem' allows
not only the image of a ship's prow to develop but also that of an
erect penis. His 'sword' continues this; and a further sexual image
of dreadful power comes in with the image of the die. For 'stamp'
has the same Elizabethan vulgar meaning as 'press' and 'strike',
and with 'death' as orgasm, 'mark' again as vagina, and 'took' as
sexual possession, the sense of rape and predatory sex becomes
far more important than that of mechanization. If we remember
how Falstaff and others use 'thing' to mean the sexual organs, we
will realize that the 'thing of blood' need not connote the inanimate: what is presented in this image is the rapist's sexual organ
covered in the blood of his violence. The well-worn sexual puns
on 'motion' and 'dying' see this terrible sentence through to its
end:

> His sword, death's stamp,
> Where it did mark, it took; from face to foot
> He was a thing of blood, whose every motion
> Was timed with dying cries.   [II. ii. 105–8]

Thereafter, the entry into the 'mortal gate' has the same latent
sense as 'Man-ent'red', 'came off' would have the same sense of
orgasm for an Elizabethan as it has for us, and the return of the
basic copulatory verbs in 're-enforcement' and 'struck' makes it
clear that a single act of possession has far from satisfied the
predator. 'Now all's his' registers that possession with an approp-
riately monstrous tone, and then, after a short pause of semi-
conscious exhaustion, his senses start working again, with
'doubled spirit' ('spirit' meaning 'semen'), drawing more attention
to what the re-quickening of the fatigate flesh is really about.
Then, with 'battle' and 'spoil' having their part to play, the
speech closes not with what Cominius thinks he has described — a
picture of valour in all its magnificence as the chiefest virtue —
but with an overwhelming sense of ugliness, predatoriness and
ecstatic violence depth-analysed as the Roman way of transferring
the energies of the erotic into fanaticism and war. War, as one of

Aufidius' servants will so blithely put it, 'in some sort may be said to be a ravisher'.

It is a marvellously complete and realized insight into the psychology of the Roman ethos, and the metaphors which carry it are handled by Shakespeare with exquisite tact. There is no over-heated insistence on it (as there might be in D. H. Lawrence at his worst) and it is not seen as providing as exhaustive and clinical diagnosis of Rome (as it might be in Freud at his worst). But it is there deep and formative in his conception of Rome, able so often to give painful depth to the play's picture of de-humanized political and familial repression as of the essence of Rome's dynamics. It helps create and elucidate the sense of frigidity which surrounds the marriage of Marcius and Virgilia, and that other kind of frigidity, exultant and with a trace of the hysterical in it, which comes out in Marcius' description of Valeria as 'chaste as the icicle'. It is vital, of course, in the creation of Volumnia, who has proudly engineered the oak-bound brow and the 'mailed hand' of the 'man-child', and who admonishes the wretched Vigilia to appreciate the spouts of blood are more beautiful and exciting than a woman's breasts. And it is there above all in the relationship between Marcius and Aufidius, reaching its climax with Aufidius making a mistress out of Marcius after they have been united together in a passage which reads like a grotesque parody of a betrothal.[4] In it they achieve an ecstatic, physical union of the kind of which Aufidius has dreamed and which Marcius was earlier seen to try on a slightly embarrassed Cominius. In their ecstasy they claim a union more intense than that of sex, built upon their everlasting hate.

It is there also in that key word 'boy' which so agonizes Marcius at the end of the play, with its fearfully accurate charge that all this man-child strength and predatory virility has nothing to do with real adulthood. It is there too in a number of continuously activated puns on words which link war with sex — swords, targets, gates, deeds, standing, advancing, heat, strength, arms, spoils, points, and all forms of bodily encounter. At any moment the metaphors which carry this profound under-view of the Roman ethos are ready to testify to the ferocity of Roman repression, by opening doors into their subconscious of which the Romans themselves are entirely unaware; as when Volumnia praises her hero-son with

> Death, that dark spirit, in's nervy arm doth lie,
> Which, being advanc'd, declines, and then men die;
>
> [II. i. 151–2]

or when Cominius exults that 'ladies shall be frighted' to hear of the man-child's deeds, but, finding themselves 'gladly quak'd', will have appetite for more.

This Shakespearean 'wanton' language of punning does mishievous underground work behind the lines of Rome's formal rhetoric. As it does so it gives us the whole basis of the repressed and repressive Roman ethos of which Marcius is a quintessential representative. And it also gives us one of the most important ways in which Romans appropriate the being of Marcius to their own fantasies and derive vicarious gratification from exulting in his virile powers. They thrill themselves by naming his deeds and pondering the excellences of his strong and bleeding body. They dream themselves into close physical contact with the exciting aggressiveness of his manly person:

> Methinks I hear hither your husband's drum;
> See him pluck Aufidius down by th' hair.   [I. iii. 29–30]

And in the sweaty pother of their desire to eye him, they manifest pathetic traces of substitute satisfactions which he is required to provide:

> our veil'd dames
> Commit the war of white and damask in
> Their nicely gawded cheeks to th' wanton spoil
> Of Phoebus' burning kisses.   [II. i. 205–8]

Their hero is thus a necessary object for the solace of the repressed.

3. Extolling the blood

That is Rome's *general* ethos and the *general* and normal use it has for him. But there are further particularities, the first of which concerns Volumnia, and the matter of ethnocentrism.

Roman ethnocentrism is firstly a matter of the city at large, and its imperial assurance of its own magnificence; secondly it is a matter of the patricians, and their assurance as to the magnificence of their class; and thirdly it is a matter of a particular patrician house, 'the noble house o' th' Marcians', with its own ambition to be the most magnificent of them all. All this fanatical attachment of Rome to its own system, trebly intensified, is concentrated onto Marcius through the agency of his mother. It is the first of two very specific ways in which the Romans appropriate his person to their ends.

Marcius, as scion of this noble house, must furnish first the family, then the class, and then the whole city, with living proof of their own excellences. In being the 'honour'd mould' in which Marcius was 'fram'd', Volumnia focuses this aspect of Rome's culture with the greatest intensity. But as we see it in her, and see it so horribly and so totally replacing all maternal feeling in her, we are not only concerned with the vanity and perversity of an individual. Again, it is not 'what happens to George', but what happens in the state of Rome of whose essential nature this particular George is a peculiarly unattractive manifestation. Her appropriation of him is at the centre of the three circles, where the fanatical enthnocentrism of the city and the patrician class focus with highest intensity in the flamboyant and hard-faced vanity of this 'mad' and 'mankind' old aristocrat.

The dreadful tones of this vanity are given in her opening scene with Virgilia, where we are apprised of what is not merely her *readiness* for making the 'good report' of her son her 'issue', but her *enthusiasm* for it, since it hardly feels like a renunciation. The grossness of this enthusiasm comes through in her '*freelier rejoice* in that absence' and '*pleas'd* to let him seek danger', in which we begin to catch a tone which is both vital to her and something of an archetype in Shakespeare's idea of evil. The tone is rapturous, exultant; it consists in the glamour which a concentrated will feels itself to possess, and in the possessor's sense of a tumultuous, limitless and stream-lined power to shape and manipulate others without resistance or impediment from their independent beings. It is in this tone that she will reach the height of her ecstasy with

> I have lived
> To see inherited my very wishes,
> And the buildings of my fancy.   [II. i. 188—90]

And it is a spirit which, when it is frustrated and the buildings do
not come out according to the fancy's designs, will give her that
petulant rage — as when Marcius' independent person seems to
get in her way:

> Do as thou list.
> Thy valiantness was mine, thou suck'dst it from me;
> But owe thy pride thyself —   [III. ii. 128—30]

and then that self-consuming fury in which she is steeped when
her will seems finally to have been defeated:

> I would the gods had nothing else to do
> But to confirm my curses. Could I meet 'em
> But once a day, it would unclog my heart
> Of what lies heavy to't.
>
> Anger's my meat; I sup upon myself,
> And so shall starve with feeding. Come, let's go.
> Leave this faint puling and lament as I do,
> In anger, Juno-like.   [IV. ii. 45—8; 50—3]

The intensities of evil involved in this appropriation of Marcius
can hardly be underestimated. But it is evil in a peculiarly
Shakespearean sense, evil as a psychological condition which is
obscene and egotistical, at one moment tumultuously energetic
and at the next locked against itself in frustration, rage or despair.
It always has to do, as with Volumnia here, with what 'unclog'
suggests — a blocking up of those channels through which the
vitalizing powers of the kinetic world might flow up into a mind
not so obsessed with will and ego, not so furiously bent upon
its own social enterprises. We have seen some of its tones already
with Iago, and now these in Volumnia, less workmanlike, more
beglamoured than his, partake of the same nature — his pluming
of his will being akin to her thrilled delight in the power of her
blood. We shall find similar tones in Angelo, in Claudius, in Lady

Macbeth, and in the evil party in *King Lear*, amongst whom Goneril also talks of 'the building in my fancy'[5] being torn down as her own furiously willed social enterprises run up against impediment.

But until we get to the Macbeths and to Goneril and Regan, we are dealing with this Shakespearean evil in a social-specific rather than archetypal setting. In Volumnia it is the ruthlessness of the will and the fury of a rapacious ego; but it is also the idealism and enterprise of her class, with the need and the determination it has to project such fantasies, not just for Iago's individual reason of pluming up his will but for the collective Roman reason of advancing its ethnocentric pride. It is for the ideological satisfaction of her family, her class and then her city that she contemplates the isolated splendour of the heroic son. And it is for this *representative* enterprise that she is rewarded with Rome's acclamation:

> Behold our patroness, the life of Rome. [V. v. 1]

The 'charter to extol her blood' which Volumnia has in the form of her son, is the centre of all these dynamic functions of Rome's life.

His fate is one which we must consider in the light of this comprehensive social demand made of his person. The pathos and anguish of Marcius who suffers this pressure most poignantly is simultaneously a feature of interpersonal life (her practices upon him) and of general social life (the practice upon his helpless person made by Rome's ambitions and ideals). Through her (and she is a perfect intermediary for it) Rome practises its ideals upon him with piercing intensity — its ideal of the aggressive glamour of Stoic endurance:

> You were us'd
> To say extremities was the trier of spirits, [IV. i. 3—4]

and its ideal of unconquerable hardness:

> You were us'd to load me
> With precepts that would make invincible
> The heart that conn'd them. [IV. i. 9—11]

What Rome and Volumnia do to Marcius can take the full force of that word 'load'. And the life is crushed out of him by these received 'precepts' just as surely as it is crushed out of Ophelia when she is loaded with the precepts of her father. Rome's 'precepts' are such as to impose the patterns of this culture on personal and family life with fierce absoluteness allowing no areas of tolerance; and Rome creates, out of the emotions on which it preys, an atrocious fanaticism in terms of which the hero has been asked to shape his emotional life.

We know of course how he fares under this demand; but before discussing that it might be useful to note what it does to his wife. For during the course of the play we see this culture operating on her through Volumnia, just as it always has done upon her husband. What we see is the bullying of the Roman ethic as it goes to work on the timid and insufficiently 'mirthful' young woman; and, contrary to what some rather hopeful critics have said about her resistance to Rome, we see this bullying demand achieve its ultimate success. Virgilia is cowed into silence by its brashness at the start of the play; but by the end Rome has found itself another victim. By then she has eventually been moved to join in Volumnia's vituperations against the mob with

> What then!
> He'd make an end of thy posterity. [IV. ii. 25—6]

And she has also produced as Roman a reason for procreation as one could wish for:

> (I) brought you forth this boy to keep your name
> Living to time. [V. iii. 126—7]

It's a small point; but nothing quite so finally establishes Rome's capacity for defeating 'nature' and canalizing all emotion into an aggressive concern with 'posterity', 'name' and extolling the blood.

4. Menenius and his god

A second feature of the social psychology of Rome involves Marcius in what is virtually a religion, and here it is Menenius, his 'father', who plays the role of chief intermediary. In this appropriation of his being, Rome uses Marcius to salve its conscience and deliver it from its *mauvaise foi* by having him act with what it conceives to be a moral authenticity beyond an ordinary man's daring. Menenius is most apt to use him in this way, and to organize others to do so.

Menenius, most wordly of the patricians, needs contact and identification with Marcius to solace him for the venalities of that worldliness. In his own life he dare not live out the ideal in the unsullied perfection in which he dreams it; he must prevaricate with his ideal and serve his time negotiating with the hated plebeians. But in the life of the ideal 'son', the 'father' can experience vicarious gratification from seeing the ideal lived in all its uncompromising absoluteness. That is why he is always so ready to whoop for joy when the ideal proves itself; and why he feels abject and ashamed of himself when the pressures of daily life have made him faithless to his god:

> We lov'd him, but, like beasts
> And cowardly nobles, gave way unto your clusters,
> Who did hoot him out o' th' city.

> 'Tis no matter;
> If he could burn us all into one coal,
> We have deserv'd it.   [IV. vi. 122–4; 137–9]

Menenius introduces the derisory and the ridiculous into our sense of Rome. His actual view of the plebs is identical with that of the rest of the aristocracy — he loathes them as 'apron men' and 'garlic eaters' — but the story of his prevarication with that opinion, and of his attempts to conceal it behind his politicking, is both frightening and absurd. It is frightening because he is so ignorant of what he, like the rest, has done to Marcius; but it is also absurd because of the ridiculous postures that an absolutism gets itself into when it falls to wordly dealings. He is what is sometimes called a 'realist'; but the ridiculous pathos of his fate is an example of what happens to that sort of realism in a world whose forces are as potent as those in Shakespeare's tragic vision.

The progress of the play splits Menenius into two. He is the patrician idealist who worships his god, and the cynic who pretends to faithlessness (and hence actually is faithless) because the world makes it politic to do so. We are introduced to both versions of him at the start — to the patrician who relishes that heady talk about the Roman state whose course will on, and to the cynic, who wheels out the first of his pieces of instant political wisdom in the form of the fable of the belly. Too many critics have been more impressed than are the plebs by his 'staling' of this 'pretty tale'. But as it is presented here, it comes through as a weary and quite unsuccessful chicane by means of which Menenius is scarcely able to make much progress with the audience he so prides himself on being able to lead: 'you must not think to fob off our disgrace with a tale', 'Y'are long about it'. And the scene which is brought to an end by the arrival of the fire-breathing Marcius is essentially an unproductive nonsense in which Menenius is beginning to make a fool of himself.

With the unprepossessing tribunes he gets himself a second audience, and the banterings of the 'humorous patrician' achieve here a little vitality. But there is still something both sad and comic about this parade of himself as being so well versed in the ways of the world, and about the trivial, verbal victories it enables him to win. In the end this second audience, again unimpressed by him, undermines him rather spiritedly with the accurate summary:

> Come, come, you are well understood to be a perfecter giber for the table than a necessary bencher in the Capitol.
>
> [II. i. 75–7]

It is again a somewhat sad and ridiculous figure, fairly well out of his depth, who shakes off this unresponsive audience with a Pandarus-like accolade for the ladies, in whose company he can relax in a life of quality and indulge his uncomplicated enthusiasm for the wondrous doings of his god.

Many critics of the play are, as I say, inclined to over-estimate Menenius, particularly with regard to the fable of the belly. But when we look at it in its actual and unflattering context we must think otherwise. It is, in reality, the maladroit fumbling of a self-confessed 'man of the world', like those other political theories he is inclined to advance for the occasion when the plebs need 'fobbing off' again — the theory of the diseased limb ('to cure it easy') and the theory of the rough but well-meaning soldier ('bred i' th' wars' and thus 'ill schooled/In bolted language'), neither of which gets very near either to the truth or to political success. What Shakespeare has really done with this character is to create a fine tragi-comic picture of a very ordinary and recognizable way of being 'civilized', 'moderate', and 'realistic', illuminated with the full powers of his derisive under-view in all its helplessness and venality. This double Menenius, with his god and with his faithlessness, and unable to abandon either, is an ordinary man of bad conscience fumbling his way through a world whose dynamics he in no way comprehends. In the end that world plays its last great derisive trick on him, when we see him once more handing out his wisdom to the world — 'he no more remembers his mother now than an eight-year-old horse' — which is a total misrepresentation of a finale that he has missed.

Prior to this we have seen him as religious organizer of the cult of Marcius, but in ways which suggest that it is a very degenerate religion. He has been master of the patricians' revels (with all those interjected acclamations of 'worthy' and ''noble') and harassed PR man for a temperamental star ('mildly', 'calmly', 'temperately'). And the only upshot of it all has been the terrible snub handed out by the son/god to the father/votary who sends the sinner back to Rome with a cracked heart. In a way he knows what he has done by denying the faith — 'When we banished him we respected not them' (the gods) — and he feels the shame of the act. But at no point does the true absurdity of his 'realism' get through to him. We last see him, on the ladies' triumphant return, forgetting the snub, forgetting his own complete misunderstanding of the situation, and getting back delightedly into his old role, organizing the rituals of celebration.

It is all sad-absurd; but that doesn't mean that it doesn't take its toll of the man who must be god to this degenerate religion. He must live as they dare not. He must be in actuality what they can only behold in dream. While they can live in the actual and not very wonderful city of Rome, he must inhabit the institutional fiction of it which they have in their minds. He must excite them with displays of an excellence to which their earthbound souls cannot and dare not aspire. They know the need to live in the actual world; but they also cannot give up the 'religious' necessity for having one man amongst them who is, as Menenius says, 'too noble for the world'. They have no way of understanding the contradictory pull of those two needs and of facing their irreconcilability, but are simply tugged back and forth between acclamation and rejection in what, fundamentally, is a tragic absurdity.

5. The 'integrity' of Marcius

That is how Rome creates, uses, practises upon and frames to its requirements the hero of the play. In him Roman repression and erotic transfer have their most intense focus; and he must extol their blood and salve their consciences. Only in *Hamlet* does Shakespeare ever depict the appropriation of a man by social demand in so complete and hideous a way. But Marcius, unlike Hamlet, has no resistance. He defines himself in the purest Roman terms, never getting outside the structures within which they have shaped him, never getting off the tracks upon which they have set him to move. As a result he never really becomes a 'person' in any proper sense of the word. Inside the ideal Roman there is not a person at all, but 'a kind of nothing', whose much vaunted integrity ('mine own truth') is nothing more than a bundle of precepts of quintessential Romanness, given to him by his mother and accepted by him completely.

It is here that the tragic irony and piercing pathos of the man is to be found. Inside all the vaunted integrity and personal inviolability is a non-person, a mere function of Rome's dynamics. The apparently most authentic man is in fact a near-automaton. The active hero is just a passive product of Rome's repressive praxis. Inside the vast pretence there is nothing. Inside his independence and solitariness ('O me alone', 'Alone I did it') there is extreme dependence and vulnerability. Inside the great man of strength is the 'boy of tears'. The play's gradual 'opening up' of this hero is a terrible and painful thing. We are made to feel Rome's pressures driving piercingly into him and pushing the bewildered victim to his eventual ruin. He owns nothing of himself. His hatreds are compulsive, and his pursuit of honour and his bravery involve little more than a primal, flamboyant violence which is the unconcious expression in him of the thing that Rome has made. His progress through the play has a single, inevitable and compelled thrust about it, as he seeks out an ever more perfect realization of the absoluteness to which he is bred.

Throughout the great central scenes, where the action moves towards his banishment, we experience the naive incomprehension of the ideal Roman as he witnesses the vacillation of actual Romans — his bewildered silences, his equally bewildered eruptions of hatred and sarcasm, his constant desire to turn the world back to those basic Roman polarities of purity and baseness in which alone he can comprehend it. He can only live when these polarities present themselves in all their simplicity — so that the fate of being hurled from the Tarpeian rock is one which he virtually relishes, for in it his fictional Rome would set up an eloquent symbol. And on the famous 'I banish you' he has created the needed extreme, by defining the whole of the actual town as 'non-Rome' so that he alone can confront it in simple magnificence and purity.

This whole movement to 'I banish you' has the force of the inevitable about it. He has gradually cast off so much as 'non-Rome' that only this final singleness can now satisfy him as pure. He has defined the impure in terms of disease ('tetters', 'measles', 'scabs') and dirt ('Bid them wash their faces/And keep their teeth clean'); he has defined it as low-life and domesticity — the life of those who 'sit by th' fire and presume to know/What's done i' th' Capitol'; he has defined it as animality; and he has defined it as agedness, womanishness and immaturity — the immaturity both of boys and of virgins. Gradually, as the ideal Roman spirit has striven to create a world simple enough for it to inhabit with confidence, it has been compelled to reject almost every way of being human — and hence to banish the whole city. There could be no more convincing dramatic presentation of the social genesis of a fanatical ideal.

Once out of Rome he can do nothing but find himself a new Rome, and one which will pick up the force of this single and inevitable movement until he reaches his apotheosis and they have 'godded him'. He then sits in gold, a non-man, an 'engine', a 'battery'. All that is done in Antium merely completes what was started in Rome. A society at war can afford to leave the god-hero undefiled by its faithlessness, because it is thus that it needs his inspiration. It is here that his being can achieve its highest momentum, 'dragon-like' in its 'sovereignty of nature', wanting nothing of a god 'but eternity, and a heaven to throne in'.

It is at this point that Shakespeare pricks the bubble and sends the play to its grotesque ending with his double humiliation at the hands of his mother and then of Aufidius. The sense of the grotesque is made out of what is tragic and ridiculous, for it is both tragic and ridiculous that it should be 'most mortal' to this god-man to be so played upon by his mother, and then chided as a 'boy' by his erstwhile 'lover' and fellow-roughneck. The end of the play is, and is meant to be, ugly and bathetic — with the body of a hero and god stood on by a gangster, who then experiences a tender emotion and begins to mouth elegiac platitudes. Only the admixture of Shakespeare's determined compassion, and the insight into Rome which creates that compassion for the human wreck that Rome has made of Marcius, can keep the whole 'unnatural scene' from being a fit subject for the god's laughter.

But it is the 'unnatural scene' with which we are left at the end, and not with the life of a hero presented in isolation. It is the unnatural scene of Rome, a nature-fearing society, which inevitably produces this grotesque catastrophe out of the workings of its social dynamics. What we are left with is the sense of a culture which can have no knowledge of any 'world elsewhere', and which, demanding and getting complete attachment to its own value-system, poisons the life of itself at the roots. Rome is thus an extreme case of Shakespearean 'culture as Law'; and Marcius is a man made by Law, and by nothing else.

4

The puritan city of Vienna

The dreadful and curious thing is that men, despoiled
and having nothing, must long most for that which
they have not and so, out of the intensity of their
emptiness imagining that they are full, deceive themselves and all the despoiled of the world into their
sorry beliefs. It is the spirit that existing nowhere in
them is forced into their dreams. The Pilgrims, they,
the seed, instead of growing, looked black at the
world and damning its perfections praised a zero in
themselves.

William Carlos Williams: *In the American Grain*[1]

1. Law and fear

Measure for Measure has been dubbed a 'problem play', but
there are two very good reasons why it may have caused
trouble through no fault of its own. Firstly, it is created at that
point in Shakespeare's vision where the comic and the tragic
models overlap, so that it involves a difficult conjunction of
tones — the compassionate and the derisive — which can very
easily be confusing. And secondly (and more simple-mindedly) it
is about both sex and religion — subjects which are not remarkable for summoning forth lucidity and detachment in people who
are asked to consider them in this play's penetrating depth. These
two aspects of the play would, it seems to me, be quite enough to
account for the confusion, offence and annoyance it has often
given its critics and audiences; and to account also for the way in

which so many critics have preferred their own ideas and their own tones and, ignoring the text, have felt licensed to promulgate independent theses about sex and religion — usually ones of a severe Christian-moralistic kind in which the Duke, as a speaker of wisdom, appears as a prominent positive.[2] And it would also account for the fact that many critics, as the exacting experience of the play has overwhelmed them, have found fault with the author, usually for losing patience or stamina after three Acts. I think that it is at least worth experimenting with the view that the difficulties may well be our own, and that the play itself may be all right.

Like *Othello* and *Coriolanus* the play again presents the terrible psychological weaknesses of a culture, and consequently a group of people who are injured by the absence in their world of any terms and values with which it is possible to develop into satisfying adulthood. More like *Coriolanus* than *Othello*, it is again about a repressive culture, and one whose repression creates idealisms and fanaticisms. And, peculiar to itself, it is about that kind of repression which stems from the defensiveness of fear, and which clings fearfully to Law as a defence from what are felt to be the unpalatable aspects of the kinetic world — which include, above all, sexuality.

Something of this sort is often said about Angelo and Isabella; and the damage it does to them is indeed magnificently set forth in the play. But it seems to me to be finely studied in the Duke as well; for he too is both an injured and a frightened man, speaking a language which is often edgily meticulous and laced with strong undercurrents of terror and outrage. I begin with him because he has so often been the centre of the most curious misinterpretations of the play. And the best starting point is his speech on law and order delivered to Friar Thomas at the beginning of the third scene:

> We have strict statutes and most biting laws,
> The needful bits and curbs to headstrong steeds,
> Which for this fourteen years we have let slip;
> Even like an o'ergrown lion in a cave,
> That goes not out to prey. Now, as fond fathers,

Having bound up the threat'ning twigs of birch,
Only to stick it in their children's sight
For terror, not to use, in time the rod
Becomes more mock'd than fear'd; so our decrees,
Dead to infliction, to themselves are dead;
And liberty plucks justice by the nose;
The baby beats the nurse, and quite athwart
Goes all decorum. [I. iii. 19–31]

It is his first major declaration of principle in the play; and I think it is a very ugly one which repays close attention.

The Duke sees justice as a savage animal; also as that kind of metalled power ('bits and curbs') by means of which animal vigour may be held in restraint. He first sees this restraint as required against the vigour of youth ('headstrong steeds'), then, as his excitement mounts, against those even younger (wayward children) and finally, in what surely cannot be other than an absurd, paranoid fantasy, against babies. His vision of a baby beating a nurse because 'strict statutes' have· been neglected would be laughable, if it were not also so frightening. But it is frightening (though still absurd) because it has so suddenly and hysterically issued from him in what has been a very rapid escalation from that commonplace complaint against the rampages of youth on which he started. We would have to be very credulous about Shakespeare's belief in 'order' not to find an element of the grotesque in his anger against the indecorousness of sucklings. And we would have to be very insensitive readers not to perceive the essential rhythm of the speech as consisting in a sudden and unexpected rush towards such anger. What has happened, as the language has slipped from the Duke with its own momentum and sped to this bizarre apotheosis, is that the Duke has been 'carried away'. He has been carried away by a set of irrational terrors, syllogistically linked, which cause this regression from a complaint about the headstrong young to a sterile protest against what is registered in the image of the baby and nurse – the bases of life itself.

As the Duke's fears accelerate away with him he drops a series of tell-tale words to whose implications of violence and cruelty he seems deaf — 'prey', 'stick', 'terror'. And he has also dropped an equally important phrase — 'liberty plucks justice by the nose' — on which we sense, for the first of many times in the play, how much of this man's prickly sense of his own dignity is involved in his idea of order. We begin to sense how he feels himself menaced by mockery and levity; and as we sense that, it is as well to be mindful (even before Lucio appears to cock his snooks) of the high regard that Shakespeare normally has for that kind of comic vitality which subverts dignified and self-elevating designs. Once again what will not be a comic play begins with a *senex*, but one who is handled as untraditionally as was Brabantio. By the time this speech is done we have been taken deep into a realistic, psychological examination of him. We have noticed a certain waspishness in the first scene; and a tendency to speech-making, disclaimers notwithstanding. And now we begin to see these things rooted in the psychology of a small man from whom there can issue a violence much bigger than himself.

2. A man despoiled

This parody of a comic play develops the psychological portrait of the *senex* to a formidable degree — a *senex* who will never get out of the way to let the pattern of release unfold, but who bustles around within the enclosing walls of the city driving the messages of its Law into the fettered minds of its inhabitants. His next appearance is as the comforter of Juliet, and we get here another important aspect of his involvement in the repressive and the repressed — the offensive externality with which he conducts himself in personal exchange. His very disguise is in itself offensive, bringing as it does a lie into the heart of personal and painful disclosures and confronting the need and vulnerability of a suffering person with deception. And his language too has this externality about it, with the cool formality of his self-announcement, his careful self-justification, and his emphasis on the license to which his (false) religious credentials entitle him. All this makes his wish to look into the torments of the imprisoned smack of insolent prying, and there is a similar insolence in the cold comfort for the wretched Juliet which he inserts between his various arid statements about ministration and instruction:

> I'll teach you how you shall arraign your conscience,
> And try your penitence, if it be sound
> Or hollowly put on.   [II. iii. 21—3]

His words never flow in discourse with Juliet. Instead, there is only the withdrawn calculation of a tight-lipped man, the hallmark of whose attentions to others is crassness. There is a zero of emotional response in him, a moral philistinism which is felt as radically offensive. This philistinism, an ignorance about the human mind and emotions, creates the offensive ease with which he assumes the right to 'minister', 'teach', 'try' and 'instruct', all of which are major human activities requiring the most profound scruple. But everything about the Duke's language and behaviour declares that he has no sense whatever of what such scruple would mean.

We next see him offering similarly barren ministrations to the similarly wretched Claudio, with the famous 'Be absolute for death . . .' The speech has often been seen as containing a severe but poignantly admirable Christian-Stoic wisdom, but it looks to me like a continuation of Shakespeare's psychological portrait of this cold, petty and frightened man. For the speech is exactly what would be taken to be a great wisdom, severe but poignantly admirable, by such a man.[3] As he enforces this wisdom upon Claudio with all his measured, argumentative insistence, he is basing his justification for repression on a contempt for the possibilities of life. The speech offends against every possible kind of vigour and any imaginable positive value; and it offers a self-abnegating indifference as though it were a high form of acceptance or spiritual resolve. It plays a slick game with one's sense of life's difficulties and disappointments, and if one seriously thought that Shakespeare was 'behind' it, one could only react with something of Samuel Johnson's distaste:

> I cannot without indignation find *Shakespear* saying, that *death is only sleep*, lengthening out his exhortation by a sentence which in the *Friar* is impious, in the reasoner is foolish, and in the poet trite and vulgar.[4]

But the triteness and vulgarity belong of course to the character, not the author, and the earnestness with which this man of books offers them as wisdom to a young and suffering mind is a further index of his desolation. He is exactly what Williams called a 'despoiled' man; and as first Juliet and then Claudio give him thanks for his doctrine, we are seeing how 'men, despoiled and having nothing' may 'deceive themselves and all the despoiled of the world into their sorry beliefs'.

By now the Duke is fully launched on his projects for the correction of the world, undeflected from his designs by any knowledge that he would have to geld and splay all the youth of the city in order to do it. It is the juristic conquest of nature which he is about, in his Socratic way — though it is not a matter of wilful brutality, for he remains, in this desolated Socratic fashion, a well-meaning man. But his designs and practices are inhuman because they depend for their realization on a perpetual disregard for the moral, even the sentient, status of others. He has a quick facility for absolving himself from normal moral hesitation ('the doubleness of the benefit defends the deceit from reproof') and, with the assurance that this gives him, he finds it easy to commit any kind of violation on his fellow beings, regarding them as objects to be organized into the patterns he has ideated. In the name of the realization of his fantasies, his whimsically inhuman dreams of order, law, decorum and dignity, he feels himself licensed to lie, manipulate and bamboozle, responsive only to the neat execution of his designs. And so he works his way steadily through the play to the last grotesque scene, where all his fantasies come true in a rush of manipulations and lever-pullings, by means of which he imagines that he has corrected the world's waywardness, tempered his justice with an admirable mercy, and brought the play to its moment of festive social reintegration.

It is ghastly; but there have been many readers of the play who have not found it so. They have not only found the Duke admirable, but so admirable indeed as to share only with Prospero the distinction of having a play all to himself where, as nowhere else in Shakespeare, a single character is placed above all dramatic comment. Perhaps it is his 'inscrutability' which does it, enabling

him to satisfy a need which has its role to play in the formation
of much religious belief and which may still have a strong,
residual existence even in non-religious minds — I mean the need
to believe that the apparent contingency of the world is only
apparent, and that behind its contingent appearances, virtually
imperceptible to the clouded gaze of mortals, stands an inscrut-
able proclivity to order, of which it is wonderfully relieving to
have evidence. However it may be, an uncritically approving view
of the Duke has been widespread, so it may be necessary to detail
here those aspects of his performance in the latter part of the
play which would seem to me to disqualify him from having any
such role, and to make the business of the 'release', 'order' or
'reconciliation' which he leads at the end of the play one of
savage parody.

There is, then, the terrifying casualness with which he sees
Pompey consigned to what Elbow assures him will be his death;
the prickliness with which his offended dignity makes him so
irked by Lucio's chatter about the Duke's alleged 'feeling for the
sport'; his brittle conviction of his own virtue, and of the crosses
it makes him bear; and the annoyance it is to him to feel that
other people may have a less exalted view of his severe excellences. Then there is the spiritual poverty out of which comes his
warning to Mariana to beware of the emotionally rousing effects
of music; his cruel impatience with Isabella's natural grief at her
brother's 'death'; the barbarity with which he treats Barnardine,
whose head may be so casually removed, and who may be
dismissed with a sense of triumph as 'unfit to live or die'; and the
delight with which he perceives that Barnadine cannot upset his
plans because the head of Ragozine may be sliced off with equal
facility — 'O, 'tis an accident that heaven provides!'. Then we
have that callous self-importance which will let him keep the
happy truth from Isabella until he feels ready to deliver it; and
the tortuous prolonging of the agony which he permits in the
final scene — a scene in which the unpleasantness of his severity is
exceeded only by the unpleasantness of his mercy and pardoning,
which are caricatures of real generosity, lacking in all amplitude
and vitiated by the sense we get of his projection of a flattering
picture of himself thereby as merciful in his moments of power.

The grating quality of this last scene is not a product of Shakespeare's having lost interest and limped to a convenient finish. It is something which makes me think of Kafka, who was also a master of the mingled pain and comedy of the grotesque. Kafka's great story *In The Penal Settlement* has a lot to say about *Measure for Measure*. In the long agony of this final scene, the idea of festive social regeneration is subjected to parodic derision as we watch the man of Law carve out the designs of his fantasy on the sentient flesh.

Such, it seems to me, is the career of a man whose psychology Shakespeare has presented with beautiful consistency throughout the play. In him, the living flexibility of a stable man is replaced by the thin determination of a frightened one, and the determination runs, straight, direct and unimpeded as no live mind can, towards the end that he has willed. But we must be clear as to Shakespeare's difficult and complex tone, because, for all the parody-element in the play, for all the laughable and derisory quality of much that the Duke does and says, nevertheless this small and cold man is not put before us as a butt for satire or ridicule. We are made to experience the mental life of him too keenly for dismissive gestures, and are made too uncomfortable in his commonplace presence to afford that kind of scorn which is full of confidence and free from pain. He is not just Adam Overdo, for all that he shares that Justice's distaste for the creatural-physical world and his desire to straighten out the bendings and undulations of the world in a pattern of nice lines. He shares with Angelo and Isabella certain characteristics which may be called 'puritan', but he is a more commonplace and more depressing kind of puritan than they — not a zealot, with a strong passional nature locked behind bars in dread, but sober, cautious, businesslike, philistine and well-meaning. He is a man (to revert to Williams' word) 'despoiled', for whom the energy, mobility and variety of the kinetic world are a perpetual threat and a perpetual offence.

I can see no other way of taking the Duke. My reading of him is 'naturalistic'; but it must be so because the play's psychological realism is so intense. The shaping presence in the play of a conventional comic model does not mean that we should simply

ignore the countervailing pull of this psychological realism;
rather that we should experience both forms in all their contrariety and see how this great play lives upon their clashing
tones. The case of the Duke gives us the most extreme and
continuous example of this clashing. The whole meaning of him is
carried by the way in which the acrid irony of Shakespeare's
'realism' is made to play its havoc with the confidences and
assurances about social man and his codes which the comic model
traditionally embodies.

3. Fanatics

The two other puritans, Angelo and Isabella, have not caused so
much trouble. Both are psychological studies of minds in the grip
of an icy zealotry which is repressed passion, and it has been well
understood how Shakespeare makes us experience their mental
life with poignant closeness. Their confrontations in the second
and fourth scenes of Act Two are among the very greatest things
in Shakespeare. They are not unlike, both in kind and intensity,
the closest scene between Hamlet and his mother — where again
there will be the desperate fight that each has with the other and
with himself. A brief consideration of the two characters will
complete my analysis of the play's dealings with the spirit of
puritanism as it goes about its tragic-derisive critique of order and
Law.

In my discussion of Volumnia in the last chapter, I began to
suggest that there was a peculiarly Shakespearean idea of evil,
seen as consisting essentially in the ruthlessness of the will. The
obscenity of her ego-mania had its relation with what was there in
Iago's pluming up of his will, and was a social-specific example of
that idea of evil which reaches its archetypal state in the
Goneril-Regan-Edmund party of *King Lear* and in the Macbeths.
Angelo is another member of this complex, but he introduces
something which was not there with Volumnia and Iago, but
something which is vital to an understanding of this Shakespearean complex as a whole. This is the sense of unutterable
misery and final impotence which this evil contains.

I hardly think the character of Angelo could have been better handled. It is a masterly achievement of psychological sympathy that this character, even at its most vicious, should, without sentimentality, be capable of calling forth above all things an acutely painful sense of his *unhappiness*. A less tactful, less scrupulous, less compassionate mind could not have made Angelo's criminality anything but vile – unless it sentimentalized him or approached him with an over-warm rhetoric. The fine thing here is that no such sentimentality is required to keep our sympathies actively engaged. We thus get what we will get again with Macbeth – an unsentimental compassion for the unhappiness of a mind which is cut off from the sustaining vitality of nature by having, in Angelo's case, forfeited itself to what he calls 'the manacles of the all-binding law'.

This is a matter of individual psychology; but the interior life of Angelo is again something which is a part of a specific social context. Angelo is an integral part of a strict hierarchy of obedience in Vienna, running down from Duke to Executioner, through Deputy, Lord, Provost and Constable. His first words in the play are 'Always obedient . . .'; and just as he views himself as a passive instrument of the Duke's will, so he will expect the same submissive instrumentality from those who stand beneath him in the structure of social command. To him this structure of command is an impersonal system which an individual may not influence. Thus 'It is the law, not I . . .'; and thus the anxious Provost is admonished that his personal fears and worries are irrelevant to the working of the system: 'Do you your office, or give up your place'. And thus too the law's victims are spoken of in a tone ('See you the fornicatress be remov'd') and with a nomenclature ('Your brother is a forfeit of the law') which make them mere objects of which the system will efficiently dispose.

But Angelo does not experience this impervious structure of command as barbarous. Its impersonality is invested in his mind with the excellent qualities of dispassionateness and neutrality; and also with a sense of the required firmness of discipline which is admirable and difficult of achievement. All this means that the crushing instrumentality that the system demands of its servants is given a familiar and menacing emotional veneer which has been finely observed by Shakespeare. The exacting discipline is seen as a test of character ('Let there be some more test made of my mettle . . .') which then brings its magnificent rewards, without the servant having to feel that his modesty has been defiled ('. . . Before so noble and so great a figure/Be stamp'd upon it'). The long wait for the right to power, the declared unassumingness of the modest servant: both make power, when it eventually comes, seem like a merited reward. And because merited, therefore peculiarly licensed. Angelo is dehumanized by the process — the metal to be stamped, in the image he used — but that brute fact is beglamoured for him as it gives way to a sense of his own satisfying modesty, and a sense of the glory which can be achieved nonetheless, when so humble an instrument proves itself capable of the most exacting tasks. I think this goes to the social-psychological heart of many kinds of puritanism and zealotry. We are watching the social genesis of a characteristic mixture of self-subjection and a restrained thirst for eventual glory, in which first self-righteousness and then ruthlessness are created.

And ruthlessness it certainly is. We do not see Angelo again until the next Act; and by then he is using the Duke's language for law — 'fear', 'terror', 'birds of prey' — but with a cold insistence which far exceeds in passional power the Duke's virtually 'accidental' use of such words. This insistence is revealed again when we see that he knows, as the well-meaning Duke didn't, that the law is necessarily imperfect, that a jury may contain 'a thief or two/Guiltier than him they try'. But while the Duke's well-meaning ignorance would never have given him such an insight, Angelo, in possession of that knowledge that ought to be humanizing, remains undeflected from his course. The consequent violence of which such ruthlessness is capable (since no new insight could now make it hesitate) is caught in the peculiarly ugly and inapposite image in which he expresses himself on the subject of the law's imperfections:

> The jewel that we find, we stoop and take't,
> Because we see it; but what we do not see
> We tread upon, and never think of it.   [II. i. 24–6]

Either way, seized or trodden on, the 'jewel' will see no light, and
it is no surprise when he exits from the scene with the easy,
casual violence of

> Hoping you'll find good cause to whip them all.
>
> [II. i. 131]

Between here and the denouement there are the scenes with
Isabella; and in the first of these, before he gives his sensual race
the rein, we have the stubborn instrumentality of his 'It is the
law, not I' and his 'that I cannot do', and also the apotheosis of
the disciplinarian's cold zealotry. This comes in his big speech on
the newly-wakened law, which again picks up the Duke's words
and again gives them new insistence:

> The law hath not been dead, though it hath slept.
> Those many had not dar'd to do that evil
> If the first that did th'edict infringe
> Had answer'd for his deed. Now 'tis awake,
> Takes note of what is done, and, like a prophet,
> Looks in a glass that shows what future evils —
> Either now or by remissness new conceiv'd,
> And so in progress to be hatch'd and born —
> Are now to have no successive degrees,
> But here they live to end.   [II. ii. 90—9]

It is a kind of *raptus* or ecstasy. While the idea of the law as an
animal of terror had slipped from the Duke and 'carried him
away' with a momentum of its own, the awakening to supreme
power of this evil magus is one over which Angelo keeps his
control. It is a cold exhilaration in which power, felt as the
supreme mystery, is seen to be able to work its way down to the
quick of nature's processes of generation ('conceiv'd' —
'hatch'd' — 'born') and stop them short.

That is the extreme of Angelo's evil, and of 'the manacles of
the all-binding law' set up in determined hostility to the natural
world. But the strength that Angelo dreams in himself at this
moment of black fantasy, generated only by the will, has, like
Macbeth's, no real durability. It is a strength which is really a lack,
a power which thrives upon continual repressions which cannot

feed him. It is immediately after this that the hardened will begins to break, and Angelo finds himself inundated with Such sense that my sense breeds with it', and the need to 'feast' upon Isabella's eyes. The thought-model out of which this has been made is similar to that which we have noticed in *Othello*. There the thin skin of Venice's elegance, which refused all recognition of the under-nature of the foul toads, could only feel itself to have been befouled and contaminated as that world made its demands. So here the brittle puritan mind can only experience the movement of sense and breeding in loathsome forms:

> but it is I
> That, lying by the violet in the sun,
> Do as the carrion does, not as the flow'r,
> Corrupt with virtuous season . . .
>
> . . . Having waste ground enough,
> Shall we desire to raze the sanctuary,
> And pitch our evils there? O, fie, fie, fie!
> What dost thou, or what art thou, Angelo?
> Dost thou desire her foully for those things
> That make her good?   [II. ii. 165–8; 170–5]

It is the helplessness, puzzlement and self-disgust of that which must make us talk of Angelo's *unhappiness* rather than merely of his evil. His helplessness before what he will call 'the strong and swelling evil/Of my conception' (where again we see that 'nature' can now only come through to him as befouled); the helplessness which will make him look back on his entire Law-bound life as a sterility ('sere and tedious'); and the helplessness of his belated knowledge that 'Blood, thou art blood' — all this registers not just viciousness but also misery. And it registers it powerfully enough to make the impression subsist throughout all the absurd, pathetic twistings and plottings to which he will resort when, feeling himself dispossessed of 'necessary fitness', he fights for a pleasure which he thinks will redeem him from the agony of his own barrenness. All his subsequent talk of 'filthy vices', 'saucy sweetness' and 'the destin'd livery' of feminine sexuality is felt to stem from this unbearable knowledge he now has of himself. He

is, like the Duke, 'despoiled'; but, unlike the Duke, he is made to
know it, to feel keenly how it

> unshapes me quite, makes me unpregnant
> And dull to all proceedings.   [IV. iv. 18—19]

At the end it is still his misery we feel as the busy Duke
catches him too in the 'Alexandrian net' of his Utopia. Once the
truth is out Angelo collapses immediately into resignation before
the 'dread lord'. He begs for 'sequent death', but has a marriage
foisted on him instead. He craves death again, but receives a
pardon as nasty as the marriage, and a brute order to 'Look that
you love your wife'. Understandably he doesn't risk another
word. He has lived by the Law, glimpsed something else for once
in his life in a black and befouled form, and now is consigned by
the Law to live by the Law again. To his pain is added this
derisory fate, which takes away from him even the dignity which
he might have achieved in confession and a noble readiness for
punishment. It is as unsentimental and terrible a portrait as one
could wish for, of a life prevented at every stage by Vienna's
preposterous belief that the social world will be made beautiful if
only nature can be stopped working.

Isabella is simpler. The literature of the Jacobean age abounds
in such maidens, daughters of Cynthia and Britomart engaged in
an heroic, defensive struggle for virtue in a fallen world of
blackness and corruption. But none of these heroines, except
Middleton's Beatrice-Joanna, ever emerges as fully as does Isabella
from a purely iconographic function in a myth of Purity and
Depravity. In her, Shakespeare has embodied the same sceptical
view of the idea of heroic and clamourously declared chastity as
did Montaigne in the great essay *Upon Some Verses of Vergil:*

> When I heare women brag to have so virgin-like a will and
> colde minde, I but laugh and mock at them. They recoile too
> farre backwarde.[5]

Montaigne, who disliked the idea of purity for its 'fierceness', and
who thought that real virtue was 'a pleasant and buxome quality',
saw in this kind of chastity a 'cruel contempt of our natural
store', which, given the nature of the actual world, could never

achieve its will unless 'nature herself were gelded'. Or, as Shakespeare made Pompey put it, unless the law intends to 'geld and splay all the youth of the city'.

It is with this rare, sceptical and not at all uncharitable calm, that Shakespeare handles the fatally tempting Jacobean theme, of glorious chastity in a world of corruption, that centres in Isabella. The portrait begins with the presence of the comic model doing its work against her, for her first appearance with Francisca is remarkable not only for Isabella's chilling desire for 'a more strict restraint' than even a nunnery can offer, but also for the familiar ripple of comic ridicule that attends the announcement of the sisterhood's elaborate rules:

> When you have vow'd, you must not speak with men
> But in the presence of the prioress;
> Then, if you speak, you must not show your face,
> Or, if you show your face, you must not speak.
>
> [I. iv. 10—13]

It sets up the same kind of expectation as do the vows, statutes and observances of the Lords of Navarre; and from this critical perspective, intensified by the play's turn into the tragic-derisive rather than the festive-comic, the figure of Isabella never escapes.

It is not of course simply her chastity which is criticized; nor does it quite register the real centre of Shakespeare's critique to draw attention to the often-quoted passage which suggests her repressed eroticism:

> were I under the terms of death,
> Th' impression of keen whips I'd wear as rubies,
> And strip myself to death as to a bed
> That longing have been sick for, ere I'd yield
> My body up to shame.   [II. iv. 100—4]

It is not the chastity itself so much as the clamourousness with which it seems to her a sufficient proof of excellence that alerts Shakespeare's suspicion (as it does Montaigne's); and what is really wrong with Isabella is not to be got from the admittedly alarming notes of that single speech but from her entire performance.

She does make a number of valuable statements in the play on the subjects of human pride, cruelty, hypocrisy and vulnerability, and does, with the assistance of Lucio's promptings, put up a vigorous resistance to Angelo. But there is something which runs even through the best of her, even through her bravest declarations and denunciations, which vitiates the human quality of them too and binds in this part of her performance with her more obvious hysterics and waspishnesses. There is always something high-pitched, shrill, 'with an outstretch'd throat', something overly sententious, even in her better moments, something which makes Angelo's 'Why do you put these sayings upon me?' contain not a little of my own feelings when confronted with her in this mood. She runs so quickly to assertive, epigrammatic wisdom as the mode in which her morality flows best that I detect always something fervid and overwrought in her. She speaks, or shrieks, in these moments as though with a compulsive relish for the moral certainties she is enunciating, and as though with a brittle need to have such certainties, and with a certain rejoicing when an opportunity for their promulgation presents itself. When brave *sententiae* are called for she knows her part, and leaps upon it with relish determined to play it to the full.

I think that we hold back, with a kind of embarrassment, even from the insights that these pronouncements contain – the 'man, proud man' tone is a rhetoric which makes one wince a little. It works at a level of thin and heightened generality which can never be quite adequate to any specific situation which might prompt it. It jars slightly in the specifics of dialogue and confrontation, as though Isabella can only speak with fluency when relieved of the burden of entering into the flux and reciprocity of interpersonal dialogue. And it connects with her chastity – its clamorous heroics and the suppressed passion which it all seems so shrilly to govern – because we wonder why she resorts to these precepts instead of looking Angelo in the eyes.

The famous 'more than our brother is our chastity' is as terrible as it is, not so much because of what is said but because of the way it is said – without sorrow, without a sense of tragic conflict, but with an air of exultant proclamation. And the same is true of her reaction to Claudio's plea that she should trade her

virginity for his life. It is possible to prefer an honourable death
before a dishonoured life and to make the idea of chastity
central to the honour involved; but not in these tones – not
when the reaction to 'Sweet sister, let me live' is a self-righteous
rant about bestiality and incest, a side-glance at the purity of her
family-tree, and an exhibition of petulant contempt:

> Die; perish. Might but my bending down
> Reprieve thee from thy fate, it should proceed.
>
> [III. i. 145–6]

It is this 'proclaiming' quality of the chastity-hysteric which
interests Shakespeare, and which impresses him no more than it
does Montaigne. No wonder Isabella shares the Duke's predilec-
tion for the elaborately staged and wrought *coups-de-théâtre* of
his miraculous Justice-bringing. And no wonder she ends the play,
in the derisive comedy of the last scene, with such good, vamp
acting in the name of Virtue. Mariana picks the right assistant
when a second big plea for Justice and Mercy is called for:

> O Isabel, will you not lend a knee?   [V. i. 440]

And we know of course that she will be delighted to proffer the
services of that much-practised joint.

4. Introjection and resistance

Such are the manacles which this all-binding puritan law puts on
the minds of the three main characters of the play, so that they
'deceive themselves . . . into their sorry beliefs'. But to 'deceive
themselves *and all the despoiled of the world* . . .'? The play deals
with this also, in those who introject some or all of Vienna's basic
mores, chief among whom are Claudio, Juliet, Mariana and
Escalus; and also in those who resist – Lucio, Barnardine,
Pompey – but whose resistance is sadly delimited by the suffoc-
ating atmosphere of this city whose central image is given to us in
a dungeon.

What we get in Claudio, Juliet, Mariana and Escalus is the
reduction of ordinary human 'decency' to a pathetically inadequate charade by the pressures of this awful social praxis. In

Claudio an un-Viennese knowledge of life's preciousness flickers for a moment in the prison speech about the 'sensible warm motion' and the 'delighted spirit', and the speech plays a big part in creating the play's continuously tender sense of the vulnerability of that preciousness in a world that is so hasty with the axe. But such thoughts do not run deep in Claudio. The man who, as prisoner, complained of 'too much liberty' was already deep in Vienna's psychosis, introjecting the nature-hatred which is Vienna's norm in the image of 'rats that ravin down their proper bane'. The abjection which is wrought in him so swiftly by the Duke's 'Be absolute for death' sees Vienna triumph over the 'delighted spirit' with awful ease. And it is the same with Juliet, whose entire role is taken up with confession of sin, abjection, readiness to learn penitence from the moribund Duke, and something of Vienna's nastiest tone — *pleasure* taken in guilt and renunciation:

> I do repent me as it is an evil,
> And take the shame with joy.   [II. iv. 35–6]

The romantic young have clearly not escaped the trammels of their city's culture without severe macerations.

Neither have the 'ordinary', 'decent' middle-aged. Mariana is 'always bound to' the Friar-Duke who has been giving the consolations of philosophy and some warnings against music to her patiently suffering soul; and her passive participation in the bed-trick, and in the elaborate unfolding of it, fully deserves the irreverent commentary it gets from Lucio. Her readiness to suffer herself to a standstill — till she becomes a 'marble monument' — has much of Isabella's gift for shallow histrionics about it; and the farcical wedding into which she enters at the end is a triumph of mediocrity getting its laws and forms in order.

And Escalus is perhaps saddest of them all. This ordinary instrument of the civil service is pathetically out of his depth in Vienna. He lurches ineffectually back and forth between consent to Angelo's schemes for general whippings and a contrary desire to play the genial Justice Clement. Just as Menenius' clown-bantering could cut no ice in Rome and had about it none of the comic strength of its origins, so Escalus gets buffeted about the

streets by an unsavoury bunch of persons who can talk faster
than he can. One of the excuses he is moved to offer on behalf of
Claudio is that he had 'a most noble father'; and when such
powerful arguments as this fail with the determined Angelo he
tends to have recourse to pious hopes – 'forgive us all'. What he
calls his 'modesty' prevents him, as far as we see on the stage,
from labouring his decency quite as hard as he claims on the
prisoner's behalf; and he is certainly not slow to lay by his
gentleness and call for 'bolts' and touzings joint by joint on the
rack when the dignity of the State and its Officers is slandered by
a turbulent 'priest'. By the revelations of the last scene he
confesses himself 'amaz'd', but the quality of his astonishment is
not such as to prevent him setting store, in his final words, by
learning, wisdom and 'temper'd judgment' – this after the play
has let him witness the catastrophes wrought by bookish and
emotionally restrained men. Critics who have agreed with the
Duke in finding 'much goodness' in the man would seem to have
missed the sustained disrespect for his ineffectuality, obsequious-
ness and sheer foolishness which Shakespeare has clearly built
into the play.

That is one way of living in Vienna – by being 'decent'; but
the play has seen finely how, in the stifling atmosphere of the
city, ordinary decencies inevitably involve introjections and
macerations which reduce the decent to, at best, passive
mediocrity and, at worst, active complicity. It is only in those who
are not decent that anything of life is to be found at all. The rest
of the city is what common vitality can only be when it is
debarred from decency by the latter's degeneration. Nature,
banished from Vienna, comes back on an old jade. Lucio and
Barnardine are not noble embodiments of the 'teeming foison' of
which the former once speaks; and Pompey certainly isn't. But
they have a will to live which is greater than that of anyone so far
discussed, for all that Vienna deflects it into a fantastic, an animal
and a putrid form. They are pot-bound versions of nature's
kinesis; but that still means they have something which clayey
vessels do not.

Pompey, whom one may take as representative of the urban
jungle, has the valiant opportunist heart of one that fancies

himself 'a poor fellow that would live'; and, in a world which may
suddenly shackle him 'at the wheels of Caesar' and then require
him to cut off heads to redeem him from his gyves, his trade in
the pleasures of the tavern and the whore-house hardly seems the
grossest of crimes. It is at any rate not a life which will prevent
even this undistinguished mind from the excellence of that 'poor
opinion' wherein he echoes Montaigne on gelding and splaying; or
from what, in this puritan city, sounds like the rather accurate
wise-crack about pro-usury laws being more harmful to 'merriment' than is his life. He is no Falstaff; but the Falstaff who
entered Vienna would have been compelled to fall to his prayers
long ago unless he had developed these more devious, less
prepossessing manners.

One must feel similarly about the remarkable Barnardine. He
has a strong symbolic presence in the play, a creature from
Vienna's lower depths, dismissed by the Duke as 'unfit to live or
die' — which puts him, whether he likes it or not, quite outside
what Vienna is prepared to regard as a human being at all. So the
fact that he holds tenaciously and without fuss to the continuance of his creatural existence is a not entirely unadmirable
response. Compassion alone could not have created so strong and
unsentimental a symbol of the life that Vienna crushes. It is
Shakespeare's most profound and sceptical wit, with the element of
derision fully at work within it, that makes Barnardine's simple
refusal to have anything to do with Vienna's idiot law so much more
telling a thing than (say) the clamorous protestations of Isabella.
When he rustles his straw, more of the play's critique of the
Law-bound is created than would be by a bookful of her noblest
precepts.

And then there is the equally profound wit of the creation of
Lucio — a wit which again resists any temptation to believe that,
in a culture of such comprehensive and aggressive banality, the
delighted spirit might still exist in unmodified excellence. He is
not excellent; but shifty, shallow, pranking, boyish and, of
course, immoral. But too few critics have had the charity to see
that such are the highest forms that a real vitality, a real wit and a
real potential will take in Viennese circumstances. There is a lot

that is worth having in his simple preference for 'the foppery of freedom' as against 'the morality of imprisonment'; and also in his braggart wise-cracks about grace and the ten commandments which, in Vienna, support a barbarism. And there is a good, quick knowledge of that barbarism in his witty and accurate remarks about the 'snow-broth' Angelo and 'the hideous law'.

In addition to his wit there are also notes of real kindness and lyrical tenderness which are heard only from him. His capacity for knowing what is beautiful and precious in life is momentary, but real — caught in a remark about Claudio:

> thy head stands so tickle on thy shoulders that a milkmaid, if
> she be in love, may sigh it off,   [I. ii. 165—6]

in his rebuke to the Duke:

> what a ruthless thing is this in him, for the rebellion of a
> codpiece to take away the life of a man   [III. ii. 106—7]

and in his response to Isabella's weeping for her 'dead' brother:

> O pretty Isabella, I am pale at mine heart to see thine eyes so
> red.   [IV. iii. 148]

This latter contrasts nicely with the Duke's own response which precedes it:

> Command these fretting waters from your eyes
> With a light heart.   [IV. iii. 143—4]

There is a fitful and sentimental decency in him, as well as a sceptical wit; and there is also that urgency, openness and unabashedness (contrasting well, for example, with Escalus' fatal modesty) that comes out in his urging of Isabella to press harder her case for Claudio. He is 'fantastic', he is 'wanton', he is 'frivolous'; but in Vienna such things are rare and valuable tokens, as the festive comedies will again remind us, of profound and life-giving impulses which Law cannot contain. His dancing impudence and unseriousness in the last scene are still carrying the best protest that anyone makes against the macabre procedures which are there grinding to their unlovely apotheosis. And when

he is captured by the Duke's marriage-machine, the philistinism
of Order has in some sense done its worst deed, for his on-going
and spontaneous eccentricity was the biggest guarantee that the
play presented against the triumph of order over the delighted
spirit.

5. *The play as a 'whole'*

Cannot this be taken 'whole'? Is it not possible to see the
coherence of the vision that has created it? And to see how that
coherence consists in a conjunction of derision and compassion
which Shakespeare makes by parodying the comic model, thereby
keeping in our minds the accommodation to life's variousness
which Vienna makes impossible? It is 'difficult', because the
clashings of the tones of derision and compassion are hard to
keep in chromatic balance. It is also difficult because easier
ways of reading it lie to hand: vote for the Duke or for Isabella,
to name only the most likely candidates for partisanship, and the
complexity of the whole thing need trouble one no further. But if
we decline to vote, the deadliness, but at the same time the
absurdity, of the Duke's coerced Utopia will come out in all its
clarity.

The play comes fittingly to its dramatic completion in the last
scene – a ritual of the despoiled, presided over by the Duke's
well-meaning ignorance. The corrective rationality of the Socratic
spirit here produces its triumph, as a suffering populace is
marshalled into order with ever less to say for its sorry self. It is
grotesque and laughable; but I find that the play can combine
these qualities with the deeply compassionate sense of waste and
loss which receives its fullest expression in the great figure of
Angelo. It is the last, nasty, ludicrous word to be said about
Vienna that even the tragedy of Angelo's destitution is nipped in
the bud. His misery must continue, smiled on as a great
redemption by his peers, who thereby save themselves from
having to witness the traumatic destruction of all that their
puritanism is. The play, with Angelo at its centre, is a
Schopenhauerian tragi-comedy *par excellence*:

our life must contain all the woes of tragedy, and yet we cannot even assert the dignity of tragic characters, but, in the broad detail of life, are inevitably the foolish characters of a comedy.

[*op. cit.*, p. 322]

5

The comedy
of Troilus and Cressida

Behold distraction, frenzy, and amazement,
Like witless antics, one another meet.   [V. iii. 85—6]

1. A problem of tone

Like *Measure for Measure, Troilus and Cressida* has been a
'problem play' obstinately refusing to cohere, for many critics,
into a single dramatic experience. And for even more it has
obstinately refused to conform to their general sense of the vision
and values of the mature Shakespeare. It has seemed disjointed
and disconcerting in itself, and also something of an intractable
oddity in the whole *oeuvre*. Opinions have differed wildly, with
very few critics giving a sense of being at ease in this particular
part of the Shakespearean world.

The great exception is Rossiter, who sees the play clear and
whole and is fully on terms with what he sees. Rossiter was the
greatest of all critics of Shakespearean tragi-comedy. He was a
critic for whom the idea of tragi-comedy was the key to the
whole business, the key to that uniquely Shakespearean vision
and those uniquely Shakespearean tones which have baffled and
offended less tough-minded readers and grated upon the ears of
those who like major drama to be less full of mischief. Rossiter
relished irreverence, and was quite clear that it was not the same
thing as nihilism. He relished contradiction, and knew that it was
not confusion. And he knew that Shakespeare was, with
Montaigne, the greatest Renaissance master of that vigorous
scepticism which strikes life out of the observation of paradox,

discontinuity and contradiction. In his lecture on *Shakespeare and Wordsworth* he defined one of the great creative capacities of Shakespeare's mind as:

> that capacity, behind wit, of being able to catch at things from abruptly contrasted points of view, and to snap them together in a pun or a paradox.[1]

He knew that this created a poetry which, unlike that of Wordsworth, could always be read without 'a willing suspension of — derision'. And he knew, and knew clearly and without strain, that the mind which included the perspective of the derisive in its sense of things was a *more* and not a *less* humane mind than that which had no room for it — more humane because more capacious, tougher, less sentimental.

The critic who saw Shakespeare's humanity and creativity like this has written the finest essay on *Troilus and Cressida* that we have. He is the one critic for whom this play is a vindication of his general view of Shakespeare, not an uncomfortable exception. And that is because he has gone closer than anyone else to the essential tones of the Renaissance paradoxical mind, and particularly to that strong, comic tone which includes the element of derision. In my view, an incapacity to get into this tone and absorb its powers without strain accounts more than any other single factor for misreadings of Shakespeare — which tend to make him more solemn, more reverent, more 'Christian', more conservative and more orthodox-Elizabethan than he is. And such misreadings have often revealed their maladroitness most spectacularly when at work on this play. Rossiter has this tone right, and sees its crucial importance not only in the mind of Shakespeare but also, so it is intimated, in the mind of Montaigne and in the mind of Donne, many of whose most joyously derisive verses are still too often handled with the same solemnity which has produced the poorer readings of this play.

So, for *Troilus and Cressida*, we need to learn this tone, which might perhaps best be done by having an eye on Montaigne and Donne for assistance. And we need to see how, structurally, it arises from the same vision which makes the other plays, remembering as we do so that we will encounter something of the tone again, with its high and fierce comic exuberance, in the two great tragedies of the traumatic, *Hamlet* and *King Lear*. We need to appreciate fully how the scurrilous, the irreverent, the wanton under-view, the derisive, all live in Shakespeare's mind not as the servants of something inhumane, or 'black', or 'problematic', but as a normal and essential element in his capacious tragic vision. And we would do well at this point also to have in mind what I have called the derision, the scathing and caustic merriment of Schopenhauer, whom Nietzsche was right to associate with Montaigne and right to describe as a 'cheerful' thinker, since the capacious honesty of which his derision and merriment are tokens is a matter of the exhilarating and the liberating. If we draw these elements together we shall begin to get to the greatness of *Troilus and Cressida*, and to an understanding of its important and quite 'orthodox' place in the Shakespearean scheme of things.

For *Troilus and Cressida* seems to me an exhilarating and liberating play, a high-spirited, exuberant and, in Nietzsche's sense, 'cheerful' play. It also seems to me a play which springs quite clearly from the general vision of the tragic world, in its deep connexions with the world of comedy, which I am exploring. If we look back at the plays so far discussed we shall see that the *idée maîtresse* of Shakespearean tragedy connects quite easily with the structure of this play and with its 'problem' tone of fierce and hilarious derision. In figures like Cassio, Duke Vincentio and Caius Marcius we have seen examples of Shakespeare's thinking about men trapped or locked in the limiting inflexibility of a culture's mores, lacking in any consciousness of ambiguity, relativity or flux, and unable therefore to mediate into an achieved social being more than a fraction of the life of nature in themselves. And in the fervid fears and hatreds of Othello, the agonized sense of 'Blood, thou art blood' in Angelo, and the furious impelled violence of Marcius, we have seen examples of the havoc made by the pulse of nature's energies in men who would have it that, for a civilized mind, such energies did not exist. In each case there grew, out of the contradictions between Law and nature, between the consciousness of social men and the wild world within and without them, the blindness, destruction and waste of tragedy.

That schematic summary of three very great and very different plays should in no way confuse us as to the variety and subtlety of Shakespeare's building upon the model. But it should help to make clear that certain ideas or images of culture and nature were vitally important in the mind that produced this richly varied group of plays. The idea of culture as something 'blocking', something stubbornly inflexible, is vital to it. So, secondly, is the idea of nature's kinesis, outside the walls of cities and inside the minds of civil men. And so also, thirdly, is the idea of a kind of pride, or fatal confidence, with which civil men attach themselves to their culture's mores and frame their limited lives within its terms, unaware of the raw chaos of vicissitude upon which they so vulnerably live.

In addition to these three, the twin themes of love and violence are peculiarly poignant ones for a mind which thinks like this: both exist at points in the lives of civilized men where the furious pulse of kinesis enters their patterned world with the maximum capacity either for destruction or creativity. The two are deeply significant and deeply connected. Such connexions are explored in the violent sexual jealousy of Othello, in the vengefulness of Angelo, and in the terrible sexual puns of the war-poetry of *Coriolanus*; and they are also active in the conception of plays as different as *Romeo and Juliet* and *All's Well*, where, in tones which run the whole gamut from lyrical acclaim to sardonic anger, the nature of something like 'lustiness', both sexual and violent, is Shakespeare's continuous subject of meditation – a dangerous, volatile quality, but vital and desired by the 'lusty gentlemen' of the first play and the 'sinewy sword-men' of the second, before haggish age steals on and wears them out of act.[2]

These five things are clearly of very great significance in the vision of the mature Shakespeare. The inflexibility of culture, the fury of kinesis, the vulnerable pride of attachment, and the twin energies of sexuality and violence: all five carry a strong charge of meaning as they coexist in his mind. All five are vital to his metaphysic; and all five are vitally present in *Troilus and Cressida*. In this great comedy of derision most of the vital features of the mature tragic vision are present, shaping a play whose laughter,

like that of Schopenhauer, turns its 'cheerful' attention to an
under-view of human societies and civilized consciousnesses which
is as comprehensive and radical as that of the tragedies themselves.

2. Cheerful derision

From the beginning of the play until the appearance of Calchas in
III.iii Shakespeare's derision and high-spirited laughter seems to
me to hold more or less unimpeded sway. The ridiculousness of
that which, from another perspective not too far distant, might
have been tragic is, I think, patent and total. And even after
Calchas' menacing requirement that he be paid for his treachery,
Shakespeare's ribald exuberance is never driven out, even though
we now have something more coldly dreadful in the play's mix.
You cannot get to either the play's comprehensiveness of vision
or its essential humanity without a full response to this comedy.
Without a full sense of its powers the play will dwindle to the
status of some dark, solemn and uneasy tract about 'appearance
and reality', or some such; or even to the status of a dark night of
the dramatist's immature soul (he was approaching forty) which
had not yet emerged into the Boethian light of Cordelia's grace
and redemption.

The jaunty Prologue begins the play's merriment, refusing as it
does to take any of the forthcoming heroics seriously and veering
instead between the tone of a fair-ground barker ('come and see
the marvels and the heroes') and an unimpressed bystander ("tis
but the chance of war'). And when the play proper begins, the
high, irreverent nonsense starts at once as Shakespeare runs
incongruously together the heavy obscenities of Pandarus ('grinding' and 'kneading') and the protestations of a young ass, Troilus,
who throws out a brief Petrarchanism about 'cygnet's down' and
then tries to cut some kind of Orphic figure with his 'Peace, you
ungracious clamours!'. It is a familiar Shakespearean juxta-
position – Mercutio to Romeo, the Nurse to Juliet, Iago to
Cassio – but handled here in so comically reduced a way that the
absurd and the hilarious can be its only outcome. When Troilus
exits to 'the sport abroad', his protests already half forgotten in

the fine fling of that phrase, what we have essentially seen is a modish youth to whom the world of comedy will duly deliver its rebuff.

I.ii is still obviously a part of this comic world, where the protestations of the high meet the scepticisms of the unimpressed — from the great description of Ajax ('gouty Briareus'), via that ludicrous dimple on Troilus' chin in his encomium of which Pandarus seeks to win the heart of a fair maiden, to the procession of heroes which is high farce and jaunty nonsense. And when we meet the Greeks in I.iii the comedy becomes sublime. Never has political rhetoric been so mercilessly guyed. It is a council of the inept and disaffected, stuffed to the chops with grievances they cannot digest, yet still trying to talk big, still clutching hopelessly after the magniloquent phrase and the magnificent gesture or sentiment; while all the time the ghost of Patroclus' reported 'scurril jests' (which he 'breaks' like breaking wind) is made to haunt their strutting footsteps in a rude pageant of their dignities. Never did the supposed 'abilities, gifts, natures, shapes' of men of self-confessed excellence come in for such ribald and high-spirited disbelief. There is no Swiftian sting to this comedy, nor any of the Elizabethan satirists' somewhat vengeful fury about the whipping of hypocrisy. It is comedy liberated from the service of a partisan cause and liberated from any overweening or overworked sense of personal disgust or personal revenge. From this play, which has so often been seen as 'troubled', 'problematic' or 'transitional', there seems to me to emerge a beautifully clarified voice of pure comedy, pure laughter. It is the laughter of an exuberant intelligence which is its own value, making its disinterested (and devastating) commentary on the protestations of a group of men who seem to themselves to be the heroic embodiments of a culture's finest achievements.

Ulysses, with the famous speech on Degree, does not escape the scene's all-embracing derision. He, like Agamemnon and Nestor, is an over-excited inventor of vasty metaphors and reverberating orotundities of phrase. Like them he is a man full of self-importance and a sense of his own dignity, in which capacity he leads the chorus of complaint against the scurril jests and fusty stuff which are so bad for their images and so injurious to their spleens. There is something strangely desperate, smacking of 'any port in a storm', about the desire of many critics to exempt him from the play's comic scrutiny. He has been praised as a conservative idealist (chiefly for the Degree speech), as an intelligent man, and as a pragmatic realist. But there is every reason for feeling that Shakespeare was not so naive a believer in the Degree ideal, especially in the crude, vamped and rhetorical form of it which Ulysses here affects to espouse. And as for intelligence and political realism: one can only reflect that it would not take a remarkable I.Q. to con the likes of Agamemnon and Nestor into a hare-brained scheme which pandered to their sense of heroic leadership; and that political realism is something which is normally praised for sharp diagnosis and the consequent getting of results, while the results in this play are not very wonderful and the diagnosis, if it can in any way be felt that Ulysses means what he says, is clearly a nonsense. (It would be a very trivial and reductive reading of the events of *Troilus and Cressida* which concluded, with Ulysses, that what the Greeks lacked was leadership and a hierarchy.) No, Ulysses is part of the scene's high sport, as is Aeneas, that rather *passé* issuer of challenges, and Nestor, the even more *passé* taker-up of them, whose weary, chivalric fopperies move this great scene to its final phase.

The second Act continues the fine comedy. Thersites' wise-cracking at the expense of the 'mongrel beef-witted lord' Ajax, and Achilles' snorting at Hector's silly challenge ("'tis trash') prepare us for the next great set-piece, the Trojan council, with the appropriate measure of scepticism. And when that scene comes (II.ii) we again have something on the stage to which we cannot properly respond unless we see how Shakespeare's ribaldry has marked it as, first and foremost, ridiculous.

Even in the good sense that Hector speaks before the famous *volte face* there is a good deal of heavyweight and clumsy vocabulary (Shakespeare in this play is the master of verbiage) which marks him as the amusing figure who, as we already know, was the author of the challenge just dismissed by Achilles as 'trash'. His famous realism —

            the will dotes that is attributive
    To what infectiously itself affects,
    Without some image of th' affected merit —

                                            [II. ii. 58—60]

is realism; but it is also a matter of a soldier trying to
philosophize, and floundering under the unaccustomed mental
strain just as surely as Agamemnon did when he earlier gave vent
to a precept or two of Stoic cast. And the Hector who calls
Cassandra's raving 'high strains/Of divination' is already that man
of unwisely exalted whims who will soon be crossing the floor to
join his 'sprightly brethren' and grace the rest of the proceedings
with his empty-headed sense of fair play.

    But the great and central comedy of the scene comes from
Troilus, ably assisted by that elder brother and somewhat
degenerate roisterer Paris. The heart of this comedy, as always
with the high-flown language of Troilus, lies in the way in which
the language of idealism, which wants to soar, keeps making
abortive little flights before crashing heavily to earth. Contemplating the idea of kingship his mind reaches vaguely for glorious
images of the transfinite, but can only come up with one which
suggests unequalled corpulence — 'a waist most fathomless'. When
he reaches the most transfinite of all subjects, love, the 'theme of
honour and renown' itself, he stumbles into those unfortunate
images of luxury, soilure, staling, digestion and trade which give
the scurril lie to his adolescent fantasies. And in this central
speech ('I take today a wife . . .') his whimsical Petrarchanism is
further pageanted by the accidental *double entendres* which
muddy the desired translucency. His 'enkindled will' is not nearly
so innocent an instrument of yearning as he would like; and the
image of the noble Paris sailing to Greece where he 'touch'd the
ports desir'd' is a wonderfully pudendal slip of a kind which riots
through much of the play's language at large. It is on the way to
being the language of the 'fair rape' and the 'ransack'd queen'
which characterizes the empty lasciviousness of his elder brother,
who is now doubtless past caring about the wallow of his words.
And as the scene closes, Troilus' hope for a general canonization
of their glorious selves still keeps the drama at a level which calls

more or less unequivocally for Shakespeare's most subversive disbelief.

II.iii sees absurdity running almost to madness. Prefaced by Thersites and the 'fool positive' Patroclus, the Greek lords once again enter with their petty jealousies and doltish recriminations set off in all their folly by King Agamemnon's large talk — his ponderous self-aggrandizement by means of the royal 'we', and the carefully elaborated magnanimity whereby 'appertainments' shall be graciously let by, notwithstanding the fact that the socially impossible Achilles has 'sent' his messengers. Achilles' proposition that the plotting nobles are only out for a constitutional adds more hilarity to that which is caused by their pretentious rhetoric and the childish giggling with which they accompany their stratagems. The boorish Ajax, good Greek that he is, tries to frame a few *sententiae* with a bearing upon the values of humility and sociability, and strikes thereby some marvellously unlikely postures. And the elaborateness of plotting and rhetoric, by means of which Ulysses and the rest try to make this unwieldy carcase run to their will, reflects derisively as much upon them as upon him — like so many minuscule Meneniuses bustling round an even less lovely Marcius. Our response to this sort of nonsense can only be a deep sense of absurdity, governed as it all is by Shakespeare's finest high spirits which eventually push both scene and act to a superb climax:

> *Ajax:* Shall I call you father?
> *Nestor:* Ay, my good son.   [II. iii. 250—1]

It continues unabated through III.i and III.ii. Pandarus apes courtly graces and the servant apes Pandarus; and the gracious scene of Lord, Lady and Servant which this introduces is again a set-piece of high farce in which the language of courtly-Petrarchan adoration can carry only the wheedlings of a flatterer and the frivolous licentiousness of a bored middle-aged couple. The young lovers, who have the unenviable task of following this performance, are clearly well on the road to the same banality, with Troilus once again leading the way with those cumbrously physical efforts at lyric flight and those inadvertently sexual *doubles entendres*. His 'ruder powers', inapt for soaring, turn his ecstasies into fantasized wallowings. The pudendal 'eye of majesty' and the bawdy 'will' (formerly 'enkindled' and now 'infinite') misgovern with scurril jest all these attempts at courtly graces.

Then, as I said, it changes. In Calchas' demand for payment we have the first entirely unfunny development. We now realize that all this nonsense is going to be paid for in real human suffering as he sets out his claim for his 'little benefit'. It is a real and very ugly world in which that claim is made, and the straw men who have made the play's farce and grotesquerie to date are not going to be able to inhabit it without breaking. The comedy does not cease here, nor will there be any 'problem' for the play as it takes this new tonal element into its mix. We will still have the hilarity and farce of the Greeks punctiliously snubbing Achilles; there will still be splendidly irreverend wisecracks from both Achilles and Thersites; there will still be the *aubade* of the lovers, greeted by the cold morning air and the 'ribald crows' which set more conventional expectations in amusing disarray. There will still be Ajax bawling and Hector being a good sport. And there will still be the theatrically engineered pieces of high nonsense, like the cry of 'The Troyan's trumpet' which Rossiter picked up for its wicked punning; or like the call of the Greek trumpet which precedes it — a glorious summons to a glorious combat which is answered by total silence since the Trojans seem to have stayed in bed too late and aren't ready yet.

But now there will also be an increasing sense of tragic absurdity, and of the catastrophic crash-course upon which these people's waywardness, frivolity, stupidity and pretension have set them all. This sense arises more and more now from beneath the farce and boisterous hilarity, but it commingles beautifully with the play's comedy, not to make it a 'problem' but to make it a masterpiece of Shakespeare's sense of the conjunction of the tragic and the absurd, the catastrophic and the ridiculous. His sense of tragedy and his sense of comedy are, as we have seen, structurally linked at the deepest level. Each springs from his knowledge of the myriad contradictions which exist between the coursing and volatile life of the world's Will and the obstinate structures of men's Representations of it. The contradiction and discontinuity between these makes one laugh precisely at what is funny in this play — pretension, false confidence, blindness, elaborate codes of language and behaviour, and the wish to 'transcend' the world's physical and contingent turbulence. Neither Greece nor Troy, particularly as they are locked in the archetypally futile obstinacy of this protracted war, can equip a human being with the means to hold his character and life in flexible stability. Instead their citizens profess codes, strike postures, giggle and grin stupidly, rant mawkishly, fly whimsically after ideals and theories, strain after emotional effects. And, like Achilles, 'batter down themselves'. It is the comprehensiveness of this abject human failure which is the source of all the play's Schopenhauerian derision; but the source also of that tragic tone which, from III.iii onwards, reminds us increasingly that men are going to pay for all this ineptitude, even with their lives.

But we laugh. Even after III.iii as this sense of destitution and tragic waste grows stronger and stronger until we reach the play's horrible ending — we laugh. Or we should laugh, if we have read Shakespeare's high-spiritedness properly. Derisive laughter on this scale is integral and vital to the experience of the play. We endure and cast off what this play reveals just as surely by our laughter as, in *King Lear*, we endure and cast it off by sorrow and empathy. Laughter too brings its metaphysical solace. The kind of laughter that *Troilus and Cressida* promotes is a recognition of profound dislocation, not an insensitive protection from it. It is a laughter which contains one's willingness to see into this hopelessness comprehensively, just as the sorrowing empathy for which *King Lear* calls is a seeing and knowing, and hence a liberating sorrow. The mind which does not know how to laugh comprehensively at *Troilus and Cressida* is likely to bring to *King Lear* a quality of sorrowing which is more sentimental, less seeing and less intelligent than that for which the play actually calls. The laughter which Shakespeare has created here, having its connexions with orders of comic-derisive vitality to which both Hamlet and Lear rise in their traumas, is a tough but in no way an inhuman thing, and it ought not to be problematic. Morally it is subtle and fine; you don't quite have the right to empathize with the trauma of the King in *King Lear* if you have not also embraced the comprehensiveness of disbelief which is the source of this play's fierce merriment. Certainly the later play could not have been written by a mind which did not contain the laughing kind of creative intelligence which this one embodies.

3. Energy and blockage

We are laughing, then, at men in love and men at war; and our laughter is in its way as comprehensive and as full of difficult seeing as our tragic sympathy will be in *King Lear*. The derision of this play burrows its way as deeply and as knowingly and as awkwardly under many a comforting notion about the civilized mind as does *King Lear*, and we shall come away from the experience of it with a deeply chastened sense — chastened here by laughter — of the littleness and fragility of the human mind in a vastly powerful and volatile world. It is the case, as Coleridge put it, that 'the terrible by a law of the human mind always touches on the verge of the ludicrous'; and that knowledge, which will be needed again to understand *Hamlet* (think of Polonius), just as we have already needed it to understand *Measure for Measure*, is something which this play has in its every nerve — which brings one back to the matter of the play's congruence with the general metaphysic of Shakespearean tragedy.

One may best begin to explore this congruence by noting how this play, which presents us with botched men, coagulated minds, bored and torpid vacancy, is also a play in which the coursing energy of the kinetic is constantly present. Much of the play's language bears witness to the presence of strong energies writhing beneath the surface of the mind, unacknowledged by the speaker and capable of erupting to make havoc. A good deal of this is sexual and is to be found in 'Freudian slips', already mentioned in the case of Troilus, whereby characters make statements which they feel to be straightforward enough but which, through pun and ambiguity, open deeper into their subconscious than they know. This scurril and wanton commentary on their protestations bespeaks potencies they know not of, and potencies which can therefore disrupt in comedy just as surely as they disrupted the Courtesy-world of Venice in tragedy.

Again it begins with the Prologue, with the Greek ships arriving at Troy to 'disgorge their warlike fraughtage', which fraughtage, being a cargo of 'princes orgulous' with 'their high blood chafed', sets going in us the kind of laughter which will respond to the numerous, unacknowledged puns about sexual activity which corruscate through the play. I have mentioned Troilus and his enkindled will and the ports desired, and also the pun on 'eye' as vagina. Ulysses produces a splendid example of this latter when he tries to arouse Achilles by telling him that

> things in motion sooner catch the eye
> Than what stirs not,   [III. iii. 183—4]

and the joke in this is repeated many times during the play — its laughter rippling through Troilus' Petrarchan pomp about the 'eye of majesty' and through Cressida's speeches to Diomedes ('The error of our eye directs our mind', 'Minds swayed by eyes are full of turpitude'). What is happening on puns of this sort is that language is being made to record kinds of energy which are basic to the business of being a human adult, but to record them as they swarm uncontrollably beneath the surface of a rhetoric which cannot give them admittance into social life. Pandarus' dirty jokes are no vehicle for gathering such energies into the human world. We get from his jokes, as from these puns, the sense that these people are adults of full human potential, but adults who are always frittering that potential away or leaving it untapped. We go behind their torpor, their instability and their mawkish physicality, into those energies which fail to come through in them except in a state of disorder, flippancy and dilapidation.

If one looks at this 'record of energy' in its language one sees how strong is the play's embodiment of that kinesis which they cannot realize in themselves. The business of thinking is a matter of live growth — Ulysses talks of the 'young conception' forming in his brain, Pandarus of the business which 'seethes' in his mind, Cressida of thoughts which 'like unbridled children' become too 'headstrong' for their mother. Fighting seems also to draw upon strong currents of energy — recorded in Hector's 'roisting' challenge and his riding 'hot as Perseus' through the Greek ranks, in his 'blaze of wrath', in Troilus' 'heat of action' on the battlefield, and in the 'bridegroom's fresh alacrity' with which the Trojans are urged by Aeneas to follow Hector into war. The language of their flirtatiousness is likewise nimble and hot-blooded – the 'merry Greeks', 'swelling o'er with arts and exercise', suspiciously expert in 'subtle games' and suspiciously 'prompt and pregnant' to the 'high lavolt', walking on the toe like the pert Diomedes; and on the Trojan side Cressida herself, 'glib of tongue' and with 'a coasting welcome', a woman in whom the 'wanton spirits' seem to 'look out/Of every joint and motive of her body'.

Love (or lust, or sex) is constantly described in terms which evoke this energy. It is a 'firebrand', 'hot passion', a 'feverous pulse'; it is 'raging appetites', 'coals', 'hot blood' and 'hot deeds' – something which clearly does possess the power to 'undo us all'. It is the racing of blood in veins, the 'quick sense' of sexual awareness which possessed the god of war when he was 'inflamed with Venus' and which seems to impregnate the very towers of Troy 'whose wanton tops do buss the clouds'.

These are characters who have the 'lustiness' of the young in *Romeo and Juliet* and *All's Well*. Their drinking is a matter of heating the blood, their war is a maelstrom of 'hot digestion' and 'heaving spleens'; Ulysses compares the rushing competition for fame with 'an ent'red tide', Nestor envisages the exemplary power of heroism in terms of vigorous bodily movement and working limbs, and the 'enchanting fingers' with which Helen will unbuckle Hector's armour tingle with voluptuousness. It is a very high-energy world that they inhabit in which we are never far away from a sense of furious bodily motion in muscle and blood.

And yet, of course, the impression we take from the play as a whole is not one of energy, but its opposite. It is the impression of blockage, not energy – of weight, bulk, mass, limit, thickness, stagnation. It is the stagnation of Achilles, the 'ox', the 'lion-sick' man, the 'sleeping giant', the hart that 'keeps thicket', the 'great bulk' who may 'overbulk' all the Greeks, draped in the 'amorous fold' of Cupid which weighs heavy on his neck, 'entombed alive'. Or it is 'blockish' Ajax, 'a man into whom nature hath so crowded humours that his valour is crushed into folly', a lumbering oaf full of pent-up violence which strains to get itself expressed in his bellowing to the trumpeter:

> Now crack thy lungs and split thy brazen pipe;
> Blow, villain, till thy sphered bias cheek
> Out-swell the colic of puff'd Aquilon.
> Come, stretch thy chest, and let thy eyes spout blood,
>
> [IV. v. 7—10]

but strains in vain since, as we have noticed, all that the bellowing produces as answer is a derisory silence. Or it is the thickened and ugly language of their efforts to speak grandiloquently. Or the lumpy grossness of their would-be courtly graces. Or the fear of Troilus that the act of love is 'a slave to limit', bounding his desires within frustrating barriers. It is their cloddishness and their clumsiness, that stupidity of theirs which makes Thersites feel that they would draw their 'massy irons' to cut a spider's web. It is that which is expressed in sum by Agamemnon's image of knots in wood:

> As knots, by the conflux of meeting sap,
> Infects the sound pine, and diverts his grain
> Tortive and errant from his course of growth.   [I. iii. 7—9]

There is sap enough in them, but it will not flow straight and it will not nourish. All is 'tortive and errant', 'bias and thwart'. For all the living pulse of energy that is in them, indeed *because* of it, but because also of their inability to let it flow nourishingly through them, these are people twisted and knotted, creaking and becoming hulks. The very power of kinetic life seems mischievously to turn back on itself and produce, under intolerable contradictory pressures, ugly and misshapen forms. As Antony will say when the fire of Egypt seems burnt out:

> Now all labour
> Mars what it does; yea, very force entangles
> Itself with strength.   [*A & C* IV. xiv. 47—9]

Or, to pick up a phrase from Troilus, we have a world 'constring'd in mass'.

These images of blockage and constriction, set against the

language of volatility, give us in essence the way in which this play is built upon the Shakespearean model. All nature's vitality runs frustratingly against the obstacles that human minds have put in the way of its progress. Held down by the dead weight of these men's banality it cannot grow and flourish. So it twists back upon itself in knots, or convulses through the crust of their stupidity to produce outbursts of violence or desire over which they have no control. As it twists and turns so they are pushed hither and thither in reckless frivolity, one minute full of crackpot bravado, the next minute slothful or frustrated, and always haunted by the knowledge that it may sweep them along again or shatter their insubstantial beings by its force. Eventually, as Thersites sees, it will drive them all down to the condition of which he, although the most conscious man, is also the most destitute representative: sterile violence, envenomed anger, disease.

It all ends in hideousness and absurdity, as 'ugly night' descends with its 'dragon wing' over a battlefield where Troilus on the one side and Achilles on the other are merely men impelled by ungovernable fury. Troilus will set himself to raise 'goblins' of frenzy in the imagination of Achilles to keep himself from feeling his own 'inward woe'. And Achilles, roused at last (but not by Ulysses' stratagems), is a figure of hellish violence catastrophically different from the hero Ulysses is still envisaging. Ulysses greets his awakening with:

> O, courage, courage, Princes! Great Achilles
> Is arming, weeping, cursing, vowing vengeance.
> Patroclus' wounds have rous'd his drowsy blood,
> Together with his mangled Myrmidons,
> That noseless, handless, hack'd and chipp'd, come to him,
> Crying on Hector.   [V. v. 30—5]

But while he sees in this a great hero we see something else: the emergence of this slow, massy, violent and lumbering bulk (and note 'weeping' too — a magnificent touch) as the logical last product of a diseased and misshapen world. The heavy relentlessness of the second and fifth lines of that quotation give us the hideousness at the heart of this play's study of the absurd. The monstrous Achilles is the apotheosis of the play's vision of violent massiveness as the product of kinetic energy twisted and knotted against itself.

4. The 'lovers'

Those images give us the essence of that maelstrom of the absurd which this exuberant comedy reveals within and behind the grand protestations of two disintegrating cultures. Every life that is lived in this play is lived ludicrously, and lived also on the brink of traumatic dissolution. Wavering uncertainly between high-blown idealisms and gross physicality these are people frittering themselves away amid the shiftings and slitherings of vicissitude. It is the psychosis of the bewildered: and as the mayhem continues this general bewilderment, this general sense of human life as the helpless victim of external pressure, becomes a dominating presence in the play. A little couplet from Troilus early in the play touches whimsically on this note:

> sorrow that is couch'd in seeming gladness
> Is like that mirth fate turns to sudden sadness. [I. i. 39—40]

Pandarus strikes it too when he recalls that

> there was such laughing! and Helen so blush'd, and Paris so chaf'd; and all the rest so laughed, that it pass'd,
>
> [I. ii. 159—61]

wherein we see a flimsy riot of little emotions brushing through a group of characters, and then — 'it pass'd'.

Nobody ever really confronts this vicissitude by which they are all assailed; nobody meets it with the energy of an actively experiencing mind. It simply steals over and through them, like the 'envious fever/Of pale and bloodless emulation' which Ulysses sees creeping aimlessly over the Greek ranks; or it inhabits their empty minds like the 'pettish lunes' which Agamemnon sees in Achilles; or it riots in them close to madness like the 'bloody turbulence' of Andromache's dream or the 'brain-sick raptures' of Cassandra. Paris besotted with sensuality, Achilles besotted with vanity, and Nestor besotted with a mixture of senility and chivalry are all of the authentic breed. So is Troilus,

> Like a strange soul upon the Stygian banks
> Staying for waftage,   [III. ii. 9—10]

and so is Cressida, who ruminates darkly about the 'kind of self'
she has which resides with Troilus, but who knows that she can't
trust that self, and who ends her bewildered meditation on it
with:

> Where is my wit? I know not what I speak.   [III. ii. 147]

In nobody is there anything but centrelessness and drifting; and
none of the brave oaths and resolves, none of the brave postures
and rhetorically espoused schemata, can keep them upright as the
ground shifts beneath their feet. So

> What's past and what's to come is strew'd with husks
> And formless ruin of oblivion.   [IV. v. 166—7]

The 'love' of Troilus and Cressida must be seen in such a
context. In the ardent playing of a moon-struck role Troilus
seems to be reaching desperately for some kind of centre, some
kind of self-meaning, though beset constantly by the fear that he
will derive from love not self-possession but self-loss. And the
otherwise wordly Cressida enters into love with Troilus as if
hoping against hope (and against her better judgment) that, in
such a world, the desired stability will somehow be more than a
fleeting fiction. As with the language of Othello and Desdemona
(but here ludicrously) we know that love cannot be made in these
terms. Neither the adolescent idealism of Troilus nor the thin and
precociously beglamoured worldliness of Cressida can provide
any sort of medium for sustaining an adult passion. In some
fleeting and unheeded sense they know it too, seeming (in III.ii)
to galvanize themselves into a false belief by means of the
over-played vowings and apostrophes whereby they try to make
the fragile bargain feel as though it had some substance.

The solacing glamour of love is clung to for the 'significance' it
seems to offer; and clung to desperately when, as they must
separate, they still preserve for themselves the dream of being
'made real' by this insubstantial passion. Troilus makes it seem

big with words:

> And to this hand when I deliver her,
> Think it an altar, and thy brother Troilus
> A priest, there off'ring to it his own heart,   [IV. iii. 7—9]

and Cressida reacts like one for whom the fleeting moment of
apparent human significance holds an opportunity for dreams of
self-meaning which are too exquisite and too rare not to be
enjoyed to the full:

> Why tell you me of moderation?
> The grief is fine, full, perfect, that I taste,
> And violenteth in a sense as strong
> As that which causeth it . . .
>
> My love admits no qualifying dross;
> No more my grief, in such a precious loss.
>
> [IV. iv. 2—5; 9—10]

They speak as people for whom love is a magnificent and rare
imagining full of a romantic glamour which can release them from
the trivia of Troy and of themselves. For Troilus, belief in this
glamorous fiction has become an ingrained habit; and Cressida
uses the belief to trick herself out of the *ennui* of her worldliness,
squeezing the last drops out of the sweet fiction when the chance
presents itself.

All this Shakespeare handles with supreme poise. The
ludicrous haunts everything that they say. Troilus' wallowings,
Cressida's efforts to convince herself that she is other than the
triviality she so irredeemably is — both are full of a folly and an
absurdity which is constantly busy exposing the romantic and
glamorous myths. Yet both are also sad-absurd, pathetic —
Troilus sometimes poignantly and tragically so. For, as with
Othello in Venice, there is a sense in which they *have to be* like
this to live in Troy; or a sense in which, having lived in Troy, they
could not be otherwise. There is an awful sense in which this is all
that Troy has to offer — a myth of love, a myth of war, both
beglamoured and neither seriously believed, but the weary game
of believing them needed as solace to the bored and vacuous.

Their elders — Paris, Helen, Pandarus — live the game as a game, knowing its littleness yet, in the littleness of themselves, fully adjusted to it. But Troilus and Cressida, a new generation with more exalted expectations and less accommodated worldliness, live the game as if it were capable of becoming real and bringing its promised glamour into substantial life.

For that trick, played upon them by the emptiness of Trojan life, they will pay dearly. Cressida will be practised upon with ease by the skilled Sir Diomed who is made cynically expert by his sure knowledge of what the words of the game really mean. And Troilus, who is too complete and naive a victim of the game ever to be capable of a salutary insight, will 'swagger himself out on's own eyes' when the real meaning of the game is made palpable. As his idealism meets its rebuff in V.ii the fiction breaks and the reality of the game comes clear: beauty does not have a soul, souls do not guide vows, vows are not sanctimonies, sanctimony is not the gods' delight and there is no 'rule in unity itself'. But that is too comprehensive and traumatic a series of insights for such a one as Troilus to embrace, for 'Never did young man fancy/With so eternal and so fix'd a soul'. The credence in his heart and the esperance so obstinately strong render that kind of knowledge intolerable; and so it is shut out by the rush of unceasing savagery and vengefulness which sweeps him (and the whole play) from here to the end in a single movement.

5. Laughter and cathartic knowledge

The gods, of course, sit upon their thrones and laugh at Troy, which presents their sense of comedy with as unnatural a scene as that which Rome offered at the climax of *Coriolanus*. A sublunary audience will temper its laughter with a chastened recognition of its own absurder self. But, Troy being littler and less fearsomely pressing than Rome, much of that divine mirth must still inform a fully alert response to the play, even on the part of a mere mortal.

For there is a kind of laughter which is as aggressively self-confident as the mind which made this high-spirited sport with human ineptitude, but which still nevertheless embodies receptivity and intelligence rather than insensitive dismissal. The energy of its derision is part of an on-going capacity for life and exuberance, and without it the endless compassion for which Shakespeare's androgynous mind has always been found remarkable would be far more otiose and cloying than it is. Negatively capable he may be; but there is also in his mind a strong charge of positive life and judgment which is given full comic licence in *Troilus and Cressida* to wreak its joyous havoc with the banalities of two absurd cultures as they flounder along the surface of nature's kinesis.

A mind without this sort of power could not have written *King Lear*. It could not have seen what is seen in *King Lear*, and if it had seen it it could only have been stunned into silence by the terror of what it saw. Without this confident and positive power it would have been unable to be as free from illusion about the status of mind and culture as it had to be to create the world of the great tragedies. The laughter which gets its quintessential manifestation in *Troilus and Cressida* is as essential to the tragic vision as that determined compassion which enlists our sympathy with the characters of tragedy howsoever far into destructiveness, criminality or madness they may be driven. The uncompromising intelligence which is in this laughter's wit is the very thing which opens into that tragic world of madness and destruction — which first reveals it, knows it, and then inhibits it. In addition it is something which contributes to one's stamina in surviving it.

One side of it is sardonic, sceptical and disbelieving, inclined to maul the pretensions of mind and culture as savagely as they are mauled here (or in the writings of Montaigne). Another side of it is spirited, buoyant and joyous, as again Montaigne is in the midst of the ruins his imagination has made of his available world, or as is Donne in the world left to him after his passionate ribaldry has had its way. In *Troilus and Cressida*, and in those considerable parts of the great tragedies where this humour is to be found again, the laughter of sardonic disbelief and the laughter of bouyant high-spirits are beautifully tuned together. Together they give us a play whose under-view of the mind's pretensions is as profound, sustained and humane as is that of the 'purely' tragic plays.

6

Denmark and its Prince

> Objections non-sequiturs, cheerful distrust, joyous
> mockery — all are signs of health. Everything absolute
> belongs in the realm of pathology.
>
> Nietzsche: *Beyond Good and Evil*[1]

1. Empathy or diagnosis?

With *Hamlet* we come to a third play which has repeatedly been
found problematic and confusing; and critical responses to it have
shown extraordinary variations. As I consider the ways in which
it has been read and produced I find that it seems to operate on
audiences and critics alike with such power that, as with *Measure
for Measure*, they cannot take it 'whole'. And I also find that it is
felt to be rather exclusively about Hamlet, about the Prince of
Denmark, and not about the Denmark of which he is Prince. Most
interpretations of the play incline towards seeing it as about Man
in The World, not a particular man in a particular part of the
world; and most, as the wholeness of the play is lost, are either
exaggeratedly empathetic or exaggeratedly diagnostic.

My own view is that the play is whole, single; that it does
generate a complex and lucid unity of the empathetic and the
analytic; but that it will only do so when we give Denmark, as well
as its Prince, the same sustained attention as did its author.
Hamlet without the Prince of Denmark would still be a very great
play indeed. The imaginative creation of Elsinore is as great and
important an achievement as the creation of the man whom
Elsinore tortures. The social-psychological coherence of Shakespeare's tragic vision is manifest in this play as well.

There are basically two ways of misreading and lessening the play by taking Hamlet out of Elsinore. The first gives us the popular romantic Hamlet, produced by a response in which the powers of diagnostic judgment have been overwhelmed by the call to empathy. According to this view Hamlet is Everyman, we all have a smack of him in us. He is a noble and above all beautiful sufferer, a single centre of purity amid the corruptions of The World. He is a truth speaker with his limed soul struggling to be free, a would-be setter of out-of-joint joints, a blighted courtier and blighted lover from whose lips fall, without great effort, gems of wisdom — a snapper out of unconsidered insights. He is also an ineffectual genius, appealing to what we might feel to be mute and glorious in ourselves, whose faults only serve to make him the more irresistibly human, the more irresistibly *us*.

This view is, of course, deeply sentimental; and the sentimentality principally resides in a self-beglamouring desire to feel like Hamlet on the cheap. The sentimental romantic sees the play as an opportunity to cast himself in an attractive role, that of the beautiful sufferer, where he can come out with all those insights about paragons of animals and quintessences of dust — but without having to be as mentally agonized as Hamlet is and without feeling himself subjected to the searching moral scrutiny to which Shakespeare has in fact exposed his hero. The romantic Hamlet is a fiction of those who believe in the heroic goodness of suffering beautifully. Like all fictions of that kind it forgets that suffering is also painful, so that the actual Shakespearean character, the apprehension of whose mental agonies makes me think of Strindberg or Kafka (for the relevant intensity), is neatly transposed into a self-image which it is comforting and flattering to project.

The other way is the way of the diagnostician, who is not sentimental, who is usually very intelligent, and who is in no way overwhelmed by any temptation to empathize. The worst of such diagnosticians have merely been grumpy moralists of a decidedly conservative cast who clearly think Hamlet wants his bottom smacking; but the best of them warrant very serious attention. Eliot (with the famous case about horror and disgust), Santayana (who is not impressed by Hamlet's 'bickerings and lamentations'), Wilson

Knight (who finds the hero's sarcasm 'unnecessary') and L. C. Knights (who finds him malicious, defensive and self-centred) are all major critics with a critical vocabulary which is quite properly analytical.[2] They have made major inroads into popular and romantic empathies which cannot simply be ignored. If I now criticize Knights' essay 'Prince Hamlet' (as a representative work) it is because it sums up the anti-romantic case extremely well and must therefore be confronted by any reading which wants to make further progress.[3]

Knights' case is that Hamlet's wit is sterile, destructive and malicious; that his animus towards others is the self-indulgent gratification of a neurotic; that he dwells upon the subject of lust with a fascinated insistence deriving from a general spite against the flesh; that much of his madness is a mere self-protective gambit (he 'finds the cloak of madness congenial'); and that he has 'the obstinate self-centredness and suspicion of a maladjusted individual'. Knights further maintains that such a character not only gives the lie to the romantic case but that it also diminishes the status and moral desirability of the play because (he picks up Eliot's case here) Shakespeare has not really 'objectified' or 'got outside' his character. He is still awkwardly involved with him, with the result that the audience becomes awkwardly involved in its turn. Thus:

> *Hamlet* can provide an indulgence for some of our most cherished weaknesses – so deeply cherished that we can persuade ourselves that they are virtues – but it is incapable of leading us far towards maturity and self-knowledge.
>
> [pp. 86–7]

The case is powerfully argued and convincingly documented. As far as I can see the ordinary romantic case cannot survive it. But, that bathwater gone, I think it is possible to get back the baby.

Knights' case, and the general diagnostic way of reading which it exemplifies, seems to me wrong in three ways. Firstly I think that it makes a radical selection from the things that are actually there in the play – the defensiveness, the fascination with lust, the cloak of feigned madness etc. – and then looks at that selection of things with static and abstracted interest. The dynamics of the social practice in which this defensiveness and fascination are created are completely ignored, as are the association of both qualities with very different and much more laudable things — the defensiveness is cousin to resistance and critical insight, the fascination is cousin to horrified and quite sincere disgust. The cloak of madness is also a selection — for it leaves out the real torment that is there, and it also leaves out what seems to me a very important characteristic of the traumatic, namely that it has to be entered, in a way consciously, as a refuge from unendurable suffering (as Schopenhauer saw madness) and as a place where the mind may recompose itself safe from the external world's attacks upon it. In *Hamlet*, as in *King Lear*, Shakespeare sees madness in this kind of dynamic way — which not only renders the vocabulary of static diagnosis reductive but also (not incidentally) calls back some of our capacities for sympathy.

Secondly, I don't think it is at all true that Shakespeare has failed to 'get outside' his character. There is a way of 'feeling with' him which is quite different from awkward involvement, romantic indulgence, with sympathy escalating into empathy and that into identification of a beglamouring kind. It is here that we need Elsinore, as with Othello we needed Venice, for Shakespeare's creation of the Elsinorean context is so firm and sure that we can 'feel with' Hamlet as a particular and specific individual, created by a specific and individual culture, and then trapped by its limitations. Our sympathy, as with Othello, is then fully integrated with our critical-analytic awareness of what those limitations are, what they do, how they are and are not resisted. This recreates the wholeness of the tragic experience, giving us back the play which static diagnosis so disastrously reduces.

And thirdly the case seems to me, quite simply, uncharitable. This stems from an insufficient response to the actual hideousness of Elsinore, given in the play, which is not just a vengeful fiction of a 'neurotic' mind. And it stems also from a moralistic impatience with individuals who are tortured and crippled by suffering, revealed by the vocabulary the case employs — in which the 'maladjusted individual' can be so confidently and normatively compared with 'maturity'.

The two ways of reading — empathetic and diagnostic — tend to divide the play between them. Of the two I prefer the romantic reading, vitiated even as it is with sentimentality and indulgence. With a view like this we can get somewhere. We can enjoy the play (which many of the diagnosticians clearly don't) and, being moved by it, we can preserve some sort of emotional outgoingness, some readiness to sympathize if only in the debilitated form of that which sentimentality is. What we cannot do is be very intelligent about it, let it instigate any really serious thought — which is where the diagnosticians step in. But a real reading of the tragedy will, I think, look like neither of these. It is possible to take it whole, to integrate its invitations both to empathy and to judgment, to undergo the whole, vast, painful experience of the thing. And that depends on experiencing Elsinore as well as the Prince.

2. *The mores of Elsinore*

The bases of Elsinorean social practice are manipulative, expeditious and politic, a matter of espionage and the political use of man by man against man. Just as in *Othello* all social relationships were intruded upon by the practice of suit and lobbying so here personal relationships are even further invaded by spying and setting on — what Polonius calls, with casual unawareness, 'the trail of policy'. The King is the centre of this world, the major manipulator, who works like the controller of a huge chess-board. He plots the movements of all the pieces upon it, charts and predicts with auspicious care, gambles against catastrophe when he has to, his behaviour as king and as man dominated by the desire to keep one move ahead. Behind every move are the twin fears of Shakespearean social man — personal fear and the fear of public disorder. He experiences Hamlet as a peculiarly problematic feature of his opponent's play, who disconcertingly veers across the board in haphazard and unpredictable ways, disrupting all the well-known defensive strategies. The King's Hamlet is one who will not obey the rules of play. He will not listen to appeals to behave 'normally', and is thus full of an incomprehensible volatility and dangerous possibility which needs to be checked, stifled or removed from the board. This latter is the final desperate act of self-preservation to be employed when the 'turbulent and dangerous lunacy' of Hamlet has escaped everything that his 'lawful espials' and 'quick determination' can devise for its containment. At this juncture and extremity 'Diseases desperate grown/By desperate appliance are relieved'.

This is not simply an attitude to Hamlet, nor is it attributable to his being a murderer who doesn't want to be found out. It is not so limited or specific a phenomenon; rather it represents the King's and Elsinore's normal way of dealing with social life. It is an attitude which decides to live life entirely within terms of efficient manoeuvring, and it operates through a chain of command and obedience of a peculiarly sinister kind. It is not the visible command-chain of Viennese law, which can sophisticate its inhumanity with the notion of severe impartiality. Nor is it a mechanism for maintaining stratification and distance which has anything of Venice's elegance. Nor again does it sophisticate its command-structure with the glamour of caste as does the Rome of *Coriolanus*. Each of these can, in its way, create *values*, which, as they are accepted and internalized, make some sort of social cultivation possible. The Viennese can believe in moral severity, the Venetians in elegance and courtesy, the Romans in courage and heroic idealism — all of them partial but not entirely negligible things. But the acceptors of the Elsinorean norms can believe in nothing. They must accept a total reduction of personal life to valuelessness, becoming thereby, like Rosencrantz and Guildenstern, 'the indifferent children of the earth'.

Where those three other cultures demanded that interpersonal relations should always be modulated into their terms, where they will be limited, and perhaps tragically so, Elsinore demands simply that everything should submit itself to the brutal intrusion of, and annihilation by, 'policy'. It is the incarnation of 'order' at the level on which Ulysses enunciates it and Duke Vincentio tries to create it, but now, relieved of their rhetoric and thus unbeglamoured, it is incapable of rising to any value worth the name. The logical last product of this order, the final, farcical, hideous-absurd specimen of Elsinore-man is Osric. And, at the

other end of the social scale, the rhetoric and ritual of Kingship,
built upon an odious structure of 'windlasses' and 'assays of bias',
is a bloated and vulgar parody of a social achievement, whose
unpleasant tones we catch in the King's state-rhetoric, now
oleaginous:

> we beseech you bend you to remain
> Here, in the cheer and comfort of our eye,
> Our chiefest courtier, cousin, and our son   [I. ii. 115–17]

and now grandiose:

> The King shall drink to Hamlet's better breath,
> And in the cup an union shall he throw,
> Richer than that which four successive kings
> In Denmark's crown have worn.   [V. ii. 263–6]

Beneath it all is the steady, tight-lipped calculation of this
fear-driven man and the ready pliability of his instruments, all
bent on enabling the Elsinorean mind and state to 'keep itself
from noyance'.

The play can leave one in no doubt that socialization at this
level, a culture of this kind, is a crime against the possibilities of
life. This network of craven instrumentality can be accepted as
social life only by those whose attitude to the psyche is so
reductive, fearful, hostile or ignorant that the continuous attack
upon individual psychic or imaginative life which Elsinore makes
can be felt as normality. It is a culture, like that in *Measure for
Measure*, whose keynote is philistinism, though here we have only
the dismal, 'despoiled' side of Vienna's philistinism and none of its
idealistic zealotry. In *Hamlet* the modes of philistinism's permanent combat with the kinetic energy of the mind and 'nature' are
presented with marvellous completeness.

3. The life of King Claudius

It is in the nature of this completeness that it is not presented as a
generalized *condition humaine* but is given, in all its detail and
variety, in all the chief characters in their different ways.
Claudius, Polonius and Gertrude are full social-psychological

studies of different kinds of philistinism – the play is that large, and its presentation of Elsinore that intricate. The life of Claudius in whom the idea of philistinism is given peculiar human poignancy, is virtually material enough for a play in itself. The progress of that life is worth following carefully. It reveals many of the most important aspects of Shakespeare's comprehensive vision of socialized man.

His life seems to me to move through five stages in the play. In the first we see his mind living in that condition of sedulous balance which he keeps up in his state-rhetoric. Discretion is balanced against nature, defeat against joy, the eye is 'drooping and auspicious', there is 'mirth in funeral' and 'dirge in marriage', 'delight and dole'. No one emotion is to gather any more strength than would permit its being effectively cancelled by the presence of its opposite. A philistine mind moves in tight and watchful meticulousness over the surface of psychic life, keeping down any forces which might lie below. And in the same tone inter-personal relationships, which might bring strong emotions out into social life, are reduced to formal and contractual requirements:

> the survivor (is) bound,
> In filial obligation, for some term
> To do obsequious sorrow. But to persever
> In obstinate condolement is a course
> Of impious stubbornness.   [I. ii. 90–4]

The second phase is something which is reminiscent of Duke Vincentio and Brutus. The reductivism is rationalized so that, when one's expectations of life have been sufficiently lowered, the cancellation of respect for the individual psyche seems normal and reasonable. Just as Brutus used his 'philosophy' to fore-arm himself against the deaths of those he loved, so Claudius (though with a mind less subtle and, of course, an intent vitiated by strategy) offers his version of the fortification of the mind by patience. Learning the lesson of 'This must be so' will make it mere 'peevish opposition' if, when a loved one dies, we 'take it to heart'.

In this phase of the life of Claudius we begin to feel something pathetic in his crassness. We begin to feel, as we will many times in the play, that there is something in the crudity of it, an oafishness, an ignorance, which we cannot experience with any singleness of moral accusation as merely 'vicious'. Shakespeare's refusal of any merely diagnostic tone reaches here too; and it does so again when the pathetic Claudius imagines that he may have done enough with these platitudinous prescriptions to persuade Hamlet to 'think of us/As of a father' making the same ludicrous underestimation of the powers of human attachment as did Brutus in hoping to win the friendship of Antony by means of sweet reasonableness and an appeal to a bundle of abstract virtues. At a later stage in the play we still feel the pathos of this oafish ignorance running through his request that Rosencrantz and Guildenstern

> Get from him why he puts on this confusion,
> Grating so harshly all his days of quiet. [III. i. 2—3]

There is enough in that of a commonplace cheeriness which wants people to snap out of their quirks and get back to a happy normality to keep up the note of the pathetic even when he is at his most menacing.

The third phase brings him through brooding to the edge of despair as he senses the weakness of his efforts to contain psychic life in himself and others. As with Angelo his language at this part of the play records the basic fear of the living mind, of the 'hatch' of the melancholy which 'sits on brood' in Hamlet and of the danger which 'doth hourly grow/Out of his brows'. In imagery like this he is sensing, with fear, the power of that fertility and productiveness in the mind which he has striven to contain; and the determination to put 'fetters' round the dangerous turbulence is not advanced with much confidence. It gives way at once to his frightened effort to pray, where the habit of fettering itself is felt as a preventative affliction:

> heart, with strings of steel,
> Be soft as sinews of the new-born babe. [III. iii. 70—1]

In this crisis of terror, where the psychic vitality which had once been dominated with nervy assurance is felt to have an unstoppable movement of its own, Claudius' only comfort is from the *mauvaise foi* which is an important feature of Elsinorean

philistinism. It is not unrelated to Brutus' 'riding out' the
phantasma of the traumatic, and consists in a morally enfeebled
effort to hope against hope that 'all may be well', that the
insurrection will come to an end, and that his manipulative
tampering with psychic necessities will have no come-uppance.

In the fourth phase the come-uppance seems inescapable and,
in deep crisis, what has been repressed or ignored seethes towards
the surface with its own kind of demand. It is here that we get
the Claudius of desperation and panic as the manipulating mind
cannot move fast enough to keep all its mechanisms of control
adjusted to contain what is pushing up from beneath. His
language in this part of the play is full of references to turbulent
pressure within and beneath — 'like the hectic in my blood he
rages'; 'O, this is the poison of deep grief; it springs . . .'; 'When
sorrows come, they come not single spies,/But in battalions'; 'the
people muddied,/Thick and unwholesome in their thoughts and
whispers'. At this point the man who has been habituated to the
denial of psychic life seems about to be cracked open or swept
away by powers with which he cannot deal, hardly having learned
to know what they are. The mind which saw grief as an
'obligation' requiring public observance 'for some term' is simply
overwhelmed by the existence of sorrows in battalions. And the
mind which had been assured of its capacities to enclose and
contain the forces of psychic vitality now begins to intimate, in
the imagery it uses to picture such containment, that the very act
of containment itself is one which sours and poisons life at the
root:

> like the owner of a foul disease,
> To keep it from divulging, let it feed
> Even on the pith of life.   [IV. i. 21—3]

It is from this low point that the horrifying fifth stage of
Claudius' life takes its thrust. The philistine mind, led to the
brink of the traumatic but capable of experiencing life's kinesis
only as threat and menace, clamps down all its controls in one last
bid to 'keep itself from noyance'. With the return of Laertes in
IV.v Claudius enters into the fifth and final phase of his life. It is
a last supreme effort of the will in which he touches unpleasant

potencies of the kind which Angelo sensed within himself when he
too had wound down to some sense of 'the pith of life' (the
'sensible warm motion') and then felt, with cold pleasure, that he
could stop its workings. Claudius as ever is more stupid, more
cloddish, less keen in mind and sensibility than Angelo, but his
performance here with Laertes partakes of the same perverse
enjoyment of his own *sang froid*.

The famous remark abut the 'divinity (that) doth hedge a king'
is a gambler's boast in which he is taking reckless pleasure in what
suddenly seems to him to be his invincibility. The public
elaborateness with which he sets up the stakes has the characteristic delirium in it, a racing excitement about power which is held
in check and grossly enjoyed:

> If by direct or by collateral hand
> They find us touch'd, we will our kingdom give,
> Our crown, our life, and all that we call ours,
> To you in satisfaction.   [IV. v. 202—5]

There is a thrilling sense of power in this large-mannered calm, as
there is again in the consciously majestic tone of

>   You must not think
> That we are made of stuff so flat and dull
> That we can let our beard be shook with danger,
> And think it pastime,   [IV. vii. 30—3]

where he conceives of this new-found power as that kind of feline
ferocity which can afford to lie at ease and strike down those who
annoy it with disdainful blows. In this mood he is akin to both
Angelo and Volumnia, at the classic Shakespeare nexus of
delirious evil, in that he now feels that he can project enterprises
in his mind and bring them into being with perfect execution, the
lives of others offering no resistance to the shaping power of his
will:

>   I will work him
> To an exploit now ripe in my device,
> Under the which he shall not choose but fall;
> And for his death, no wind of blame shall breathe;

But even his mother shall uncharge the practice
And call it accident.   [IV. vii. 63—8]

This thrilling sense of an unlimited power to control has now
taken over in his mind from the panic-striken sense of weakness
in which he had, shortly before, felt himself the victim of sorrows
in battalions and of ungovernable forces — like slander,

Whose whisper o'er the world's diameter,
As level as the cannon to his blank,
Transports his pois'ned shot.   [IV. i. 41—3]

That is the life of Claudius before he meets his doom when the
great *tour de force* for which he gambles goes awry at the end.
But there is one further, peculiarly pathetic thing about Claudius'
fifth, power-crazed phase. I have compared the cold excitement
of the will which is involved in it with the ruthlessness of Angelo;
but there is also something else, pathetically different and highly
characteristic of this play where so many of the things which are
most terrible are also most ludicrous. Angelo, in this condition of
excitement of the will, is anything but funny. Neither is
Volumnia. But the *raptus* of Claudius is comic-pathetic in
comparison with these. There is none of the exhilaration of their
perverted idealism in him, and his final zest, like the general
philistinism of his character, has a strong element of the sadly
banal.

For the spirit of Claudius reaches its highest momentum when
he enters with Laertes upon that sad little *folie à deux* on the
subject of Lamord, the great horseman and fencer. For a few
moments they both lose themselves in the midst of their plottings
to enthuse about athletic prowess:

King.   but this gallant
Had witchcraft in't; he grew unto his seat,
And to such wondrous doing brought his horse,
As had he been incorps'd and demi-natur'd
With the brave beast. So far he topp'd my thought,
That I, in forgery of shapes and tricks,
Came short of what he did.
Laer.   A Norman was't?

King. A Norman.

Laer. Upon my life, Lamord.

King.   The very same.

Laer. I know him well. He is the brooch indeed

And gem of all the nation.   [IV. vii. 84—94]

This little exchange is often cut in production, but it never should be. It says everything about Elsinore and the sad stature of its King. For once something has genuinely caught his imagination, inspiring him to wonderment and to the 'forgery of shapes and tricks'. It is as if he had seen magic, something in heaven or earth not dreamed of in his philosophy. A quick-fire and live conversation sparks up for once, Laertes joining him with those delighted extravagances about brooches and gems. For a few moments the Elsinorean imagination catches fire — but only to apotheosize the *summum* of manhood as consisting in athletic agility whereby a man can appear 'incorps'd and demi-natur'd/With (a) brave beast'. With what wicked and deflationary comedy does the imagery of that cut through the mental range of Elsinore-man! It is manliness in the sense of which Claudius was speaking when he told Hamlet it was 'unmanly grief' to mourn his father in excess of normal social requirements; or manliness of the kind of which Laertes is the play's foremost embodiment. It puts the final derisory touch to the grotesque tragi-comedy of the King's life and makes a caustic mockery of Elsinore's pretensions to being considered seriously as a culture at all.

4. *Polonius*

That the play's examination of the philistine mind should be made in a tone which modulates so easily from the hideous to the comic-pathetic is a consideration which leads one naturally to Polonius. The entire creation of him is consonant with the creation of the Elsinore he is so admirably equipped to inhabit. It is all done with a perfect balance between the terrible and the ridiculous. Everything Polonius says and does is at this point of balance, where we perceive, relaxedly enough, the nonsense and silliness that he is, but simultaneously perceive, in a way which is anything but relaxing, the awful effects of what he does. If we laugh at him the laughter will soon be soured by unpleasantness; if we begin to make a moral judgment on him the portentousness of the exercise will be qualified by our sense of the ludicrous minuscule on whom we are commenting. There is nothing evasive or prevaricating about this tone; it is a lucidly sustained ambiguity whose doubleness puts a marvellously precise edge on what the play finally has to say about him.

His variety of the philistine is principally presented in his famous precepts for the control of headstrong youth, his pedantry, his preciosity as regards social forms, his expertise on all matters connected with Art and Life, his ability to encapsulate everything in commonplaces, his crass assurance and his equally crass blindness when the assurance is shown to be fatuous. All this is funny – except when we see that, as it combines with his readiness to act upon his convictions with setting on, spying and overhearing, it creates a restriction and subjection of life which, but for Shakespeare's exquisite restraint, would be almost obscene. We have gone through humour to this point of recoil from him by the time he is despatched, when he has become the noxious listener to private and intimate agonies, venturing upon his task with the equally noxious excuse that the situation demands

> some more audience than a mother,
> Since nature makes them partial.   [III. iii. 31–2]

The outrageousness of his precepts, prescripts and offered tags of wisdom consists in their wilful reductiveness and the stops that they put upon the vital and the kinetic. For Polonius, thought itself is dangerous until it has been shaped and measured; open and expressed friendship is a vulgarity; clothing must not be 'fancy' or 'gaudy'; a woman's response to her wooer must contain nothing 'free and bounteous'. Some of the imagery in which he embodies these notions tells a very revealing tale. The live mind is again an object of mistrust, with its 'new-hatch'd' and 'unfledg'd' impulses; and the 'green girl' who is his daughter sees the connotations of the adjective playing awkwardly back upon the man who thinks it merely connotes a disqualifying lack of experience. He is likewise peculiarly deaf to the revealing implications of his own financial metaphors ('tender yourself more dearly', 'scanter', 'higher rate') and of the metaphor in which he conceives of the greater freedom of those who have the double advantage over Ophelia of masculinity and social superiority — they have 'a larger tether'.

Again most of this is funny — we know how to laugh at this sort of bourgeois non-descript. But it is also serious and nasty enough, particularly because he conceives of himself as licensed by his paternity thus to advise, prescribe and enforce, with the mean little self-justifications of 'you do not understand yourself' and 'I will teach you'. For this licence, practised ceaselessly on Ophelia, is exactly what causes madness in her, just as it helps to cause it in Hamlet. Ophelia is not allowed to create her own self, to interpret and mediate her own world and thus give it cognitive consonance. Instead she is the recipient of ready-packaged concepts, told what to think and what to feel. It is thus that no real self can ever develop in her, so that, like Desdemona and Virgilia, who have been socially practised upon in the same way, she is made helpless when difficult experience is thrust upon her. What Polonius does to Ophelia is the play's most detailed presentation of that denial of self-hood, that constant busy-body shaping and interpreting, which Hamlet protests against with his

> You would play upon me; you would seem to know my stops; you would pluck out the heart of my mystery . . .'Sblood, do you think I am easier to be play'd on than a pipe? Call me what instrument you will, though you can fret me, yet you cannot play upon me.   [III. ii. 355—64]

It is thus that the vileness of Polonius emerges from within the very thing which makes him so comic and absurd. All his ludicrous exhibitions of pedantry and expertise, his mouthings of clichés and commonplaces, his observations and definitions — all imprison the mind's potential range in littleness. And he then enforces that littleness on others with tireless scurry and bustle. His mind has greater range than that of Claudius, with what might in other circumstances have been an attractive kind of curiosity in it; but the end and aim of the curiousity here is that it burrows its way into the lives and minds of others, and takes the life from them to shut it up within his formulae. He can for example recognize (as Claudius never could) that there is 'method' in Hamlet's madness, and that it gives rise to insights that 'reason and sanity could not so prosperously be delivered of'. But the recognition is totally inert. Hamlet's insights are immediately wrapped up in ready commonplaces which get no nearer than Claudius' oafish incomprehension to actually 'taking in' what they contain, and his estimation of the status of 'reason and sanity' (which means his regard for Elsinore's idea of the normal) is in no way qualified by his seeing a superior perceptiveness in Hamlet's abnormality. The attachment to what Elsinore calls normal is complete; the curiosity has been reduced to a meaningless little bustle round the edges of it.

5. Gertrude

Gertrude is the third great centre of the play's presentation of Elsinorean philistinism and its attack upon mind and sensibility. Her main importance for this stage of my analysis is that she exhibits the morally debilitating *mauvaise foi* with which philistinism is accepted and introjected. She has, as Blake would say, 'become what she has seen' — accepted Elsinore's version of life with more or less passive surrender and made the remnants of finer consciousness in herself more or less innaccessible to her ordinary awareness. When keener awareness is pressed upon her by Hamlet in the great closet scene she knows (as Claudius would not) what he is talking about. Under this pressure 'damned custom' is not quite 'proof and bulwark against sense'; but in the ordinary circumstances of life, where such moral cauterization is not in process, the surrender to Elsinore has been successfully accomplished. She no longer has the moral vitality to be aroused by the atrocities she sees it commit. She is a perfect portrait of what Eliot meant by the moral and psychic torpor whereby

> the enchainment of past and future
> Woven in the weakness of the changing body,
> Protects mankind from heaven and damnation
> Which flesh cannot endure.[4]

And Shakespeare's unfailing sympathy with that enchainment and weakness is great enough, for all his unflinching analysis of her, to give the portrait the same fine restraint as we saw in the presentation of Polonius.

Her performance up to the closet scene is one of ordinary compassion for the 'too much changed son', disturbed only by one ominous mention of 'our o'erhasty marriage'. But it is an inert compassion, combining as it does with the sort of moral blindness which will not see the evil of spying and prying, which will join Claudius in those hopeful philosophizings which characterize *mauvaise foi* ('all that lives must die' etc.), and which, in the desperate circumstances of this tragedy, will make her as helpless to understand or intervene as the others. She comes to the great scene with Hamlet as a sort of *femme moyen sensuelle* who is suddenly asked to operate at a moral depth which she has accustomed herself to neglect. So that when she is asked to look at that depth without recourse to the 'flattering unction' which would normally 'skin and film the ulcerous place', her reaction must be one of terror:

> O Hamlet, speak no more!
> Thou turn'st my eyes into my very soul;
> And there I see such black and grained spots
> As will not leave their tinct . . .
>
> O, speak to me no more!
> These words like daggers enter in my ears;
> No more, sweet Hamlet.   [III. iv. 88—91; 94—6]

She finishes the scene in a state of distraction and exhaustion, with no way of dealing with what she knows is there.

She then passes the rest of the play ever more suffering inundations of grief and guilt ('One woe doth tread upon another's heel,/So fast they follow') but unable to derive from them any energy or impulse which would make this suffering more than inert. She is in that characteristic Elsinorean state of riding out the storm and hoping for the best, a state of *mauvaise foi*, disablement and indifference, which is once beglamoured with the name of 'cool patience' when she recommends it to Hamlet.

Though she once has the capacity to see something of worth in Hamlet's madness — something 'pure' like a rich 'ore' among 'metals base' — her ability to do anything with this insight is minimal. And at the end, in the almost intolerably painful scene in the graveyard where the barbarously 'maimed rites' of Elsinorean Law are the hideous background to Hamlet's suffering, it is to the idea of this inhuman patience that she returns:

>   thus awhile the fit will work on him;
> Anon, as patient as the female dove
> When that her golden couplets are disclos'd,
> His silence will sit drooping.   [V. i. 279–82]

Whatever compassion she may still feel has now no further use. She is powerless to react with anything but acquiescence to the sense of wilting and forlornness ('drooping') in those lines, reduced as she now is to a condition of moral and psychic exhaustion scarcely more resilient than that of the Ophelia she had described as 'incapable of her own distress'.

6. A waste land

In all these cases of the play's presentation of the psychological and moral incapacities of philistinism Shakespeare's restraint is impeccable. There is no punishing exposure, no ruthless desire to track down viciousness; and a great deal of both compassion and humour goes into this steady, unerringly intelligent and lucid presentation of very ordinary human failings as they prove catastrophically inept in the face of difficult moral demand. Cocooned in the acquiescence and indifference which Elsinore breeds, the three major Elsinorean adults flounder and blunder their way into troubles which they hardly comprehend. There is little point in the kind of response which tries to isolate sins and apportion blame, to ask questions about who knew about the murder and whether the Gertrude–Claudius marriage is incestuous. The real 'crime' in which all these characters are involved is that of participating without protest in a social normality which is hostile to the most essential needs of consciousness. It is a crime of not seeing and not knowing, of surrendering their humanity to a waste land of zero possibility where anything alive enough to stir the dull roots is alarming, whether felt within themselves or others.

The rest of Elsinore is balefully similar. Laertes, the idiot boy, the mindless philistine athlete of Elsinorean manhood, lives the vitalities of youth with all the crassness of the sporting type and man about town that he is. His Polonius-like precepts for the wretched Ophelia — 'Fear it, Ophelia, fear it my dear sister', 'Be wary then; best safety lies in fear' — see a new generation adopting the banal codes of their elders without demur. And the unimpressive figure that he cuts as an alternative to Hamlet, sweeping to his revenge with heroic relish and no hesitations, should be noted well by those who think that Hamlet's 'failure' lies in his indecision.

Horatio is a 'decent' man, a 'good' man; but he is as powerless and ineffectual as Virgilia in Rome. He has a mind which is in a way far too 'normal' to make any major inroad into Elsinore, and he is thus the kind of friend in whose company the tormented Hamlet is still isolated. He is no less frightened than the average Elsinorean by the 'toys of desperation' which might lead those who are 'desperate with imagination' into trouble. And his response to the madness of Ophelia is pure Elsinore:

'Twere good she were spoken with; for she may strew
Dangerous conjectures in ill-breeding minds. [IV. v. 14—15]

Hamlet praises his capacity for coolness — 'blood and judgment so well commeddled' — but the famous remark about more things in heaven and earth shows his awareness of the limitations attendant upon that sort of quality. It is Brutus again of whom one is relevantly reminded, as Horatio goes to work on the facts of his world with cautious empiricism ('the sensible and true avouch of mine own eyes') to shore up the stability of 'A man that Fortune's buffets and rewards/Hast ta'en with equal thanks'. It is right and inevitable that a mind of this kind, with its admirable but limiting equanimity, as far from the 'gamesome' as is Brutus, should produce as its final response to Hamlet's fate those generous, humane but fragile elegiacs about flights of angels. He is hardly more able than the rest to know anything of the depths of suffering and difficult insight which drive his friend into madness.

And it is Rosencrantz and Guildenstern who sum it all up — 'the indifferent children of the earth', 'Happy in that we are not over-happy', and ready to surrender all independent right to life in the obedient service of an inhuman nullity:

> we both obey,
> And here give up ourselves, in the full bent,
> To lay our service freely at your feet,
> To be commanded.   [II. ii. 29—32]

They work upon Hamlet not with the bustle and commitment of Polonius but with unimpassioned indifference. It is an assignment to which they are resignedly attached, convinced as they are that life in Denmark can exhaustively account for all the world's possibilities and therefore that its crushing requirements are a universal norm. They thus play their appointed parts in it with untroubled calm.

The creation of this Elsinore is a single imaginative act, for all the complexities and specificities of its detail. A coherent vision animates it. The dulled responses and lowered expectations, the blindness, stupidity and indifference are all part of a single core-culture to which each character is, in his own way, completely attached. Its political basis is in the venality of espionage and manipulation, its highest 'value' is athletic prowess, its pleasures are reduced to grossness — drink without laughter, sex without joy — and its capacity for imagination or the ecstatic is deadened by fear.

A very important image of the vision involved is given by Marcellus at the opening of the play:

> Good now, sit down, and tell me, he that knows,
> Why this same strict and most observant watch
> So nightly toils the subject of the land;
> And why such daily cast of brazen cannon,
> And foreign mart for implements of war;
> Why such impress of shipwrights, whose sore task
> Does not divide the Sunday from the week;
> What might be toward, that this sweaty haste

Doth make the night joint-labourer with the day:
Who is't that can inform me?   [I. i. 70—9]

This important speech conjures up a hum of ceaseless toil as the general, wearisome condition of Elsinorean life, where everything is sacrificed to the lowest and most monotonous demand of social obligation represented by unwilling ('impress') work. We derive from the speech a sense of dull, continuous and unrewarding effort as the life-condition of men in this society, all governed by the severe discipline suggested by 'strict and most observant watch'. If we think of the meaning of the comic model in Shakespeare, the labour which 'Does not divide the Sunday from the week' represents a completeness of social obligation which has abolished everything that is meant by 'holiday'. And if we think of what Shakespeare regularly means by sleep, with its soothing and nourishing roles in the natural cycle of life, we shall realize how the work which makes 'the night joint-labourer with the day', involves a similarly comprehensive attack on basic psychic need. The quickness of the kinetic world is here replaced by a dreary and laborious substitute-life which, alienated from the most elemental facts of nature, can produce nothing more live and energetic in human motive and action than is suggested by Marcellus' phrase 'sweaty haste'. It is Elsinore *in toto*, the centre of that single vision which so comprehensively contains all the variety of the individual lives I have so far discussed.

I don't want to imply, with this lengthy discussion of the specificity of Hamlet's culture, the uniqueness of the place, that we are therefore given here a set of human problems for our dispassionate curiosity. There is no need to assume that because Elsinore is a special place it therefore has nothing to do with other places. On the contrary, its debilitations and shortcomings are not rare, and indeed have something to do with all forms of social attachment and organization. They are in part intrinsic to the business of being socialized, in greater part than are the shortcomings of the cultures so far examined in other plays. But for all that, we cannot I think take them as exhaustively representative of all the possibilities of socialization. There is a way of experiencing Elsinore which, knowing that its mores are in part intrinsic to the very business of socialization itself, knows nevertheless that this does not make Denmark, as Rosencrantz and Guildenstern opine, 'the world'. Elsinore seems to me like a Weberian 'ideal type' — a creation of Shakespeare's mind which, contemplating the nature of socialization and the demands it makes upon individual consciousness, draws out of the whole vast and complicated process a single feature (basically it is contempt for psychic energy) and presents its consequences with fine analytic clarity.

We cannot look at the Hamlet who inhabits this Elsinore with simple romantic empathy. The romantic reading is in basic agreement with Rosencrantz and Guildenstern that Elsinore is 'the World'. It is on this basis that it proceeds to indulge the sensation of beautifully hopeless and otherworldly protest against its essential condition. Nor, however, can we look at him with diagnostic judgment, the static quality of which also assumes that Elsinore is 'the World' and that Hamlet's misplacedness within it makes him a case' of neurosis, maladjustment or immaturity. When we look at the specific social dynamics of Elsinore in all their superb detail we are simply setting up the relevant terms in which to order our response to Hamlet, to take him with the full force of his dilemma realized in our minds as Shakespeare has given it. Given Shakespeare's acute and detailed social-psychological documentation of this culture we are wasting our time, and indulging a certain laziness of response, if we merely empathize or categorically dismiss — or indeed if we mystify the whole lucid presentation with notions about Oedipus and Primal Fathers. We see, as we look at this detail, that it is a society which does much to justify and authenticate Hamlet's basic protest and to lend acute relevance to the greatest insights which he reaches in trauma. It is a society in which the 'funeral-bak'd meats' *have indeed* 'coldly furnish'd forth the marriage tables' and which *does indeed* wish to pluck out the heart of his mystery and play upon him like a pipe. And it is above all a society which commits the continuous crime of the enclosure and containment of psychic life, giving one of Hamlet's most agonized protests a fine and desperate accuracy:

O God, I could be bounded in a nutshell and count myself a
king of infinite space, were it not that I have bad dreams.

[II. ii. 253—5]

7. *The double prince*

I have suggested that both romantics and diagnosticians are
fundamentally lazy in their response to the play, and that the
laziness consists in allowing either the play's call to empathy or
its call to judgment to overwhelm that wholeness of response,
made out of both, which I think it requires and deserves. When
we come to Hamlet himself this is crucial, because fully to
experience him is a most exacting and demanding task. Perhaps
nowhere in all Shakespearean tragedy does a character require
such a continuous effort of assessment and reassessment, of
feeling and qualification of feeling, an effort of lucid ambiguity
sustained under such pressure of immediacy.

If we follow through the development of Hamlet's traumatic
reaction to Elsinore we shall see that at every point our attitude
to him needs to be created out of doubleness. We recoil and are
drawn back, we move close and are held away, while all the time
the ambiguities remain alive, breeding deeper understanding and
never giving way to that kind of inert indecision which would
create in us (as it would bespeak in the author) confusions and
uncertainties. This is a great enough play, and its hero is one of
sufficiently realized substance, to bear all the pressure of
Shakespeare's analytic mind without becoming a mere diagram.
And as we follow the analysis which that mind has made we are
not reducing the play to diagrammatics but enriching our sense of
the sureness with which it handles materials howsoever intract-
abe, and thus of the complexity which it can give a hero who is
palpably and immediately a single human being. We can afford to
follow the intricacies of this double quality in his trauma without
fear of losing the man in complications.

We experience his mourning at the start of the play as a
genuine grief at the death of his father and a genuine shock at his
mother's 'o'erhasty marriage'; but we also take it as that kind of

self-exhibition which needs a conspicuous role to provide a strong defensive exterior for the emptiness within. His talk of his father as Hercules and Hyperion is a genuine love and admiration challenging with desperate grandiloquence the squalor he sees around him; but it is also the juvenile idealization of a mind which does not want to recognize this father as having been a king (and thus a political animal) and a man (and thus made of flesh). And his general tendency to express physical revulsion represents both a real protest against the grossness of Elsinore and a hysterical reaction to the discovery that he, the gem of a court's idealisms, is also made of flesh.

Much of his humour promotes the same doubleness of response. When he pursues the ghost around as it moves under the stage there is a fine vitality in his exuberant wise-cracking about the 'old mole'; but there is also an hysterical wit exercised in beating off the pain of fearful knowledge. In the humour with which he baits Polonius, Rosencrantz and Guildenstern there is an excellent contempt for their nastiness, but also something which, because he never turns its pressure of demand upon his own weaknesses (which are caressed not a little in his soliloquies), feels also like an over-venomous defence. This comes back in the play-scene, where the aggressive, bawdy wise-cracking is splendidly full of kinds of energy unknown in Elsinore but also, of course, full of misdirected vindictiveness in that it is used to harry the innocent Ophelia. In all these moods he is reaching after richnesses of experience and perception which Elsinore cannot create or acknowledge; but he is also doing it with a recklessness which derives a goodly conceit of itself from contemplating its own daring.

This matter of self-image links with the trace of snobbery which is a counter-force to another set of his insights. His instructions to the actors, far from being Shakespeare's views on the theatre gratuitously added to the play, are finely woven into this part of the pattern. They bear witness to his enthusiasm for a vitality and lack of inhibition which he sees and yearns to possess; but they are also the rather mawkish words of a bright young man down from university and ready to teach the professionals, a cocky young fool teaching his grandmother how to suck eggs.

Similarly, his intellectuality, his declared high estimation of the value of the intellect and of art, is presented both as an admirable striving after kinds of human possibility which Elsinore feels can be exhausted by a few *bon mots* from Polonius; but it also has that strident and protesting quality which belongs to a young man who feels that this sort of talk puts him above the ruck with a certain *éclat*.

The products of that intelligence, when they come, also have the characteristic doubleness. His soliloquies witness an attempt to achieve qualities of moral scruple and depths of self-knowledge the absence of which makes the others so gross; but, as I have said, there is just a little that is self-caressive about them, something of the man who admires himself for being so wondrously complicated and conceives of this complication as a feature he shares with nobody else. And in some of those pronouncements which offer to generalize on the basis of his ponderings – 'What a piece of work is man', for example – the major part of our response is deeply respectful of the mind which has fought through to this insight and expressed it in all its difficult contrariety; but something still remains of that suspicion which teaches us to beware of this power to pronounce. He doesn't quite leap on these things with Isabella's suspicious relish, but there is an element of her brittleness there, something very different from the quietly accommodated humanity of the Montaigne from whom many of them come.

His hesitations about revenge also have the double tone. His hesitation about killing Claudius is admirable enough in itself, particularly, as I have said, with the comparison to hand of the prancing Laertes – an alternative kind of avenger for whom action holds no intractable problems. But the real hesitation is not just about killing but about acting at all, and it is here that we get the characteristic ambiguity. There is real moral compunction in it and real insight into the futility of many kinds of socially corrective action; but, contrariwise, there is also the irritating and debilitating talk, talk, talk of an obstinately self-doubting mind. And, also on the subject of action, his description of the sea-voyage and the pirates' attack is full of a childish 'I did this and then I did that' tone, just as the talk of sweeping to his revenge is so tragically unlikely to be an honest statement from this harassed mind. But the first also contains a hint of Hamlet's stifled capacity to relish the vigour of physical and decisive action, and the second looks more admirable as a kind of prayer for the release of vital powers which in him remain blocked. The same ambiguities surround the business of decisive action in the grave scene. Hamlet's leaping into the grave is an act compelled in him both by the loss of Ophelia and by the scene's dreadful exhibition of the 'maimed rites' of Elsinorean Law. As such it is an admirably powerful reaction to the affront to life which Elsinore constitutes at this moment; but there is self-advertisement and desperate role-playing in it as well, seizing on an heroic role to play to the full as a relief from the intolerable contradictions of a frustrated mind.

To respond to all these threads in the play's presentation of its hero is, as I said, an exacting task. But I find that it does not break down the character into a sequence of debating points, nor that it cannot coexist with that sympathy-commanding immediacy with which the contrarieties of his mind and social dilemma are given to an audience. The Hamlet who comes through Shakespeare's sustained analysis is whole and palpable, and the fine and poignant manner in which the analysis is maintained, interlocking sympathy with judgment, pain with comedy, exhilaration with exasperation, should give one no cause to opt out of it and concentrate on a conveniently reduced selection of its features in the advancement of a more simplistic case. It is constantly anti-reductive, and it constantly has the means to create and reveal new facets of the dynamic presentation of his mind in its social world which escape any easily reductive categorization.

The greatest of all the play's exhibitions of this anti-reductive doubleness is the closet scene. This scene, like those between Angelo and Isabella, or Volumnia and Marcius, is a dialogue of extraordinarily sustained intensity. The characters, as they fight for a justification of their lives, drive each other to the brink of hysteria in this poignant combat with each other and also in that acute inner struggle that each is having with himself. Its doubleness derives essentially from the scruple Shakespeare shows about the role of moral castigator and cauterizer which Hamlet occupies in the scene. It is a role which, given the general torpor of Elsinore and the specific *mauvaise foi* of the Elsinore-habituated Gertrude, commands one's ready sympathy; but the play is far too aware of the complexities of this sort of ferocious inter-personal engagement to allow Hamlet's self-appointment to the role of 'scourge and minister' (the characteristic Elizabethan satirist and avenger) to be a matter of any single value-judgment.

Thus, for all that we preserve a basic sympathy with the cauterization as he sets about it, we are also reminded both of the impudence and of the theatricality of one who will offer to 'set you up a glass/Where you may see the inmost part of you', of one who will 'wring your heart', of one who will confidently hold up real and counterfeit pictures of what Man is, and of one who will display not a little pleasure at the ingenuity of his own devices in envisaging 'the engineer/Hoist with his own petar'. These, the less admirable features of the role of 'scourge and minister', cut across the urgency and basic moral decency of Hamlet in the scene to take elements of our sympathy away from him and towards the Gertrude whom, in this light, he seems rather to be torturing than aiding.

And then again, doing the same work of correcting and complicating our balance of sympathies in the scene, there is that dewy, romantic, conspicuously young quality of much of Hamlet's language As we hear him talk of the 'grace and blush of modesty', of the rose which is to be found on 'the fair forehead of an innocent love', and of the grace which, seated on his father's brow, gave him

> Hyperion's curls; the front of Jove himself;
> An eye like Mars, to threaten and command;
> A station like the herald Mercury
> New lighted on a heaven-kissing hill,   [III. iv. 56--9]

we begin to see that the basic principles of the scourge and minister are not such as to equip him very well for the task of making mature and understanding moral judgments on those who are disadvantaged enough to be made of mere flesh and blood. That is not enough to warrant his dismissal as an adolescent, of course; but it does enough to move more of one's sympathies away from this idealistic young man and towards the woman of flesh and blood, whose life has been equally palpably created for us, upon whom the comments are offered.

This idealizing element is, of course, the obverse of that generalized disgust at the 'solidity and compound mass' of the world which turns Hamlet's justified (and indeed admirable) horror at the grossness of Elsinorean life in the direction of a more sterile protest against the inevitable conditions of life itself. It is this which produces the over-insistent tone in 'the rank sweat of an enseamed bed', the 'bloat king' and his 'reechy kisses'. It is over-played, the insistence arising from an inner need or compulsion as much as from the moral necessities of the situation. But again there is no need to rush from this observation to the judgment that this is 'neurotic' or 'Oedipal'. What we see here is the much more difficult and interesting phenomenon of what happens to a mind that must attempt to create itself amid the squalor of Elsinorean life, when that squalor has power and presence enough to push him over from proper disgust to general and vengeful nausea. And with those features of Elsinore in mind which are *actually* nauseating it should take no great effort of intelligent compassion to see that the effect of witnessing this 'overspill' should not be moralizing impatience so much as a heightened awareness of how intensely difficult such self-making is.

Similar considerations appertain when we consider something which is close to this over-played disgust, namely the cruelty and jeering which there is in his horror at the fact that his mother has an alive sexual appetite. There is a gratuitous jeer in 'at your age/The heyday in the blood is tame' and a nastily derisive sexual punning (on 'sense' and 'motion') in 'Sense, sure, you have,/Else could you not have motion'; and 'Rebellious hell,/If thou canst mutine in a matrons's bones. . . .' is another outburst strongly laced with cruelty and ignorance. But it is a mind in the pain of self-formation which produces these things and a mind which has been lied to by Elsinore's lived pretence that the kinetic world can and should be totally controlled by subjugation to a code of social propriety. It is thus a mind which is in no position to control those nose-rubbing insistences that rush ferociously through passages like

> Eyes without feeling, feeling without sight,
> Ears without hands or eyes, smelling sans all [III. iv. 78—9]

or 'A murderer . . . a villain . . . A slave . . . a vice of kings . . . A cutpurse . . . A king of shreds and patches'. Such things are, to an Elsinorean, fearful knowledge; and their fierce coursing though Hamlet's language is witness, principally, to the magnitude of the difficult insights which crowd in on such a mind once the nutshell has been cracked and the hitherto enclosed self is exposed without defence to the nature which before had been relegated to the status of 'bad dreams'.

To follow and do justice to the full terror and complexity of a scene like this we cannot rest on the fixed absolutes for judgment which both romantic and diagnostic readings presume. Once we stop thinking within terms of the static categories which each of those ways of reading sets up for the consideration of the abnormal mind we shall not find the exacting double tone of Shakespeare's analysis to be a source of confusion or unclarity — for which, *in extremis*, we may join T. S. Eliot in blaming the errant author. It will instead take on quite another aspect. It provides a way of approaching the irreducibility of personal life scrupulously and tentatively, yet with full analytical clarity, as something which is explicable, though never exhaustively or categorically so. And this scrupulous approach to difficult explication is a product of that quality in Shakespeare's mind which makes him see the fate of an individual life as a matter of working out its possibilities within a given, limited set of social norms. When those norms are as inhuman as they are at Elsinore the form which is taken by an effort to reach mental vitality and integrity is *necessarily* disordered and painful. The writhings and twistings of his mind, towards liberation and back into defence, towards vital action and back into torpor, towards release and back into blockage, are all part of a coherent vision of how a brave and imaginative man tries to construct a world of cognitive consonance for himself in the face of everything that the offered world of Elsinorean 'reality' and 'normality' has constructed on his behalf.

8. *A defeated trauma*

The tragic end result is a victory for Elsinore. There is hardly any
more painful moment in all Shakespeare than that in which
Hamlet renounces the validity of his efforts and enters Elsinore
on its terms. Three times he imagines he can get away with using
the dismissive word 'madness' with which, as he once knew with
all clarity, Elsinore has been in the habit of laying the flattering
unction to its soul to persuade itself that not its trespass but his
madness speaks. On the last usage he has surrendered himself:
'His madness is poor Hamlet's enemy'. From here the play rushes
to its end and his extinction in one swift movement. Involved in
an Elsinorean-athletic combat of muscle and cunning the superior
consciousness to which he had reached in his trauma is of no
relevance to him. It will receive only the kind but frail
acknowledgment of Horatio's elegiacs, after which no memory of
it or deference to its significance will survive 'The soldier's music
and the rite of war' which initiates the reign of Fortinbras.
Nothing has been learned and everything lost. The structures of
Elsinorean normality have been prized apart by a single life and
the volatilities of the world of kinesis have flared through the
cracks. Those structures now close and reset, as they did in
Venice, Vienna and Rome, and all sense of what they still exclude
is banished from the collective mind.

But the great value of what they exclude has been strongly
represented in the language of Hamlet's traumatic confrontation
with the world beyond Elsinore's enclosing structures. That
'under-view' of Elsinore, which made him

> wipe away all trivial fond records,
> All saws of books, all forms, all pressures past,
> That youth and observation copied there   [I. v. 99–101]

and seek to open his mind to more vital kinds of perception,
derives from a world of traumatic energy which is exhilarating
and terrifying by turns. As it comes through in Hamlet's language
we recognize its vitality principally by its speed or energy-
charge. This is there in the satiric language of the 'funeral-bak'd
meats' and 'who shall scape whipping' where the derisive

under-view is given zest by the whirling enthusiasm with which Hamlet sees and leaps upon it possibilities. And it is there also in that heady relish, moving fast to keep up difficult balances, which informs the remarks which topsy-turvy traditional sanctities (the 'paragon of animals' etc.) and structured social relationships ('mother and father is man and wife; man and wife is one flesh; and so, my mother'). Such language has bitterness and pain in it and it is used to taunt and jeer; but there is an unmistakable bravura in it as well, and an unmistakable radical fire which is set off in an admirable and exciting light by the offered comparison of the torpor of Elsinorean man, happy in that he is not over-happy.

This fire and bravura informs a whole range of Hamlet's statements. It comes from a new feeling of being unshackled in mind, released from the imprisoning nutshell. This volatile release expresses itself in the pursuit of difficult and dangerous knowledge free from traditional fear — 'though hell itself should gape' — and in the urgent sense that such knowledge is virtually a physical need of the human mind — 'Let me not burst in ignorance'. It expresses itself also in the lively abandon with which a vigorous life is welcomed and sought — 'We'll e'en to't like French falconers, fly at anything we see' — and in the enthusiasm with which the liberated imagination is recognized and celebrated, for its capacity to 'amaze indeed/The very faculties of eyes and ears'. It is all possessed of a crackling zest which too many readers miss in favour of the image of a brooding, ineffectual genius which has attached itself too powerfully to the play — the same zest which is there in the quick-fire joking, punning, bawdy and clown-wisdom which he uses on Rosencrantz, Guildenstern, Polonius and Osric. It has to do with much of the language of passion and wit which we know from the releasing world of the festive comedies, a language which moves faster and probes deeper than that of the social men, normatively attached to Law and discipline, upon whom it comments. It works its way down by pun and irony to levels at which its satiric deflation of socialized man must involve a quality of accommodation to the natural, the intractable and the absurd to which the patterns and norms of social life render us relatively insusceptible.

This is the level at which social priorities and distinctions dissolve in the comic-absurd of 'a king may go a progress through the guts of a beggar' and where the body of My Lady Worm is 'knock'd about the mazard with a sexton's spade'.

But, as the play makes clear in so may ways, it is one thing to talk this language of basic accommodation and quite another to live it steadily. The same vitalities which to Hamlet in this mood are intoxicating are, at other moments, frightening in their structurelessness. Then, instead of the rapidities of his sarcasm we get the *ennui* and resignation of his self-doubt; instead of the enthusiastic zip of his quick ironies we get the lingering unresolvedness of one in whom the absence of any stable value-structure now feels like the absence of any self and the absence of any motive for action. The insights of the traumatic will at one moment give psychic strengths 'as hardy as the Nemean lion's nerve'; but at the next they will weigh upon him heavily enough to break both spirit and body:

> Hold, hold, my heart;
> And you, my sinews, grow not instant old,
> But bear me stiffly up.   [I. v. 93–5]

Likewise, all the *talk* of the worm and the sexton's spade will not make him fear any less the merely animal aspects of life, nor will it make the skull of Yorick smell any more pleasing. Even the cherished freedom of imagination for which he strives will, at such moments, look like a terrifying form of possession:

> The spirit that I have seen
> May be a devil; and the devil hath power
> T'assume a pleasing shape; yea, and perhaps
> Out of my weakness and my melancholy,
> As he is very potent with such spirits,
> Abuses me to damn me.   [II. ii. 594–9]

Throughout the play it is the tragic experience of Hamlet to be held at this point of indecision, of half-achieved self-formation, of halted progress, of radical insight locked against itself in terror. The under-world of the traumatic into which he sinks contains those energies which Nietzsche saw as released to men by tragedy — 'the constant proliferation of forms pushing into life . . . the extravagant fecundity of the world will' — and Hamlet at his best is able to tap some of this energy and release its powers into the closed world of Elsinore. But at other times he cannot, or dare not, confront it, and he becomes nauseated with what he sees. There is nothing in this play, as we shall see there is in *King Lear*, which, in Nietzsche's words again, can 'turn his fits of nausea into imaginings with which it is possible to live', and in the end the world of the traumatic destroys its victim. Nietzsche's 'journey', Nietzsche's 'passing through' is blocked. Once again it is a human incapacity with which we are concerned, the inability to absorb the intractable and the absurd into normal life. Nobody in Elsinore has the capacity for ambiguity or the tragic deference to let the world of Hamlet impinge on his mind. And Hamlet alone cannot survive the wild and fantastic progress of trauma. So his lonely dream of a midsummer night retains throughout a bleak and wintry aspect.

9. Postscript — the players

There is one final point to be made with regard to Elsinore. The harder I look at the play the smaller and more enclosed Elsinore seems. The play begins with its walls and they are present in our minds throughout. Every mention of the world outside intensifies this sense of 'the house which offers no release', an enclosed, a provincial place, somewhere which is shut off, deeply symbolic of all the myopia of culture. Arrivals and departures in the play are significant movements which are not only geographical but ethical. England, Paris, Wittenberg and the open sea are *other places* — the latter three suggestive of largeness of life and expansiveness of possibility beyond Elsinore's reach. Even in the open air of Elsinore's graveyard we are presented with men who speak a language more deeply and easefully accommodated to basic nature than the inhabitants of the court within; and also with the remains of one, Yorick, whose infinite jest and most excellent fancy is suggestive of a psychic range and vitality far beyond what we see of Elsinorean capacities. The trees, weeds, water and flowers of the brook in which Ophelia drowns herself are strongly felt as belonging to a nature which is external and alien to the court's life. And so is the sea, above which Elsinore's walls tower in impregnability.

All these accumulated suggestions of a world outside Elsinore help to place the tone of the court very clearly; and one visitation from an outside world, that of the players, does this job in a very important and powerful way. Their role in the play has been much debated, and particularly Shakespeare's attitude to the melodramatic heroics of their stage language. They have some-times been held to have little to do with the main business of the play; but though the Elizabethan theatre was marvellously free of formalism, and able to make its plays swallow large chunks of rather extraneous matter, I do not think there is any-thing marginal about these players, and the rhetoric of their stage-language does not seem to me to be merely a subject for criticism. They bring into the stifling atmosphere of Elsinore intimations of a life altogether more human, and the extravagant melodrama of the Pyrrus speech has all the vital open-air qualities of the popular stage, bringing into the enclosedness of the court a freedom of expressive range and an uninhibited bravura of the spirit. The Player-King's admirable forbearance with Polonius' idiot and ill-mannered interruptions, and with Hamlet's scarcely more admirable parade of expertise and instruction, comes through as an attractively relaxed maturity. And his capacity to produce his performance at any moment and in any circum-stances is a similar token of an uninhibited kind of self-possession which Elsinore cannot create.

Hamlet knows this. They represent for him a vigour for which he yearns, a vitality of mental life whose value he enthusiastically esteems. His praise of them is a praise of freedom of expressive range, of an uninhibited capacity for outwardness and self-projection, of the unclogged mind. The player's 'dream of passion' sees him venturing with ease into areas of mental experience of which Elsinore is both ignorant and afraid: no Elsinorean could dare to manifest 'distraction in's aspect' with this kind of equanimity. And the player's ability to 'force his soul so to his own conceit', 'his whole function suiting/With forms to his conceit', is something which contrasts very movingly and revealingly not only with Hamlet's confused self which cannot conceive but also with the shrunken selves of the philistine members of Claudius' court, the creative powers of whose minds are either locked behind their fears or overwhelmed with oblivion and indifference. As in the comedies the powers of the artistic imagination are symbolic of qualities which are essential to psychic life. The 'children of an idle brain,/Begot of nothing but vain fantasy' are once again tokens of creative-imaginative powers without which the spirit is 'bounded in a nutshell'. I feel the freedom and range of that life outside the Elsinorean nutshell every time the admirable player, as enthusiastic about his art as Bottom but far more skilled, begins to unroll the marvellous, surging, unabashed bravura of his theatre:

> Anon he finds him
> Striking too short at Greeks; his antique sword,
> Rebellious to his arm, lies where it falls,
> Repugnant to command. Unequal match'd,
> Pyrrhus at Priam drives . . . .
>
> [II. ii. 461 *et seq.*]

7

King Lear:
the metaphysic of the spring

> Civilisation is hooped together, brought
> Under a rule, under the semblance of peace
> By manifold illusion; but man's life is thought,
> And he, despite his terror, cannot cease
> Ravening through century after century,
> Ravening, raging, and uprooting that he may come
> Into the desolation of reality . . .
>
> (W. B. Yeats: *Meru*)[1]

> . . . But as it was,
> A dead shepherd brought tremendous chords from hell
>
> And bade the sheep carouse. Or so they said.
> Children in love with them brought early flowers
> And scattered them about, no two alike.
>
> (Wallace Stevens: *Notes Toward a Supreme Fiction*)[2]

1. The complete metaphysic

We have examined five plays which make their social-psychological studies of the Law as it prevents the 'release' of the comic world. Each presents a society which cannot acknowledge or understand those aspects of life which lie outside its own peculiar vocabulary. Each therefore suffers a crisis of anger or bewilderment as the multitudinous life of nature refuses to conform to its *Vorstellung* of the world. The destruction of Othello and Marcius is understood neither by them nor by any Venetian or Roman onlookers. In Vienna, a bitter parody of a festive-comic play wherein the movement towards release and the enactment of a final resolution is a lie and a charade discloses to us a narrow culture still remaining fearfully at odds with the natural life which its final celebration pretends to embrace. In *Troilus and Cressida* the inability of Troy (or Greece) to support human life is total and absurd, and the pulse of the world's kinesis simply has its destructive way with men who in no way comprehend it. Finally, in *Hamlet*, we have our first case of a sustained traumatic experience of the world on the part of a man who is thrust outside Elsinore's encapsulating narrowness into the ferocious vitality of the kinetic world; and his eventual destruction, still without his fellows knowing the greatness he has achieved, still without the saving richness of nature being released into the ossified human group.

In all these cases, in tragic and proto-tragic plays alike, we see that tragedy is not an event that can be understood solely in terms of the life of the hero or protagonist. Nor is it enough simply to see his world — Rome, Venice or Elsinore — as his 'background', thus giving it the essentially secondary function that that word implies. Tragedy is a significant event in the life of a human group. It is social trauma. It offers, as Schopenhauer and Nietzsche both knew, a peculiarly profound and crucial insight into the dynamics of social/mental life. It is a critical moment in the development, or non-development, of the social life of a group, a moment of representative crisis wherein the delimiting structures of a culture are subjected to extreme pressure by virtue of the fact that they in their turn have exerted intolerable pressure on individual life.

In the festive comedies crises of a similar kind are met and survived. The structures lock, the pressures mount, and then are released in a creative way through the agency of nature. An adjustment is made, the nourishing vigour of the kinetic is received and absorbed, the generative processes of the world's will go on unimpeded by the rigidities of the Law. Ambiguity, tolerance and deference to the incomprehensible carry the vitalizing powers of the kinetic into a cultural world which, like the natural world, finds that it can permit the birth of spring.

But the five tragic plays we have considered so far are wintry.

The flowing sap of new life is a fearful and disturbing presence in the frozen ground of an old Law. The spring will not come forth in the freedom and mirth of festive-comic release and there is no gay delivery of fresh life. Civil men have lost the gamesomeness of the kinetic. The vitality of life is contained and blocked, and when it convulses through the hard surfaces that hold it down its wanton exuberance is terrifying to men who have accustomed themselves to living shut off from its forces. The life-giving powers of nature are, in these circumstances, too ferocious to be contemplated by civil men, too savage to be admitted into the rule of Law. The sap of nature seems to them like a torrent of vileness, its incivility hideous to civil minds. And because it seems like this it *is* like this. It seems destructive and wild, and hence it actually is the agent of a civil man's destruction. He has no way of welcoming it, he is not in the habit of acknowledging it. He has been trained either in complacent ignorance of its powers (as in Venice and Troy) or in militant hostility to them (as in Rome, Vienna and Elsinore).

Such a metaphysical pattern seems to me to underlie the social crises of the five plays we have considered so far. I say 'underlie' because, with the exception of *Measure for Measure*, this metaphysic, which is so visible and explicit in festive comedy, is much more succinctly woven into the thought-structures of these tragic plays. But it is there, carried by the plays' language and imagery, and by such motifs as the closed house (or walled city) and the *senex* (Brabantio, Vincentio, Polonius). And it is there too in the series of young or newly married couples whose life, in one way or another, is stifled by the Law of their elders — Othello and Desdemona, Marcius and Virgilia, Claudio and Juliet, Troilus and Cressida, Hamlet and Ophelia. In them youth is prevented from being spring. New social growth takes place without benefit of nature.

When we come to *King Lear* we find a play which is very different from the other five. What we find in it is a great metaphysical and archetypal summary of the vision of human Law of which the other plays have given specific instances. The other plays, I have insisted, are not about 'the world' but about specific parts of it where specific examples of human culture prevail. They are works of social-psychological realism. *King Lear*, unlike them but like the festive comedies, dramatizes the general metaphysic. We do not find in it the mores of ancient Britain, as we have found the mores of Rome, Venice or Elsinore. What we find is a play about general Law which is archetypal, a play in which the figure of the King is an archetypal imagining of everything that it is to be a social man. *King Lear* is about 'the world'. Its tragic crisis is an archetype of the social crises we have seen in the other plays. Its metaphysical patterning is, as in the comedies, visible and manifest in dramatic structure, motif and image. It is about cultured man, 'sophisticated' man, as Lear puts it, and the tragic dynamics of his relationship with the wild world of nature. Twentieth-century criticism has been right, as I said in my introductory chapter, to see this play as the heart of the matter; though I am less sure that criticism has yet developed the terminology for grasping the play's whole metaphysical meaning.

As this central play works itself out, motifs, themes and tones with which we have already familiarized ourselves in considering the other plays take their place in the comprehensive summation of it all that this one involves. The large-mannered and flamboyant confidence of men powerful in their own culture, and powerfully committed to its 'normality' (as we have seen it in Othello and Marcius) is here again in some of the notes struck by Lear in the opening act, where a culture celebrates itself with conspicuous vanity. Rome's claim to kinship with the gods and with the mightiest and most predatory hunters of the animal world finds its echo in Lear's arrogant cursings wherein he seeks to enlist ungovernable powers on the side of his own social enterprises. A militant culture's summary dismissal of the 'errant' or 'abnormal', to which Vienna was so prompt in *Measure for Measure* and which is Elsinore's way of dealing with Hamlet, is present in the expulsions of Kent and Cordelia which initiate the tragedy of this play, and in the later expulsions of Lear and Gloucester.

In this first act the King, like that version of the comic *senex* who returned as Brabantio, claims ownership of the life, mind and love of his daughter; and that daughter delivers the Desdemona-like speech of resistance which stirs up vengeful repugnances within him. Even nearer to Brabantio is Gloucester, that archetype of the 'citizen' with his duties and loyalties and sense of place, as the second figure in whom there is dramatized the classical Shakespearean conception of man's delimiting attachment to his Law. And the pride of the socially assured and attached meets its rebuff not only from the bravery and endurance of those who suffer its onslaughts but also from the mischief of the contingent world itself which, oblivious of human posture, will go its own indifferent way, sometimes making a grotesque mockery of the boldest pretensions.

The madness which in Hamlet was both terror and exuberance, and which was both of those things because it was released from the containments of the normal, is here again with a similar meaning and structural role. It is in the King; and it is in his Fool, whose presence constantly helps us to focus the play's under-view of the Law, and whose vigorous overturning of all stable norms brings some of the exuberant disbelief of *Troilus and Cressida* into the heart of tragic experience. And that peculiarly Shakespearean concept of evil, as the willed and thrilling appropriation of life by a spirit of furious ego and enterprise, is drawn up from the Iagos and Volumnias and Angelos of the other plays into the archetypal presentation of its essential forces which is given in Goneril, Regan, Edmund and Cornwall.

So the play seems to summarize the whole tragic world, and thereby to present us with a general vision of human order which has manifold connexions with the specific studies of social orders made in the other plays. But it summarizes even more than that, and creates its meaning out of an even greater body of Shakespearean thinking about the dynamics of social life. For if in terms of tone and motif *King Lear* draws upon the whole corpus of the tragic plays, then in terms of pattern and dramatic movement it gives us the shape of the festive-comic model more clearly and completely than any of the plays so far discussed. Returning to the metaphysical and general from the social-specific, it returns also to the structure of a festive-comic play wherein the metaphysic is made dramatically visible.

Thus we begin within a great house, where all the panoply of a culture is assembled. We are at a moment of characteristic crisis in that culture's growth from generation to generation. As in festive comedy a culture is revealing its propensity for the reduction of civilization to mere Law. And, again as in festive comedy, the most classical of all instances of the crisis of growth — marriage, and the settlement of inheritance and lineage — begins the movement of the play. This house of Law is surrounded by the wild world, into which the errant are driven or where the Law's victims seek sanctuary; and those who adventure into it experience all the tumult of the kinetic which, in the social world, was tamed or ignored or repressed.

Soon the play polarizes along classic festive-comic lines. Within the house, whence new life has been banished, socialization degenerates into what (legitimate or not) has the crude and oppressive quality of usurpation — the usurpation of order by tyranny. And outside the forces of release gather themselves, summon new adventurers out to recognize and join them, and to survive the experience of the outer world before returning to repossess the house. Act III of *King Lear* alternates indoor with outdoor scenes to bring this pattern and meaning into palpable dramatic life; and Acts IV and V see the creation in the fields of a new household, released and releasing, made up of those of the old order whose loyalty to civilization has been flexible enough to permit them to reject the Law and defer to the experience of trauma, together with the young — Cordelia, Edgar, children of the Law-givers. The festive-comic tones of joyous release, spring-time and reintegration are strongly there in the latter part of the play. As in festive comedy, but as in no other tragedy, the protagonist's experience of the wild world is witnessed with sympathetic and deferential understanding by his fellows: for once there is a new acquist of true experience from the great event. And again as in the festive comedies but as not in the tragedies, the protagonist himself is fully receptive to the meaning of his crisis and exposure, and *survives* the journey through the wild.

Until the last scene. Up to its final moments the play has followed in movement and structure this festive-comic pattern. Then, at the very moment of social reintegration, the circle is cut again by the deaths of Cordelia, Lear and Kent. The debates about the end of the play — its 'blackness' or otherwise — may be seen as a question of how much weight in the experience of the play as a whole should be given to this withdrawal or cancellation of the festive meaning. I shall take up such issues later in this chapter, but it is worth noting here that I do not think they can be adequately discussed without reference to the scene's structural position at the end of a play which has so conspicuously followed this conventional model — in other words without reference to the general metaphysic which that model embodies. Perhaps the scene cancels the festive-comic meaning entirely and leaves the end of the play 'black'; or perhaps it relates to the festive-comic pattern in other less decisive ways. Either way the shaping metaphysic is involved, carried by a festive-comic model which has been utilized and transmuted with extraordinary originality and freedom. Only a critical language which acknowledges the presence of that metaphysic can make a serious effort at interpretation of the play.

2. The lord of nature

The all-powerful and Law-giving King of the play's opening is a figure of deep metaphysical significance who has clear and strong connexions with figures from the comedies who would hand down the law of an older generation to contain the recalcitrantly independent life of the young. The citizen Gloucester, at first entailed by a crudified version of Law as brute power and then repelled by it as more flexible and humane conceptions of the civilized stir within him, is another figure whose role in a familiar and patterned metaphysical design should not escape critical attention. Of course they are both too individual to be 'explained away' by a pattern, or reduced to the status of mere cogs in a metaphysical machine. But again Shakespeare's apprehension and realization of the human significance of the pattern is far too subtle for there to be any danger of that; and criticism must attempt to emulate that subtlety, responding to Lear and Gloucester both as the dramatic individuals they so palpably are and as the players of significant roles within a metaphysic of culture and nature which here makes its great summary of the vision of the other plays.

The Lear whom we meet in the opening scene is a proud man. I say that not to draw attention to his 'fatal flaw', nor to suggest that we take what happens in this scene, or in the play at large, purely at the level of individual-moral characterization. It is not a matter of a character-trait, but of a general human characteristic which, short of mere symbolism, he *personifies* or *embodies*. (Rashness would go nearer than pride towards getting his character-note — Kent and Goneril are both accurate observers.) But it is his pride which takes the stress in another sense. He is proud in that he personifies that large and unreflecting confidence which, in the metaphysic of Shakespearean tragedy and comedy alike, is the key-note of men who are formidably, comfortably, ignorantly and dangerously attached to their cultural world, sensible both of its power and of their representative power within it. He is a manifestation of the fatal pride of Law.

We are immediately given this sense of his role in the play's scheme of things in the image of the map. He peruses the vastness of nature, to which the map of his kingdom makes reference, with that kind of leisured and weighty poise of which his opening phraseology is amply redolent — 'our fast intent', 'our largest bounty', 'a constant will'. With the map before him the vastness of the natural world can be squared, measured and divided at a finger's stroke — 'even from this line to this', 'this ample third of our kingdom' — and made to speak eloquently of its convenient bounty and beauty:

> With shadowy forests and wide champains rich'd
> With plenteous rivers and wide-skirted meads. [I. i. 63–4]

This is human culture, conscious of its power, achievement and resplendence, celebrating its amplitudes; and a King, magnificently representative of culture, relaxing and glorying in his state. As master of all this mastery he feels the wealth and splendour he embodies:

> my power,
> Pre-eminence, and all the large effects
> That troop with majesty.   [I. i. 129–31]

He knows the sanctions and the laws which he can invoke to crush the rebel Kent, summoning up their powers with massive words like 'allegiance', 'place' and 'potency'. He feels his royal self to be the centre of life, the all-in-all of the world, disdainfully capable of withholding all the qualities of civilization from the rebel Cordelia:

> Therefore be gone
> Without our grace, our love, our benison.   [I. i. 264–5]

The King, then, conceives of himself as the lord and owner of nature, and as the lord and owner of men's destinies. He can possess and dispossess at will. His lordship and mastery, and the allegiance he can demand from his subjects – all are absolute. Dismissed from this presence a human being dwindles to the status of a trivial piece of the physical world – Kent's 'hated back' and 'banish'd trunk', Cordelia's 'little-seeming substance' – as non-human as the 'barbarous Scythian'. They will be expelled to inhabit an outer, extra-cultural and non-human world of dumb, animal violence; an area of life not on the map, and hence not part of the King's 'nature', inhabited by the sub-man or beast 'that makes his generation messes/To gorge his appetite'.

What we have here is not just a choleric egotist. Magnificently palpable as a human being though Lear is he cannot simply be taken as an old man with a venomous temper. He is a real man; but he gets his *significance*, which is not the same thing as his *reality*, from the vital and recognizable role we feel him to be playing in the life and growth of human culture at large. Through the behaviour of the King we see the dynamics of the civilized world; in his judgments we feel that Law speaks; and in the fact that he is old and bigoted lies a metaphysically significant fact about culture and Law – that inalienable capacity for rigidity, ossification and defensive violence, an innate tendency to resist the rejuvenation by natural growth to which the youth and marriage of Cordelia refer.

So the King and his culture are old and law-hardened. He will permit the growth of the new only if it submits itself to the crudest version of continued allegiance to *his* Law – a submission accepted by the flashily public 'love' of Goneril and Regan, and rejected by Kent and Cordelia for whom first 'service' and then 'love' mean something altogether different. Again we have individuals; but again individuals whose actions are of the profoundest metaphysical significance, woven as they are into the great pattern which this scene creates. It is a representative, archetypal crisis in the life of culture, and nothing has contributed more to its realization as such than the festive-comic image of culture's progress through blockage to release.

As we watch the old King unfold his *Vorstellung* of the world's magnificence, and banish those who do not comply with it to the extra-cultural world of bestiality, we are watching something full of irony. Kent exits from the scene not as a 'trunk' but as a quite unfallen man of some considerable buoyancy who will not degenerate into the bruteness of the King's 'outer world' but 'shape his old course in a country new'. Cordelia too, 'cast away' and 'stranger'd' by her King and father's dismissal of her, is taken up and married by another king and led not to a wilderness but to 'our fair France'. And it is Lear himself, not some imagined barbarian, who has made his generation messes to gorge his appetite.

But the general metaphysic of the scene will again help us to be clear as to how this irony works; for it does not make for any crisply dismissive moral commentary on the errant egotist for his 'vanity' or 'pride' as such words might refer to the specific culpabilities of an individual. The scene's metaphysical patterning has made us too aware of the *inevitability* of the King's pride of attachment, and the *necessity* of its attendant defensive bigotry — an inevitability and a necessity which we know how to associate with the ageing and ossification of a culture and hence which we know how to see as supra-personal. The aged King is as much a victim of this necessary ossification as his daughter and servant are the victims of his wrath. Being king, the apotheosis of the mastery which is culture, he cannot be otherwise. Invested with complete symbolic responsibility for the Law as a whole, freighted with the full panoply of a culture's resplendence, how can he be other than the confidently and narrowly convinced man that he is? How can the agent of the Law be also the agent of deference and flexibility towards the nature which the Law must structure? How can this crisis *not* happen? He is (harking back to that distinction I made between two of Nietzsche's terms) governed by *necessity* rather than by *despotism*; and the necessity is that which his metaphysical role as ruler imposes upon him.

And so it is as a representative necessity in the difficult growth of culture that this crisis comes. He wields his power with crude violence; but that same power really *is* magnificent, and really *does* call forth unstinted loyalty, not just from time-servers, nor just in his own proud fantasy, but from a man whose humanity and uprightness will not waver throughout the entire play:

> Royal Lear,
> Whom I have ever honour'd as my king,
> Lov'd as my father, as my master follow'd,
> As my great patron thought on in my prayers. [I. i. 138—41]

Kent, who is about to tell Lear abruptly that he is 'mad', is not coining eloquences. He is giving a full assent which is never withdrawn throughout the play to the principle of civilization carried in those great words 'royal', 'honour'd', 'king', 'lov'd', 'father', 'master', 'patron'. Neither the scene's comprehensive irony, nor the play's sustained tragic exploration of human culture does any damage to the meanings that Kent embodies in such words. The irony does not therefore work purely dismissively on the self-celebration of the King and his culture. The 'pride of culture' which Lear has exhibited, and indulged in his fury, is rather something which the scene's irony works on in a purifying or clarifying way, beginning the play's long process of sifting out the Kent-Cordelia meanings of such words from their contamination of Lear's reductive abuse of them.

Lear, in other words, actually is king, master, father, great patron. In his kingship there actually is embodied an idea of culture which commands the full assent of the humane. As king he personifies and embodies 'man' in his full potential — a meaning to which such words as 'royal' and 'master' will accrete as they are used in the play. He is the essential man. His royalty carries in itself all the meaning which 'man' has as against 'beast' or 'thing' — which is to say that he personifies culture.

But, the irony of the metaphysic reveals, in the very fact that he personifies culture and is 'royal' there is latent and necessary trouble. To be so supremely the spokesman and embodiment of a culture's achievement is, in Shakespeare's world, to be necessarily prone to the blindness which I have called 'pride'. Lear embodies culture's power, and therefore also its tragically necessary weakness. The King as embodiment of culture is also the embodiment of that pride or narrowness which so inevitably slides into bigotry and thence into viciousness. This kind of attachment, unless you are as miraculously clear-sighted as Kent and Cordelia (and they are not burdened with the role of king), inevitably brings over-attachment in its train. A word like 'master' slithers towards 'tyrant', 'patron' towards 'owner', 'father' towards 'dictator'. And the idea of civilization, which for Kent and Cordelia carries a full charge of humane loyalty and obligation, degenerates into a notion of raw power which, in its ignorance, presumes to believe that it has so conquered nature as to be able to enlist its ungovernable forces on the side of its own whims and decrees:

> by the sacred radiance of the sun,
> The mysteries of Hecat and the night;
> By all the operation of the orbs
> From whom we do exist and cease to be . . . [I. i. 108—11]

The archetype of socialized man has been created, and has entered the classical tragic crisis. The traumatic journey of the Law's destruction and recreation will now begin.

3. The revolt of culture against Law

So the opening of the play is rich in metaphysic and archetype. The beginning of the story of the King unfolds the metaphysical significances of that story, bringing the metaphysic to palpable, dramatic life. The great patterns are made visible, and the great archetypal words, like 'king', 'master', 'royal' and 'nature', which will realize those patterns and give them immediacy and vitality throughout the play's duration, are launched into their dramatic life. The drama which begins with a king and his map will be a metaphysical play about social man and the natural world.

But after this first big scene, where the full panoply of culture is before us and human events make manifold reference to the general and supra-personal, the play quickly moves into the little world of the local, the private, the domestic. Edmund's speech on the goddess Nature provides a bridge, and then we are in the small world of a private citizen whose crisis will be 'domestic'. But still the shaping metaphysic is at work, and still those parts of it which come from festive comedy — like the concept of the *senex* — have their role to play in developing the significance of Gloucester's life and making his drama as archetypal as that of the main plot.

For the sub-plot of the life of Gloucester, though it is domestic, private and small, meshes in with the general metaphysical significances which the public life of King and State have intimated in the opening scene. The privacies of the Gloucester world are different in scale from the massive significances of the King's world, and the criticism which will apprehend them properly will look more like the traditional criticism of 'individual character' or 'character study'. But as we follow the life of the private citizen its relationship to the wider pattern, to the archetypal study of Law and nature to which the King's life gives rise, becomes ever more clear, and is felt as ever more *necessary* to the understanding of this local life. Gloucester in fact presents us with the play's second great archtype of social man. He is not, like Lear the King, the *summum* of all that culture is. But as an important citizen, noble and gentle, he is the bearer of peculiarly poignant and representative human responsibilities. In his language and his behaviour we get vital indices of how much culture can achieve.

In the earlier part of the play one must feel that it is not very much. He has fathered the bastard Edmund — created a man from whom the privileges of culture are withdrawn (and therefore, from Edmund's point of view, the sanctions also) — but he speaks of it in a casually racy tone which scarcely accords it this kind of significance. He makes it seem like the almost admirable slip which an important citizen is privileged to be permitted, and his reference to such qualms as it may have given him — 'now I am braz'd to it' — just catches in its tone (though there is no heavy moralistic insistence) an element of fatal disregard for life wherein one feels him to have become slightly too easily attuned to the cessation of moral sensitivity. (Kent's 'I cannot wish the fault undone, the issue of it being so proper' contains just the right tones of hesitation and generosity which meet the matter so much more fairly than Gloucester's 'braz'd'.)

He is absent for much of the major business of the first scene, not witnessing Lear's curse upon Cordelia and the banishment of Kent, though we shall see his response to it in the next scene. And when he is present in the latter part of the first scene he is present in silence. He sees the lone Cordelia receive Lear's abuse and he sees Burgundy's shabbiness; and, as he watches, the important citizen and decent servant of the state does not have a word to say for himself. It is like the modesty of Escalus, an ineffectual flabbiness too morally desensitized to react with Kent's swiftness to the misuse of power and too conscious of the Law's letters to see quickly enough what is portended by this violation of its spirit.

In the domestic scene (I. ii) we get our justification for feeling that this is not purely 'private' but a matter of society, hierarchy, status and law; and it is again the modest Escalus, but now also the weak and gullible Brabantio, who have contributed their specifics to this archetype of a decent and law-abiding citizen. The grossness which stung Kent into his immediate resolve is to Gloucester just a quirkish policy of the Great Ones who stand above an earl in the scheme of things and upon whose doings this ordinary earl (unlike the extraordinary Earl of Kent) is not accustomed to comment without a fuzz of status-induced modesty to blur him. 'All this done/Upon the gad!', and the citizen knits his worldly brow in puzzlement: that is the Escalus part of the archetype. The Brabantio part comes in when the citizen knows he is big enough to act and react in his own moral right, in matters concerning his own household and familial duty. Here the citizen knows he has rights. He has children, which means that obligations, duties and loyalties are owed to him; and in that conviction his deepest ego is enshrined. All self-meaning will be gone if a child does not give him the same love-as-duty which he gives those above him. The parental love which is knowing and feeling, which resides in an actual knowledge of the loved child as an individual, and which hence can trust that child in its separateness: this is not to be found in Gloucester any more than it was to be found in Brabantio. He gives love as a patron (the breeding of his bastard was 'at my charge') and expects to receive it back in the form of gratitude. A love-relation which has dwindled to this status will snap, as with Brabantio, upon the slightest suspicion of duty withheld:

> O villain, villain! His very opinion in the letter!
> Abhorred villain! Unnatural, detested, brutish villain!
> Worse than brutish!   [I. ii. 72–3]

And, again like Brabantio, he will later be led to the most extreme counter-withdrawal: 'I never got him'.

Like his Venetian predecessor Gloucester is quick to the self-pity of the thwarted *senex* – 'To his father, that so tenderly and entirely loves him. Heaven and earth!' He is prompt to seek redress – 'Edmund, seek him out, wind me into him, I pray you.' And he cannot live with himself until the matter is settled, for where love does not include trust security can only reside in total knowledge: 'I would unstate myself to be in due resolution'. Only thus can he keep himself from noyance. There can be no security so long as the dreadful possibility of filial ingratitude haunts him. And then, when it is 'proven', there can be no security so long as it goes without the most extreme punishment. His entire *Vorstellung* of the world is menaced if this exception to the world's known laws is not righted or removed. All his deepest fears as to the viability of that *Vorstellung* will have been hideously confirmed; for just as Desdemona's 'unfilial' act seemed like a realization of all the fears which had lived in her father's dream, so the unfilial act of Edgar will only tend to confirm the justice of his father's anxieties – the eclipses and portents which have been troubling him as intimations of the age's degeneracy.

When we meet him again in Act Two he is at his worst, a captive of the crudest meaning of Law. Braced with an inspiriting sense of the righteousness of authority, the citizen makes his being over to the agency of the all-encompassing law:

> The noble Duke my master,
> My worthy arch and patron, comes tonight;

> By his authority I will proclaim it,
> That he which finds him shall deserve our thanks,
> Bringing the murderous coward to the stake;
> He that conceals him, death,   [II. i. 58—63]

and

> All ports I'll bar; the villain shall not scape;
> The Duke must grant me that.   [II. i. 80—1]

Entailed by the Law, the citizen here reaches his lowest point. Here he can indulge to the full the self-pity which is congenial to righteousness:

> O, madam, my old heart is crack'd, it's crack'd,   [II. i. 90]

and surrender himself obsequiously to those representatives of the power of Law who are most conveniently to hand:

> I serve you, madam.
> Your Graces are right welcome.   [II. i. 128—9]

This portrait of the early Gloucester is drawn with beautiful accuracy and economy. Everything, as I say, of Escalus and Brabantio (and behind them the comic *senex*) has gone into this archetype of the socialized man who is dwindled into mediocrity (and *in extremis* real unpleasantness) by unreflecting habituation to culture as Law. It is a splendid clear-sightedness, and a rare conjunction of the specific with the metaphysically general, which has created this quintessence of such men; and which has included in that quintessence also a trace of Polonius (that fussy concern about the Great World of Policy and the oddities of the new-fangled) and Duke Vincentio (that well-meaning but ill-thought concern about the world's degenerating to a point where the bonds will crack 'twixt son and father').

But the portrait is masterly also for its restraint and its generosity. Without flinching from the fact that his mediocrity can descend to real viciousness (that is recorded of Gloucester in II.i, and I mean to stress it by linking him with Polonius and Duke Vincentio), Shakespeare has never treated him with anything short of calm and fairness. It is partly a matter of tone and dramatic presentation, wherein the waspishnesses of the diagnostic such as intrude into a prose commentary on him are avoided by imaginative sympathy. And it is partly again a matter of the play's metaphysic; for just as Lear, burdened with the necessities of kingship, could not in a sense be other than he is, so Gloucester, burdened by the necessities of citizenship, and by the necessities of the role of father in a family structure, is likewise felt to be metaphysically *inevitable*.

And so, created with imaginative sympathy, and placed in a setting where the metaphysical inevitability of his narrowness is quite apparent, Gloucester is able to draw from us much more than a critical diagnosis. We saw behind Lear's rhetoric of power to the finer language of civilization and excellence of which it was a debased version. Now we see behind Gloucester's debased language to some very real human decencies. His bumbling sense of the proprieties is faintly in touch with modesties and courteous deferences of a gentle and likeable kind. His foppery (as in the speech about eclipses and portents) bespeaks also an unassertiveness about the power of man in nature, and holds promise of that sense of human vulnerability which breeds kindness and gentleness. And, as the contrasting intelligence of Edmund will remind us, this kind of folly lacks the assertive will which can sweep aside all in-bred hesitations and make over culture completely to the spirit of Law. Thus, though his fears will run away with him and make him talk of his son being brought to the stake, he does not in fact like violence when he sees it — 'Weapons! arms! What's the matter here?'; and the punishment of Kent with the stocks, let alone the stake, brings out his sympathy and concern — 'I am sorry for thee, friend . . . I'll entreat for thee'.

As the play develops, the presence of these decencies within the citizen's debased codes makes itself gradually more felt. The story of Gloucester is a story of the reawakening of culture from within the hardened and ossified version of itself which I have called Law. His two speeches in III.iii are superbly pitched at a point of balance between the citizen's sense of what is politic ('there is part of a power already footed. We must incline to the King') and a decent man's genuine sense of outrage:

> Alack, alack, Edmund, I like not this unnatural dealing. When I
> desired their leave that I might pity him, they took from me the
> use of mine own house, charg'd me, on pain of perpetual
> displeasure, neither to speak of him, entreat for him, or any way
> sustain him. [III. iii 1—6]

As he is torn between these opposing demands there begins
to be created in him the language of Kent, which is a language of
culture in a richer sense than mere Law:

> I will look to him, and privily relieve him . . . If I die for it, as
> no less is threatened me, the King my old master must be
> relieved. [III. iii. 14—19 *passim*]

The stocking of Kent had troubled him as an impolitic way for a
Duke to handle the servant of a King, but it has also stirred
deeper scruples. Hereafter his sense of the civilities and proprieties becomes ever more responsive to the richer meanings
which the words of civility also touch.

And hence his steady growth in stature, insight and courage.
The sight of Lear on the heath — the errant expelled by Law — is
too much for the decent citizen to stomach. In his repugnance he
finds the prompting to challenge the powers which he had
obsequiously obeyed;

> my duty cannot suffer
> T'obey in all your daughters' hard commands,
> [III. iv. 144—5]

and he begins to learn whose meaning of the word 'duty' he has
espoused — 'Ah, that good Kent'. At the beginning of III.vii
where he will be blinded, the citizen finds himself seized by the
brutalities of power and triumphantly acts through the crisis of
his reawakening life. The words that he uses to carry his sense of
outrage are a moving and beautiful testament to this reawakening:

> What means your Graces? Good my friends, consider
> You are my guests; do me no foul play, friends.
>
> By the kind gods, 'tis most ignobly done
> To pluck me by the beard.

                         I am your host.
             With robbers' hands my hospitable favours
             You should not ruffle thus.   [III. vii. 29—40 *passim*]

Helpless in the hands of those who wilfully flout every humane
scruple, he makes his kindly sense of the obligations of friendship
and hospitality sustain a strong witness to the whole idea of
civilization — as Cordelia had done with her word 'bond' and as
Kent had done with 'father', 'master', and 'patron'. And as their
meaning is released from within the shell of the words so he
moves to his full stature and commitment:

    I am tied to the stake, and I must stand the course.
                                                [III. vii. 53]

Ejected in his turn he will, on the heath, be able to
acknowledge how the conveniences of culture cocoon their
beneficiaries in moral blindness — 'Our means secure us'. He will
find the strength to move through the annihilating sense of the
absurd into which his traumatic awakening plunges him — 'As
flies to wanton boys are we to th' gods' — and to be liberated into
that chastened generosity which will make him echo Lear's
egalitarian prayer:

    Let the superfluous and lust-dieted man
    That slaves your ordinance, that will not see
    Because he does not feel, feel your power quickly;
    So distribution should undo excess,
    And each man have enough.   [IV. i. 68—72]

In that speech, he will squarely confront the inhumanity of
culture when it has degenerated into mere Law and power — the
enslavement of the gods' ordinances.

So the moving story of the Earl of Gloucester, though it is
private and small, takes place within and gives detail and
substance to the metaphysical patterning which the public crisis
of King and State has set up. And the vital festive-comic part of
the metaphysic, wherein is traced a movement towards the release
and rejuvenation of culture, has been a major contributor to the
creation of his significant life. We have had the old King and the

old citizen in whom the ossification of culture has been made dramatically alive; and in the citizen's awakening we have also felt the dramatic realization of the idea of culture's release. Another small and private life — that of Albany — adds more substance to the pattern made by Gloucester's awakening; and a brief consideration of that will complete my discussion of the revolt of culture against Law.

Albany's is a small part, until at the end he steps into a major public role and a major structural role as a focus and organizing point for the resisters of the degenerate Law, which by then has become mere brute power. But the handling of his revulsion from the excesses of the Law provides an important parallel and addition to the case of Gloucester. He is like Gloucester in his weakness, his silence (throughout the first scene, for example), and in the ease with which, because of these, he can be practised upon or entailed by the thrust of evil. Like Gloucester he lacks Kent's alertness to the abuses of Law, and needs time and desperate pressure before his humane scruples will assert themselves. The progress of the awakening of his decency takes place off-stage — he is absent from I.iv to IV.ii when he will emerge 'but never man so chang'd' — but the lightly sketched movement of his quiet life adds some vital material to the play's creation of the rescue or rejuvenation of culture.

The foppish Gloucester who talked of eclipses and other premonitions was, I have argued, not simply a fool. He was also a decent man in whose foppery there was some sense of the limitedness of the human mind, its inability to govern and control the vast powers of the kinetic world. This sense, foppish or no, had a latent humanity in it consisting in a knowledge of human vulnerability. The man who feared eclipses had something which Lear fatally lacked as he invoked the powers of the gods to crush his enemies. And he had something which the triumphant wilfulness of Edmund, Goneril and Regan held viciously in contempt.

Albany, less foppish than Gloucester but with a decency which is just as weak and fitful, has intimations of the same limits. The driving will of his wife frightens him and makes him hesitate because it runs contrary to his saving sense of the limitedness of

the human mind. The rational thrust of her determination and
enterprise stirs him to anxious protest against the dangers which
he intuitively feels to lie within this sort of false presumption:

Striving to better, oft we mar what's well.   [I. iv. 347]

And he also feels intuitively that the fear which drives culture
towards the rigour of Law (the fear which we have seen in
Vincentio and Claudius for example) is pathological and reductive: 'you may fear too far'.

This sense of the limitedness of mind, and of the reductive
logic which, impelled by fear, makes over culture to the rigour of
Law, is a kind of guarantee against the pride of culture, and a
guarantee against the inhuman licence to practise and manipulate
which we have already seen studied in *Hamlet* and *Measure for
Measure* and which in this play grows at a horrifying pace when
such chastening knowledge is put by.

For the momentary voicing of these humanizing thoughts
Albany gets his key position in the play as a kind of minor
assistant to the movement which principally lives in Gloucester.
When he reappears in IV.ii he has undergone a long sojourn with
his anxieties; and the latent fineness of the hestiation which his
quiet nature embodies is now awakened in the sure voice which
speaks its rather saintly wisdom to the ferocious Goneril. He is
still in some senses of the word a 'weak' man — Kent would
probably not have had his scruple about dealing toughly with
Goneril because she is a woman. But that weakness is again
mostly a strength, keeping him (to her considerable irritation)
from the wolvish 'masculinity' of Edmund. He is not quite
'thrill'd with remorse' like the servant who revolts and kills
Cornwall, for 'thrill'd' would be too strong and passionate a word
to use of his quiet humanity. But with a calm and quiet-voiced
decency he contributes the piety of his goodness to the play's
presentation of the humane sanction involved in culture but not
in Law.

4. The delirium of evil

So the King embodies the ossification of an old Law, and the
citizen Gloucester grows out of such ossification and into a new

humanity. We have begun to elucidate something of the play's essential metaphysical shape. The play sets up culture in its excellence and Law in its bigotedness as inextricably linked things — the linkage is metaphysically necessary. And it enacts, following the festive-comic pattern, the rejuvenation of culture and the reawakening of finer civilities which were frozen in the winter of Law.

But, so far, this shape has been perceived somewhat 'comfortably'. We have not yet taken any account of the tremendous forces which are involved as social man loses and finds himself in this way and as a society makes these adjustments in its life. Albany does indeed come quietly out into the light. But Gloucester loses his eyes, nearly loses his mind, and then loses his life. Lear loses his mind and then his life. The rescue of culture by Cordelia, Kent and Edgar involves them all in griefs almost unendurable and finally claims the life of Cordelia and, it is clear, of the exhausted Kent. The play's metaphysical movements are clear enough. The ossification and re-emergence of culture can be described in this way. But the movement is in fact a terrible convulsion, and the forces involved in it are all but fatal to life itself — only Edgar and Albany of the major characters surviving it. The powers of the kinetic world are so violent that these adjustments in the life of society take place amid havoc and catastrophe. If the play has anything to do with the birth of spring then we must say that the birth of spring involves the earth in direst agony. If the festive-comic *shape* is apparent in the play then its *tone* certainly is not. The green world of psychic renewal is the storm-lashed heath, and the exuberance of the metamorphosed mind is the madness of the King 'cut to th' brains'. We must now begin to take note of the terror of the forces involved in this 'spring'. The first place where we can get a sense of this terror and power is in the play's representation of evil wherein the fury of the world's will is appropriated to vicious misuse. The second place is in the madness of the King, who experiences the agony of this convulsion 'unbonneted', without protection.

This evil, as I have said in earlier chapters, is a matter of obscene wilfulness. Social-specific examples of its tones were found in Iago, Volumnia, Angelo and (comic-absurdly) in

Claudius; here, as in the Macbeths, we have its archetype. But as in the other plays so in *King Lear* there is nothing mysterious about this evil. In the other plays it always consisted in a desire for power, a desire for invulnerability, for freedom from fear, the lust to be free of insecurity and non-recognition, the drive of ambition. It was always made palpable as social-psychology; and here too its presentation in archetype does not mean that there is anything merely gratuitous or mystified about it. It is generated, in all too credible and recognizable a way, in a seizure of power by the ambitious and the holding of that power against the protests that come from traditional humane habit and sanction. And it is most ferociously impelled into life by one whose exclusion from social acceptance and recognition make him an archetype of the Iagos of the world — the bastard Edmund.

It is in the nature of this evil that it moves always towards the hysterical, as potencies are seized upon and the seizure enjoyed in rhapsodic tumult. These hysterical notes are first sounded by Goneril and Regan in their declarations of love for Lear. Their language in that first scene is flashy, brazen and streamlined. They abandon themselves to its intoxicating glamour rather as Volumnia abandoned herself to her rhetoric of blood in which, as here, intimate devotions fell prey to will and enterprise. Goneril, who loves him 'dearer than eyesight, space, and liberty', and Regan, who is

> an enemy to all other joys
> Which the most precious square of sense possesses,
>
> [I. i. 72—3]

exult in these flamboyant extravagances in a way which involves grotesque distortions or amputations of the psyche. The senses ('eyesight') and the consonance of the mind (the 'square of sense') are ravaged by what is virtually a kind of insanity, but ravaged with a cold control (like Angelo's) which enables them to turn this performance on and off again at will. When we first meet it the spirit of evil is that of a frightening mechanism of the will which is set loose to cut its way through mental and social fabric alike.

The second feature of it that we see is its mental and political enterprise. Goneril, Regan, and Edmund are, like Iago, Angelo and Claudius, doers, fixers, calculators of opportunity and movers one step ahead. Once the mechanisms of the will have started their operators will have no rest, pushing their will-machine through manoeuvre after manoeuvre in pursuit of the desired goal of complete security through complete power. The fear of failure or chaos is a major motive for keeping this drive going. Already at the end of the first scene they are in motion:

> We must do something, and i' th' heat.   [I. i. 306]

And by the fourth scene Goneril is hard pressed by the number of moves that must summarily be executed to allay the constant fear of disorder:

> 'Tis politic and safe to let him keep
> At point a hundred knights — yes, that on every dream,
> Each buzz, each fancy, each complaint, dislike,
> He may enguard his dotage with their pow'rs,
> And hold our lives in mercy.   [I. iv. 324—8]

It will be a fast-footed opportunist who can keep up this frenzy of enterprise and manipulation — like Goneril trying to anger Lear's knights and 'breed from thence occasions', or Regan, sounding the same word as she winds the aggrieved Gloucester to her will:

> Occasions, noble Gloucester, of some poise,
> Wherein we must have use of your advice.   [II. i. 120—1]

Or like Edmund enjoying the sense of his own skill and adroitness:

> Pat! He comes like the catastrophe of the old comedy,
>   [I. ii. 128]

or, with grosser laughter:

> My practices ride easy.   [I. ii. 173]

This spirit of restless contrivance, impelled by a raging of the will and a persistent fear of failure, is inclined to break out in a familiar kind of cold anger when its drives seem to be impeded — the black and frowning 'frontlet' of Goneril which Lear chides, the furious and barren jeer of her 'mew!' to Albany, Cornwall's hunger for 'revenge' when Gloucester deserts his cause, and the fierce competitiveness of the sisters' desire for possession of Edmund. It is like Volumnia's 'anger's my meat ... in anger, Juno-like' as the rapacious ego gathers its forces to burst its way through recalcitrant opposition, and conquer the impediments to its dreams of power. Projects and conquests are figured in the driving mind, and the mind braces itself with rage to preserve intact 'the building in my fancy'.

Close to this angry tone is a tone of sullen callousness, peevish and bargain-driving, which is a vital and authentic part of the whole syndrome in so far as it too practises upon others with the desire to reduce, degrade and annihilate. Goneril has this ugly tone as she berates Lear and scowls at the 'pranks' and 'not-to-be-endured riots' of his knights, and Regan echoes the tone in her turn as she jeers at the 'unsightly tricks' of the old man's desperation. And when they are together at the end of Act Two the tone redoubles in intensity, each inciting the other to increasingly hard-faced demands as they feel their torment of him making its deadly progress.

There is always a reckless delight or pleasure in the tones of this evil, marking it as perversely passionate. It is hotly energetic and explosive. Metaphysically speaking it seems to be a deadly form which kinetic vitality can take when, harnessed by the mind, the life of nature is made to fuel the Law-bound and ego-bound will. Where culture defers to the life of nature passion does not take such a form, for the free play of nature's energy is then acceded to without fear and without the desire to possess. But the Law, lacking that deference, breeds this grotesque substitute for passion, this grotesquely destructive and self-delighting desire. Nietzsche's concepts of the Greek and the barbarian Dionysos define this spirit well, in its connexion with and difference from the full passional life of kinesis. This evil, in *King Lear* as in *Macbeth*, is Nietzsche's 'witches' cauldron' of horrible and insatiable destructiveness. And the people who live by it do so by deliberately conjuring in themselves the most terrifying aspects of the natural world, and then keeping their power over what they have conjured.

This spirit reaches two climaxes in *King Lear*. The first is in the blinding of Gloucester where sadistic pleasure and the will to degrade are given freest rein. The second is in the competitive lust of the sisters for Edmund, which is the logical end-point of the delirium and perverse passion they embody.

The blinding scene could hardly be more terrible. If we now tend to think of Auschwitz as we watch it then that seems to me inevitable and right. The sadism is there, starting with Cornwall's *relish* for the deed which first sounds the note of hectic licence and heady outrage which the scene embodies. So also is the pleasure which is taken in the gratuitous reduction of life to the mere physical-objective — 'corky arms', 'vile jelly'. The whole scene is set off by haggish chanting:

> *Regan.* Hang him instantly.
> *Goneril.* Pluck out his eyes.   [III. vii. 4—5]

And throughout its duration the cruelty of the action is constantly being stepped up in intensity by a well-savoured chorus of brutal statements:

> Pinion him like a thief . . .
>
> To this chair bind him . . . .
>
> the lunatic king . . .
>
> Upon these eyes of thine I'll set my foot . . .
>
> One side will mock another; th' other too . . .
>
> Go thrust him out at gates and let him smell
> His way to Dover . . .
>
> Turn out that eyeless villain; throw this slave
> Upon the dunghill.   [III. vii. 22—96 *passim*]

This is not just cruelty, but a cruelty which is intensified by pleasure taken in outrage. You are not quite responding to the evil and horror of this scene until you see that they *enjoy* what they do. They enjoy dismantling the man; and dismantling the edifice of humane culture to which his protests in the name of friendship and hospitality have made their moving but helpless reference.

Enjoyment and perverse passion inform the other climax of this delirium which comes in the sisters' lust for Edmund. Goneril gives herself to him thus:

> *Goneril.* . . . Wear this; spare speech. (*Giving a favour*)
>   Decline your head; this kiss, if it durst speak,
>   Would stretch thy spirits up into the air.
>   Conceive, and fare thee well.
> *Edmund.* Yours in the ranks of death.

Regan duplicates the tone and manner: [IV. ii. 21—5]

>   General,
>   Take thou my soldiers, prisoners, patrimony;
>   Dispose of them, of me; the walls is thine.
>   Witness the world that I create thee here
>   My lord and master.   [V. iii. 75—9]

It is the dramatic realization of what many an Elizabethan or Jacobean writer would call 'lewdness' — a difficult concept to present squarely as numerous examples of its appearance in Elizabethan satire and Jacobean melodrama will show. It can be a mere function of an idealizing and somewhat righteous imagination which, seeking for any opprobrium with which to blacken the enemies of Order and Good, will find the language of sexual misdemeanour or perversion conveniently to hand. But then the concept is part of a far less viable metaphysic than here — a metaphysic in which that myth of Purity and Depravity, from which I said Shakespeare had lifted and developed the figure of Isabella, was a defining element. Here, in a very different metaphysic, the concept achieves its life and the idea of evil as 'lewdness' is convincingly realized in social/sexual terms.

In Shakespeare's other presentations of this kind of malign power the sexual element has had its role to play. As here it was not *insisted upon* — one of the usual indices of hollowness and opportunism in other Renaissance uses of the motif. Rather it was confronted with a steadiness and calm which, again unorthodox in the Renaissance, did not seek to promote a righteous and rather prim sense of shock. Iago's drive towards the annihilation of Othello took into itself the language of sexual jealousy and sexual degradation with convincing naturalness. Volumnia's hysterical rhetoric too, thriving upon the cessation of ordinary womanly feeling, did not need to be strained by a partisan idealist to give it that tone of glamorously exultant desire. And Angelo's language of terror and threat drew, with equal rightness, on the yearnings and frustrations which the repression of sex by the Law had bred in him.

They are by no means all cases of the same emotional dynamics. (If they seemed so, in such different people, we would indeed simply have another Jacobean case of the easy and unexamined appropriation of a conveniently blackening language.) But in each case the clear-sightedness of Shakespeare's social-psychology has, within the terms of a different and greatly superior metaphysic, made the equation between perverted natural drives and ruthless social ambition live and hold. The ego, wishing to manipulate the human world, must also manipulate itself — thereby staving off the 'compunctious visitings of nature' which would deflect another such person, Lady Macbeth, from the directness of her enterprises. It thereby makes itself into a formidable machine for action which gets its power from a brute appropriation of one of the most volatile forces of the kinetic world — sex.

It is this that Goneril and Regan embody as archetypally as does Lady Macbeth. The forces of *die Wille* are seized upon and possessed; and as long as the possessor can keep his hold on them he will be swept along at intoxicating speed by their tumult. All the working scurry that his mind can invent will be necessary to keep that hold; but, so long as it is kept, he will experience a wildly confident exhilaration born of a sense of his own daring. This energy can be imparted thrillingly to others, as Lady Macbeth will impart it to her husband. And when two people live it together in complicity, like Regan and Cornwall in the blinding scene or Goneril and Regan in the scene which leads to Lear's expulsion, there is created that characteristic Shakespearean *folie à deux* which runs exultantly towards a grotesque parody of passion. Marcius and Aufidius, transferring sexuality into the blood and hate of battle, grotesquely parodied a betrothal; in these twin declarations to Edmund the sisters' daring and conscious outrageousness runs to similarly hideous vows in whose language of uplift and incantation the delirium of evil reaches its second climax.

5. *The trauma of the king*

That should begin to give one some sense of the power of the forces involved in this tragic and traumatic enactment of the Law's crisis. The high-energy world of the kinetic is of awesome potency. Its furies, as we have seen them appropriated by the destructive wilfulness of Goneril, Regan, Edmund and Cornwall, will make the gaiety of a festive-comic spring impossible. If there is to be spring and if there is to be gaiety then they will be agonizing, tumultuous and convulsive. There will be terror in their upsurge and unspeakable pain in the endurance of them. The release and adjustment of the social world will be violent. The wild dream of a midsummer's night will be full of thunder and the 'most terrible and nimble stroke/Of quick cross lightning' which will cut the King 'to th' brains'. The erstwhile Law-giving man who experiences this metamorphosis will be a straw in a terrible wind — 'poor perdu', as the compassionate Cordelia puts it.

We need, as I said, a sense of this violence in the kinetic world to avoid describing the play's metaphysical movements 'comfortably'. A good deal of the criticism of the play, even some of the best of it, strikes me as comfortable in just this way. *King Lear* has often been modulated into a metaphysical pattern which takes this terror away from it, and which makes what the play means by 'nature' seem a much less ferocious thing. Christian criticism of *King Lear* wherein such words as 'redemption' (the redemption of the sinning King) and 'learning' (the arrogant King's learning of humility) play a big part, has been guilty of this modulation of the play into a more comfortable metaphysic; and also guilty, in the process, of shifting the centre of our attention away from the figure of Lear and onto the figure of Cordelia. Lear himself is the key figure in Shakespeare's metaphysic. Cordelia, beautiful creation though she is, can only be felt to be 'standing for Nature herself'[3] if a more comforting, Christian metaphysic has appropriated Shakespeare's play to its purposes. The less comforting metaphysics of Nietzsche and Schopenhauer seem to me to have far more to do with it, and to be of much more use in helping us to experience the play without recourse to false solaces.

Christian criticism of *King Lear* has found it congenial to talk of what Lear 'learns' from the experience of the storm, and I suppose that he does learn. But if that takes the emphasis then I think that criticism is not doing justice to what the experience of the play palpably is. I do not believe that an audience could ever watch Lear on the heath and think 'good, he's learning'; and if we make the idea of learning central to our account of his madness then we are falsifying what it feels like to behold it and making the storm seem like some kind of productive chastisement, welcome for its improving qualities. I do not have a strong enough stomach for that. It is ominously close to Goneril's version of the matter:

> O sir, to wilful men
> The injuries that they themselves procure
> Must be their schoolmasters.   [II. iv. 301–3]

And ominously different from the good Kent's more humane impulses:

> Here is the place, my lord; good my lord, enter.
> The tyranny of the open night's too rough
> For nature to endure.   [III. iv. 1–3]

Learn he may; but the savagery of his education is such as to make me quail not a little in the presence of those who dwell upon its desirability and acclaim its capacity to bring him to 'redemption'.

Though of course he is brought to redemption, just as he learns. But redemption is, as Edmund might have said, another 'fine word', perhaps in some senses necessary but also barbarous. No doubt the shattered and exhausted old man who is carried off the heath in a litter and who cannot bear to meet his beloved daughter for the 'burning shame' which his abuse of her has bred in his excellently enlightened mind — no doubt he is a 'redeemed'

man. But one might do well to note the words used by Cordelia,
as opposed to the Christian critics, to describe this condition.
She, though she is the apogee of the Christians' metaphysic, does
not talk of the bad man's redemption but of 'the good man's
distress'; and as she hears of his sufferings her thoughts are
turned, as Kent's had been, only to plans and prayers for its relief
and not to any prim sense of the moral excellences therein
available. Again, if the idea of redemption takes the stress, there
must be a sense in which, acting as it were on Lear's behalf and
with his best interests in view, we welcome the condition to
which the thunder reduces him. Whereas the play (I feel sure as I
watch it) asks us to feel that a dog shouldn't be out on a night
like that, and that seeing an old man out in it is appalling 'past
speaking of'.

Then there is the storm itself which has also been
modulated away from what it is in Shakespeare's play by critics
with over-strong allegorical motives. I sometimes feel as I read
such critics that the storm only happens in some allegorical
universe where things have 'meanings' and are eloquent with
'significance'. The storm then seems like a metaphor, or some
kind of morally important cipher. But in the play it is brutally
physical — very wet, very cold and very violent. Even when it is a
correlative for the psychic it still has this brutally physical
directness — cutting Lear to the brains and cracking the sinews of
his mind. Again the characters of the play will point us the way,
for their views of the storm are decidedly non-allegorical — an
interesting difference from *Macbeth.* They see the storm as a storm,
no more and no less. It very definitely *happens*, in a pressingly
physical world. It is foul weather, the worst weather that Kent can
remember, weather from which the gentle Cordelia would have
rescued a savage dog, weather so awful that not even the creatures
of the night will venture forth in it. And, thus unpeopled, the
storm in *King Lear* is quite free from witches and mousing owls
and crows making wing to rooky woods and horses eating one
another — quite free (a sobering shock) from all symbolisms.

And just as we cannot therefore feel licensed to pronounce
about the storm's 'essential meaning', and should never be too
quick to modulate our response to it from the contingent to the

allegorical, so we must beware about pronouncing upon its meaning for Lear, even upon how it feels to him. At one point he gives two quite contradictory accounts of how the storm works upon him, the one close upon the other's heels. First he says it does not hurt him because the pains within render it negligible:

> this tempest in my mind
> Doth from my senses take all feeling else.   [III. iv. 12–13]

But then, a few lines later, he says that it hurts him enough to drive out the hurts within, and that it is therefore welcome:

> This tempest will not give me leave to ponder
> On things would hurt me more.   [III. iv. 24–5]

That is the chaos of a man's experience of the contingent world. It does not lend itself to transposition into the neat meanings of an allegory.

So we must beware of imported allegories of the storm's 'meaning', beware of forgetting its brute contingent presence; and beware of the callow moralism which intrudes itself into readings of the play whose metaphysic gives untoward stress to such ideas as learning and redemption. What, thus forewarned, can be said about Lear's madness? How do we really respond to the trauma of the King?

I find it convenient to divide Lear's progress through the play into five parts. The first is that which precedes the heath and his madness (Acts I and II). The second is in the great storm scenes of Act III, preluded by the Gentleman's description of him 'contending with the fretful elements' and alternating with scenes *within* the house (Gloucester's castle). The third phase, after a longish gap in which the King does not appear, is in the central part of IV.vi, preluded this time by Cordelia's description of him 'crown'd with rank fumiter' but not now juxtaposed with indoor scenes since all humanity has now come out to join and rescue Lear. The fourth and fifth phases – the return to Cordelia, and the end with Cordelia dead – belong in the next two sections of this chapter. I shall discuss the first three phases here.

In the first phase Lear begins, as I have said, as the Lord of Nature, the large-mannered, large-worded reader of the map of his kingdom. He ends it enraged and frustrated, flinging out of Gloucester's castle onto the heath. Until the very end of this phase (when, goaded to distraction by Goneril and Regan, he produces the first of his great speeches of humane insight – 'O, reason not the need . . .') he can scarcely be called a morally admirable man. And yet, nonetheless, he has never been shifted from the centre of our empathy and engagement. His performance prior to this great speech has, morally, been one of arrogance, impetuosity, bullying and self-indulgence; but as soon as such terms are listed they manifestly declare their irrelevance to what it is to experience him. This tormented old man, howsoever self-inflicted those torments are and howsoever he may inflict torment on others, can never quite be moved from the focal point of our emotional involvement with the play. Our emotional focus upon him can never be blurred by the moral commentary which his actions and words could, if one felt that way inclined, easily promote.

Even at the beginning it was so. Even as he handed out his arrogant and ignorant evil to Kent and Cordelia in the opening scene I doubt whether any audience could recoil from him with quite the same moral judgment as such behaviour would prompt elsewhere (and elsewhere in Shakespeare). Already the metaphysical necessity of his being thus was too palpable. Feeling that necessity, in his agedness and his being the Law-giver, we have felt no spur to moral protest. We have watched instead with an involving sense of the inevitability of this crisis and with a knowledge of the King's crucial position in it. And as this first phase unfolds our sympathetic focus upon the King becomes stronger. His impetuosities and rantings and cursing and threats never quite set in motion what might be called our ordinary moral awareness – unless we prefer to take refuge in the callownesses or moralism rather than become involved in the more difficult vastness of Shakespeare's metaphysic. (And most audiences do not so prefer, whatever moralistic critics may say. Lear never has any trouble on stage in drawing the necessary involvement from his watchers.)

It is, as I say, his metaphysical inevitability which creates this suspension of moral quickness. But that must be created and lived

out as something humanly palpable if it is to draw us spontaneously as the play is performed. There must be 'something about
Lear . . .', as I remember a student beginning when trying to pin
this down. And ending too, because it is difficult to put one's
finger on exactly what it is. Kent is a help — his own unbreakable
loyalty alerts and directs that of the audience. And the ranting
and quick-tempered King's very *unexpertness* in the 'politic'
handling of the likes of Goneril and Regan is an important factor
too: it is a *virtue* to be unable to come to terms with what they
represent, and it bespeaks large capacities to be unable to buckle
one's being within what even they will call 'the rigour of our
state'. As they work upon him Lear comes to seem like *raw life*,
'the *thing itself*', practised upon by human design, the naked,
squirming substance of life to which atrocities are done by
mentality and Law. And the simple fact comes clear that in all
the ragings and self-pityings of Lear in this phase of the play there
is more evidence of inalienable vitality and human possibility
than of anything else. Our impulses tell us that his desperate and
in many ways pathetic cursings are the first rumblings of that
colossal vitality which will burst upon the stage at the start of Act
III; and that the upwelling grief to whose power his mind
eventually gives way — the 'hysterica passio', the 'climbing
sorrow', the 'rising heart' — is evidence of a great and turbulent
richness of emotional being.

In all his morally 'unedifying' performances we find this
richness, this romantic life, this evidence of powers which are
what our impulses tell us they are — inalienable, in no way to be
deserted. The upwelling turbulence of his romantic life makes
him draw our unrepentant empathy throughout these two Acts. A
man who feels his guilt and sorrow as strongly as this ('No more
of that', when the Fool reminds him of his banished daughter); a
man who is capable of such defenceless bewilderment ('Who is it
that can tell me who I am?'), such bitter self-recrimination ('O
Lear, Lear, Lear!/Beat at this gate that let thy folly in'), such fury
at the wrongness of what is wrong ('Vengeance! plague! death!
confusion!/Fiery? What quality? Why Gloucester, Gloucester
. . .'); a man capable of such weeping, and of such disdain to
weep: such a man holds our empathy with a completeness which

no moral-critical reflection can in any way qualify. And as this primal sympathy with him is sustained in us we should never be in any doubt (and I believe no audience ever is) that our impulses on his behalf are right. The magnitude of his being makes the play polarize at once: his great, chaotic and turbulent humanity on the one hand, and the desert and zero of human possibility represented by Goneril and Regan on the other. The chaos of vitality that is his mind in these opening acts is just that quality which Nietzsche described in the remark from *Zarathustra* which I placed at the head of my opening chapter:

> one must still have chaos in oneself to be able to give birth to a dancing star.

At the end of this phase, when the dancing star is delivered from him in the great (and now morally great) speech, 'O, reason not the need. . . .', we have a vindication of the rightness of the impulses which have unreflectingly taken his part. Nobody is ever surprised at the sudden manifestation of this moral fineness in a hitherto not very moral man. And the very unsurprisingness of the development should confirm for our minds the point that our primal sympathies have been implying throughout: that this kind of turbulent vitality is *necessary* to human fineness. It is the kinetic life without which such delicacy and generosity as is in his speech cannot exist.

Knowing that, one's impulses have known not to desert him. They have known that if you desert him, prompted by the moral commentary that could easily be made, then you desert something inalienable. Banish plump Jack and banish all the world; or, even more relevantly, desert the cause of Antony (who, as the Christian critics have wasted no time in telling us, is also immoral and irresponsible) and an audience, like so many Enobarbuses, will simply wither and die, throwing its dried heart against the flint and hardness of its moral probity. The Lear who holds one's loyalty in these two acts seems to me like a plump Jack or an Antony. His immense vitality is a 'mine of bounty' (Enobarbus' phrase) wherein are to be found such riches as could be deserted only by 'men revolted' (Enobarbus' phrase again, and a dreadful one which seems to connote men who are revolted from the very business of being men).[4] And Lear is deserted only by men revolted — Edmund, Cornwall, Goneril, Regan, and the citizen Gloucester before he is rescued from his revolt by those imperatives of humane feeling.

When we reach the second phase of Lear's life in Act III we see this elemental vitality and this inalienable life coming to their fierce climax in his madness. The mad King of 'Blow, winds, and crack your cheeks . . .' clearly *is* elemental, a part of the tumultuous energies of *die Wille*, possessed of a fire and exuberance and recklessness and (the note is clearly there) a kind of supreme *merriment* in which all the forces of Shakespeare's kinetic world run pell-mell. Nietzsche would say that he is possessed by Dionysos, and such a way of describing him is probably more use than most. It is the magnificence of Lear in this phase that he is huge and strong enough to let those forces rage through him, vital enough to welcome and inhabit their fury, 'gamesome' enough to dance to their wild and whirling music. Outside the Law the riotous fertility of his imagination has been released, and he gives himself over to its powers with uninhibited completeness.

It is always a sense of this 'gamesome' quality of Lear that seems to me to be absent from most accounts of his trauma — a sense of his recklessness, his merriment, the devouring hilarity of his madness. But it is a laughing as much as a weeping man (the two run close of course) who incites the thunder on and relishes the prospect of its striking terror into Law-bound and guilt-stricken men. When he boasted his ownership of great and punitive natural powers in I.i he did it with solemn determination — 'by the sacred radiance of the sun' etc. — and we knew, with Kent, that he was swearing his gods in vain. Later the appeal was quieter ('Hear, Nature, hear; dear goddess, hear'); and later still it came as a desperate plea:

> O heavens,
> If you do love old men, if your sweet sway
> Allow obedience, if you yourselves are old,
> Make it your cause; send down, and take my part.
>
> [II. iv. 188-91]

Now, on the heath, he has lost this solemnity, and with it is losing all trace of the hopeless desire for personal vindication. His call to 'the great gods,/That keep this dreadful pudder o'er our heads' is newly impersonal, and as a consequence newly buoyant, almost jocund. The pudder is over *our* heads – everyone's, not just those of his personal enemies; and those upon whom it falls are *their* enemies' – the gods' enemies, not those upon whom Lear himself wishes to put the divine finger. Lear now is *abandoned.* His welcome is to the indiscriminate havoc-making wantonness of it all – which means that he welcomes, and abandons himself to, a great traumatic truth about nature and the world of Law. In a tone of joyous derision, which has everything to do with the exuberantly derisive mind of Hamlet and the exuberantly derisive mind of the author of *Troilus and Cressida*, Lear abandons himself to an experience which will release his romantic life from its encapsulation within the Law. And with this abandon and release there goes a new disinterestedness which is part of the exuberance. He is, like Nietzsche's Schopenhauer, 'cheerful'; or, as Yeats said Hamlet and Lear were, 'gay'[5]. His challenge to men to 'cry/These dreadful summoners grace' signals a triumphant arrival at Yeats' 'desolation of reality', disentangled from the hoops and rules of 'manifold illusion' which had once sustained his civilized mind.

Of the three Shakespearean tragic protagonists who experience the world of the traumatic whereby the manifold illusion is broken through, only Lear reaches this condition of complete abandonment to its vital but terrifying truth. Hamlet, younger than Lear, and alone as Lear is not, could never sustain either the exuberance or the disinterestedness to which his 'unhooped' mind was laid open – and was eventually recaptured by the hoops and rules of Elsinore. And Timon, with whom it is always useful to compare Lear, never loses the insistent note of personal vengefulness which Lear is here abandoning, and as a consequence never ascends to Lear's gamesome vitalities. His rages bear down upon his enemies with relentless hatred and, as he is overwhelmed with the disgust he feels, the joyous and disinterested derision of Lear proves to be quite beyond his tonal range. In the later play it is Apemantus not Timon who points the folly of crying the summoners grace:

> Will these moist trees,
> That have outliv'd the eagle, page thy heels
> And skip when thou point'st out? Will the cold brook,
> Candied with ice, caudle thy morning taste
> To cure thy o'ernight's surfeit?   [*T of A* IV. iii. 222—6]

Timon, even more than Hamlet, is locked and isolated within his trauma. Its overwhelming gift to him is nausea. But in this second phase of Lear's traumatic journey the reckless, wanton and released quality of his mind creates what Nietzsche felt to be the paradoxical centre of tragic experience — turning 'fits of nausea into imaginings with which it is possible to live'.

So it is always the exuberant welling up of great forces of life and reckless imagination which we feel as we watch the Lear of Act III. It comes with great pain of course — the pathos of the 'trial' scene can scarcely be exaggerated, and the world still has its terrible mischief to make with him and his lingering obsessions:

> *Lear.* Now all the plagues that in the pendulous air
>   Hang fated o'er men's faults light on thy daughters!
> *Kent.* He hath no daughters, sir.   [III. iv. 66—8]

But we go wrong if it is only on the pathos of it that we dwell, just as we would go grotesquely wrong if we thought of the essence of all this as residing in his *learning* — 'humility', or what not. The trial scene is full of pathos and unspeakable suffering. But it is also full of the hectic inventive speed of Lear's mind, his ferocious uncovering imagination, his marvellous capacity for experiencing and for surviving experience.

And it is on 'marvellous' that we should focus — with a kind of amazement that a man can have Dionysos alive within his aged frame and endure the experience with such willingness and buoyancy; and with a kind of gratitude too, since Lear carries to us and inhabits for us forces which we could not bear. If it is amazement and gratitude that govern our tonal response to what Lear is (rather than an appreciation of what he learns and how he is redeemed) I think we will be near to the heart of the matter, and, once again, near to what the characters of the play feel to be its heart. For it is just this kind of amazement that Cordelia expresses with

> Alack, alack!
> 'Tis wonder that thy life and wits at once
> Had not concluded all,   [IV. vii. 40—2]

and Kent with

> The wonder is he hath endur'd so long.   [V. iii. 316]

And it is just that sense of gratitude and deference that Edgar fixes and 'organizes' for us in the play's closing words:

> The oldest hath borne most; we that are young
> Shall never see so much nor live so long.   [V. iii. 325—6]

The third phase of Lear's life is in IV.vi. It is the central part of an extraordinary three-part scene wherein first we have 'Dover cliff', second the King making the famous 'adultery' speech, and third the killing of Oswald by Edgar in his father's defence. Lear's part of this scene might well be felt to be the very centre of the whole play.

There is first the broken and fragmented speech of Lear:

> Nature's above art in that respect. There's your press-money. That fellow handles his bow like a crow-keeper; draw me a clothier's yard. Look, look, a mouse! Peace, peace; this piece of toasted cheese will do't. There's my gauntlet; I'll prove it on a giant. Bring up the brown bills. O! well flown, bird! i' th' clout, i' th' clout— hewgh! Give the word.   [IV. vi. 86—92]

Then the pathos of the King's humbling:

> When the rain came to wet me once, and the wind to make me chatter; when the thunder would not peace at my bidding; there I found 'em, there I smelt 'em out. Go to, they are not men o' their words. They told me I was everything; 'tis a lie — I am not ague-proof.   [IV. vi. 99—105]

Then the 'adultery' speech itself:

> Ay, every inch a king.
> When I do stare, see how the subject quakes.

I pardon that man's life. What was thy cause?
Adultery?
Thou shalt not die. Die for adultery? No.
The wren goes to't, and the small gilded fly
Does lecher in my sight.
Let copulation thrive; for Gloucester's bastard son
Was kinder to his father than my daughters
Got 'tween the lawful sheets.
To't, luxury, pell-mell, for I lack soldiers.
Behold yon simp'ring dame
Whose face between her forks presages snow,
That minces virtue and does shake the head
To hear of pleasure's name —
The fitchew nor the soiled horse goes to't
With a more riotous appetite.
Down from the waist they are centaurs,
Though women all above;
But to the girdle do the gods inherit,
Beneath is all the fiends';
There's hell, there's darkness, there is the sulphurous pit —
Burning, scalding, stench, consumption.
Fie, fie, fie! pah, pah! Give me an ounce of civet good
apothecary, to sweeten my imagination. There's money for thee.
[IV. vi. 107–31]

The scene will give us the quintessence of Shakespeare's tragic
vision, the quintessence of his tragic critique of Law.

Throughout the scene Lear's central preoccupation is Law —
power, authority, kingship, culture, moral standards. He is
engaged in a characteristically wholesale parody of the pretensions of the 'sophisticated'. 'I am the King himself': the figure we
have before us owes much to that 'holiday' or 'misrule' idea
which makes its festive-comic play with the pretensions and
assumptions of the civilized. (The stage direction which has him
fantastically dressed with weeds/wild flowers bespeaks production going right to the heart of this vision.)

The speech of scraps and fragments quoted above is a series of rude pageants of the doings of the powerful, 'the King himself' in particular. It is with real astonishment, and then again with the affected astonishment of the parodist, that Lear creates perspectives from which the power of the civilized seems little and absurd. Lives can be owned with financial power — 'There's your press-money'; comments of deep human consequence can be tossed off by a strutting inspector of troops — 'That fellow handles his bow like a crow-keeper'; the trivia of kingly whims ('Look, look! a mouse') can summon up fussing attendants to whose clamours the regal calm of majesty can then put a timely end — 'Peace, peace!'; resonant challenges can be sworn ('There's my gauntlet'), summary orders delivered in the life and death matter of war ('draw me a clothier's yard', 'Bring up the brown bills'); and the lusty applause of a potentate, for whom the war is a splendid game, can be bestowed upon a good player — 'O! well flown bird; i' th' clout i' th' clout'. Salutary perspectives. But salutary perspectives created and accepted by Lear with his characteristic ebullience, without Hamlet's crippling nausea or Timon's crippling righteousness. It is wicked, derisive pageanting of those who are great within the Law, as irksome to the pride of culture as any of Patroclus' 'scurril jests', but of course much more magnificent because so disinterested. And because disinterested therefore capable of leading him through to the supreme sense of authority-as-absurdity which opens the 'adultery' speech itself:

> When I do stare, see how the subject quakes.
> I pardon that man's life.   [IV. vi. 108—9]

An amazing, a quite absurd privilege of the powerful to beckon forth or permit 'life' itself with a mere gesture.

To this fast and furious parodic revelation of difficult perspectives (yet so unwilled, so far from mere nihilistic jeering) is now added the pathos of some simple truths. Over-allegorized readings of the storm must founder on the irresistible rightness of Lear's own understanding of the matter — 'When the rain came to wet me once, and the wind to make me chatter' — wherein the overwhelmingly simple and moving truth of the case is expressed precisely by *not* making allegorical sophistries out of the wetness of rain and the cold of wind. Apprehended thus directly the elements make their great statement about culture with miraculous ease. Of course that sort of thunder will not peace at the bidding of the King; of course the King is not 'ague-proof'; and of course there is 'manifold illusion' in the pride of culture — 'they told me I was everything'. Simple truths are spoken without eloquence. The metaphysical burden of kingship gives way to this robust and direct statement of what, as soon as it is said, feels inevitable, obvious. But it is enough to be a major piece of his sustained under-view of culture's pretensions. And, in its flat unaggressiveness, enough to attest to the unique disinterestedness of that under-view.

And then there is the 'adultery' speech itself. It begins with Lear as furious parodist again, his imagination flinging to a perspective (and taking us easily with it) from which it is clearly preposterous to regard adultery as a crime. And then it turns to what has been widely taken as a tirade against the wantonness of sexual appetite of which adultery is an instance — but which is in fact something very different. Here the completeness, disinterestedness and consequent vitality of Lear's trauma is at its most manifest and most important. Within this single speech is enacted the movement *through* traumatic nausea which happens only in *King Lear* and only because of the unequalled vitality of the King — his bravery, his recklessness, the extraordinary on-going zest of 'Pour on: I will endure'.

To read this speech rightly and catch its essential movement we might compare its tone with that of the sex-obsessed nausea which runs through Hamlet's language to Ophelia ('you jig, you amble and you lisp' etc.) and Gertrude ('Rebellious hell,/If thou canst mutine in a matron's bones...');[6] or with the sexual disgust which captures and overwhelms Timon in his rages

> This is it
> That makes the wappen'd widow wed again —
> She whom the spital-house and ulcerous sores
> Would cast the gorge at this embalms and spices
> To th' April day again.   [*T of A* IV. iii. 37–41]

Lear's speech is not like that. His mind is freer, and his sensibility is not paralysed by the shock of difficult traumatic insights. Nor does he take those insights as an opportunity, to be pounced upon with relish in so far as they offer the licence to abuse or the solace of self-righteousness. His language does not lock like Timon's onto a single track of horrified and self-righteous castigation. His stature is such that even at this terrible level of exposure to the hideous his mind moves nimbly through a range of tones and feelings, devouring and absorbing the experience with the elemental heedlessness which we saw on the heath. And then coming through to be greeted by the love of Gloucester, whose 'Oh, let me kiss that hand' would have been far harder to say to Timon or Hamlet.

The traumatic insight into the arbitrariness of justice and authority with which the speech begins contains the characteristic vitality of one who can afford to be delighted by outrageous humour. And so does the latter and apparently more nauseous part of it — in the strong capacity for mimicry, parody and caricature which goes into the description of the 'simp'ring dame' with her 'riotous appetite'. It is still painful, and there is still pathos in the watching of it. But there is also that admiration or amazement at the continued surging vitality which pours into this brisk miming at the expense of the absurd and the pretentious.

It is with that in mind that I have called this the 'adultery' speech and put the word into inverted commas. For it is not really about adultery, but about those aspects of nature and man which were categorized as belonging with 'beast' and 'devil' by the highly civilized, 'sophisticated' Venetians of *Othello*. It is a speech about goats and monkeys and foul toads, and the Lear who makes the speech is disabused of the 'simp'ring' claim of culture to have banished those aspects of the natural world to which such creatures make symbolic reference. To be thus disabused, particularly for a man whose role as King had told him that nature consisted only of 'shadowy forests' and 'wide-skirted meads', is a horrifying experience — hence the rampant violence of his insistences:

There's hell, there's darkness, there is the sulphurous pit —
Burning, scalding, stench, consumption.   [IV. vi. 128—9]

But for Lear, as for neither Hamlet nor Timon, and certainly not for Othello, the horror begins to expend itself even in the telling. There is a sense in which Lear is not just expressing his repugnance in this speech but also transcending it, shaking it out of his tortured mind. The repugnance piles up into those two lines of reiterated disgust, and then collapses into the exhaustion and resignation of 'Fie, fie, fie! pah, pah!' and the moving plea for release from his torture which comes with

> Give me an ounce of civet, good apothecary, to sweeten my
> imagination.   [IV. vi. 130]

That ending to the speech is a triumph. It again calls forth wonder that a man who is savaged by that sort of insight can endure not to reduce his torment (as Timon does by turning it into vengefulness); and the reward for living the torment unprotected is the achievement of the transparent epiphanic beauty of his closing lines. There will still be the remnants of his nausea — in the stinging addition of the offer of money for the apothecary's kindness, and in the bitter withdrawal of the hand which Gloucester would kiss:

> Let me wipe it first; it smells of mortality.   [IV. vi. 132]

But the fundamental movement has been made. This is an imagining with which it is possible to live; indeed it is impossible to persist in taking it solely as horrific. For there is after all a kind of aftertaste to the speech which is far from horrific, wherein we recognize that the 'going to it' of such frail and beautiful creatures as the wren and the small gilded fly cannot simply prompt nausea, and that even the more savage-sounding rampages of the fitchew and the soiled horse cannot cripple with nausea the mind of a man whose vitality has proved equal to the wildness of the storm. And finally an aftertaste in which the significance of that ounce of civet comes clear. For while one such as Othello could not live with the imagining of goats and monkeys and foul toads, the more capaciously imaginative Lear cannot help intimating truths which single-minded nausea or horror would shut out. These are truths about nature — including the truth that a sweet perfume can be obtained from an oily yellow substance secreted from the anal gland of a carnivore and feline. Thus his horror runs its course, and thus his reckless truth-telling must run to more than the purely horrifying.

We may still wish to describe some of this in terms of learning and redemption, but I feel embarrassed in the presence of those prim, comfortable and above all disrespectful little words. I prefer to return to my sense of the basic Shakespearean metaphysic to summarize the enormous and unique significance of Lear's life. He was the Lord of Nature, and as such represented archetypally the blindness of socialized man. But, ejected from the position which would sustain the 'manifold illusion' of social power, and ejected by the inevitable functioning of the Law which he principally embodied, he proved himself also to be an elemental man. It was an elemental vitality which welled up when the 'hysterica passio' and the 'rising heart' began to thrust their way through the crumbling frame that contained them. Cast into trauma by this dissolution of his civilized world (the King's pastoral *Vorstellung* of the world's convenient bounty) he proved himself also to be an unbreakable match for its wild tumult. Like no other Shakespearean tragic hero he therefore spans the whole range of the metaphysical dualism: he was King, and he was also the elemental man who participated in the tumult of *die Wille*. It is therefore in him that the whole tension of the dualism is lived, and in his survival of that tension that what Nietzsche called the 'metaphysical solace' of tragedy is given. It is a solace – and something still in touch with the 'release' idea of festive comedy – because the possibility of a life like Lear's ends the intractable war between the two terms of the dualism. He has been King without losing his kinetic life; and he has experienced the full force of kinetic life without losing his humanity to the terror of it.

There are certain kinds of banal optimism to which this metaphysical vision of the Law and the wild world will be an affront, even without the ending of the play to make the vision as apprehended so far seem even less comforting. But the contrary view of the nihilist or pessimist seems equally small and partial as we recognize the full triumph of Lear's life, and the general metaphysical triumph which it portends, as I hope they have come out of this analysis of his traumatic journey. Nietzsche's idea of the 'strong pessimism' of tragedy seems to me to place itself usefully between these two reductive ways of looking at the play; and so also does the idea of the 'violent spring' or agony of the earth's growth upon which I have begun to touch in tracing this play's connexion with the festive-comic model. It is to those two (related) ideas that I now find myself turning as I move to the last two phases of Lear's life. We shall need to look first at those characters who rescue culture and the King from the ravages of the wild, and then at the play's last scene.

6. *The birth of spring*

In the King's madness of the second and third phases of his life we have been taken to the creative-destructive heart of tragedy, the terrible but at the same time joyously releasing centre of social man's experience of the kinetic world. In Shakespeare's metaphysic it is the trauma of the King which must occupy the key position in the tragedy. A metaphysic in which nature has the tumultuous, high-energy power of *die Wille* or of Dionysos is brought into dramatic life by a play which is first and foremost the story of this exuberantly vibrant King. It is a falsely solacing modulation of Shakespeare's metaphysic which gives the play's meaning of nature to Cordelia, and puts her instead of the King at the centre of the play.

When we look at the characters who accompany the protagonist on his traumatic journey, or who otherwise defer most completely to the qualities of life embodied in the King, a further displacement of Cordelia may (I fear) be called for. *King Lear* is, as I have said, the only Shakespearean tragedy in which there are sympathetic and understanding witnesses to the trauma of the protagonist − characters sufficiently free from rigid attachment to the Law to be able to apprehend the true nature of the tragic crisis without Elsinorean fear or Venetian blindness. Albany and Gloucester are brought out into such clear-sightedness, the servant who kills Cornwall has the humane capacity to desert the limited 'Law-meaning' of 'service' at the behest of more profound imperatives also connoted by the word. But in addition there are four characters in the play — Kent, Cordelia, Edgar and the Fool — whose whole lives are lived in flexible and unimpeded contact with humanities which are richer than Law, and who create between them a sense of 'civilization' or 'culture' which is free from the reductivisms of Law and deferential to vicissitude as Law is not.

I see no reason to give Cordelia any special pride of place in this quartet; indeed every reason not to. For it is the synergy of the group with which we should be concerned, an orchestration of their very different tones producing something richer than any one of them could be alone. She takes pride of place for Lear of course: she will become the whole of life for him, and nothing that Kent or Edgar can do can mitigate for him the horror of her death. But the simple naturalistic fact that she is his daughter seems to me quite sufficient to explain that. And if we remember that (remembering likewise that it is Edgar who has a similar intensity of significance for Gloucester) we shall not be tempted to isolate Cordelia and give her any general metaphysical status as nature's 'voice'. Her vital role is played in conjunction with three other roles, and the four are associated together in the creation of a single metaphysical movement which eventually, in the fourth phase of Lear's life, lifts the play out of winter and darkness and towards the delicate sublimities of an Apollonian spring.

The four are indeed different, but they do have one very important quality in common. Kent is banished, returns in disguise and plays out a new social and tonal role with an unhesitating facility for making such transpositions. Edgar likewise is a hunted outcast, transposed from the son of an earl first into a beggar and then into a warrior with that same facility. Cordelia is transposed from daughter to wife, from England to France, from loved one to outcast, and later from France (and wife) to England (and active rule); and she again, like the other two, moves through these transpositions of estate without hesitation or disorientation. Through all three there runs a core of humane life which does not require the securities of role-definition to support it. The Law does not define or circumscribe their beings. Their human status is not just a function of a particular social status. Their 'attachment' to the Law is peculiarly flexible; so that, tossed about by the crises of social life, they do not collapse into that characteristic disorientation which besets men whose whole entire definition of themselves has been made in terms of (say) Roman caste or Venetian courtesy. They have a peculiar capacity for being 'translated' in social role but unmoved thereby in essential being. And the fourth one of the group, the Fool, enacts in the hurly-burly of his language a kind of permanent state of 'translation' wherein more justice is done to the inevitability of vicissitude, disjunction and paradox than can ever be done by the linearities of a social rhetoric. Some brief consideration of these four characters will give us the raw material which Shakespeare makes fictile in the birth of a metaphysical spring.

Kent is a very direct man, as is given of course as soon as the play starts. It is registered in the decisive swiftness with which he states his case — 'Lear is mad' — and the determination with which, under pressure, he sticks to it — 'thou dost evil'. But there is another aspect of his strength in this scene as well — a buoyant quality with humour and mockery in it which goes with his ability to be unimpressed by the mere fact of power or greatness. It is a man who knows how to deride the notions of the great who asks Lear, in a theatrical tone of mock-amazement,

> Think'st thou that duty shall have dread to speak
> When power to flattery bows? [I. i. 146—7]

and who exits to his banishment with the parodic gesture of

> Thus Kent, O princes, bids you all adieu. [I. i. 186]

There is something pert about 'O princes' which greets the inflations of the powerful with buoyant disdain.

This comic streak in Kent is fully active in the early scenes before the storm. He has no difficulty in living to the full the abrasive vitalities of the low-life role he assumes, knowing how to use the vigorous language of the tavern on the odious Oswald, and how to stage an impudent parody of the language Cornwall would no doubt expect to hear from a minion:

> Sir, in good faith, in sincere verity,
> Under th'allowance of your great aspect,

> Whose influence, like the wreathe of radiant fire
> On flickering Phoebus' front . . .   [II. ii. 100—3]

O princes! — this is the fusty stuff that so irked the big talkers in *Troilus and Cressida*, as also is the peculiarly scurril jest which he breaks when Cornwall is clumsy enough to give him the chance:

> Sir, 'tis my occupation to be plain:
> I have seen better faces in my time
> Than stands on any shoulder that I see
> Before me at this instant.   [II. ii. 87—90]

This is no doubt 'unwise', as was his intemperate hounding of Oswald who, though odious, is unimportant. But Kent's powers are too volatile to be held within what is politic; and while intemperance might have been a fault to Escalus, Kent's sense of right springs from deeper:

> (*Corn.*)   . . . know you no reverence?
> *Kent.* Yes, sir; but anger hath a privilege.   [II. ii. 64—5]

So Kent is noble, brave, good etc. But so was Brutus. The great difference is that Kent is also 'gamesome'. He has the swiftness and vitality of which his humour is an index, and in a high-energy world like Shakespeare's such qualities are much more reliable, much more sensitive to the essentials of things than the linear and logical mental attributes of a Brutus. Of earlier Shakespearean characters it is Mercutio rather than Brutus of whom one is reminded. In the Shakespearean world such humour is both an intuitive or imaginative kind of rightness and also profoundly *undeceiving*; so Kent, undeceived as Mercutio is undeceived, is very clear-sighted about the limits of the 'wise' or the 'politic' and about the deserts of the great. One of his asides later in the play gives this another focus:

> . . . Albany and Cornwall;
> Who have — as who have not that their great stars
> Thron'd and set high? — servants.   [III. i. 21—3]

That is the insight of a humorous and sceptical man, and it is a *locus classicus* for the source of that flexibility and capacity for 'translation' which Kent enjoys. It sees him easily able to acknowledge all that is accidental, partial or arbitrary in the structures of his culture – the source of the clear-sightedness which made him know without hesitation that the King who thought he was a god was 'mad'. This comic irreverence, combining with his reverence for what is 'royal', and keeping his sense of the meaning of such a word free from any Law-bound constriction, makes Kent the adaptable and seasoned man that he is.

If for Kent we think of what is seasoned and strong, for Edgar we think of what is young and, in some important senses, weak. Edgar, described by Edmund as

> a brother noble,
> Whose nature is so far from doing harms
> That he suspects none   [I. ii. 170–2]

is weak in that he is credulous and therefore vulnerable; and it is characteristic of him that there should always be something unlikely, even grotesque, about the far-fetched schemes he embarks upon for the salvation of his father. But Shakespeare never indulges in any heroic sentimentalism about the instant Virtue, instant Uprightness and instant Resistance of The Good. As in *Macbeth*, where the fleeing princes bring suspicion on themselves and the fleeing Macduff finds that he has abandoned his family to Macbeth's gestapo, so here: the ordinary decencies of the civilized are routed with terrible ease by the fierce drives of will and evil, and Edgar, in his flight and his desperation, is a man hunted, a man preyed upon, a victim both of the hue and cry and of his own 'weakness'. The strength that his weakness gives him is the power to become so completely identified with the hunted of the world.

So just as Kent's seasoned qualities could be seen in the facility with which he translated himself into his low-life role, so the qualities of the weak and vulnerable Edgar can be seen in his capacity for being translated into so genuine a representative of all who are

> whipp'd from tithing to tithing, and stock-punish'd, and
> imprison'd   [III. iv. 131–2]

— all the victims of what Angelo called 'the manacles of the all-binding law'. To be thus able to be so complete a representative of the life which is still life, even though unacceptable to the Law, is an extraordinary human attribute. To be able to be thus vulnerable and thus hurt ('My tears begin to take his part so much,/They mar my counterfeiting'), and to be able to move so easily into complete identification with the life which, rejected by the Law, must

> outface
> The winds and persecutions of the sky   [II. iii. 11—12]

is to possess another kind of flexibility, though one very different from Kent's. It is a suffering and patient strength which, without need of form and formula, can outlast the drive of will because it is so responsive to the essentials of nature and hence so adaptively alive.

How alive can be seen in the great 'Dover cliff' scene with Gloucester. Edgar's therapy for his father here is the grotesque contrivance of a man hoping against hope in his desperation. The great life of Edgar lies in his readiness to pursue any course, however unlikely, however absurd; and also in his constant fear that such well-meant manoeuvrings might be an unallowable licence. Both aspects of this represent the enormous respect he has for what he calls the 'treasury of life' — treasury enough to warrant such extreme efforts to save it, but treasury enough also to make one hesitate (as Duke Vincentio never did) about abusing it with tricks and manipulations. Like the equally famous and equally controversial IV.iv in *Macbeth* (Malcolm's bizarre testing of Macduff) the scene depicts the havoc wrought in life by the destructive drive of Law which reduces the civilized to such absurd contrivances. But Edgar's strength — his adaptive flexibility again — is that he defeats that drive by absorbing it. Pushed wherever it will push him he still holds to his primal purposes, never driven off from his efforts, yet never so presuming a calculator as to forget his scruple about such designings.

In the end he emerges with formidable power. He has still not lost that vital self-doubt and hesitation ('Never — O fault! —

reveal'd myself unto him') but it is by now quite clear that that
sort of hesitation is far from being the opposite of strength. His
challenge to Edmund in V.iii must be quoted in full to feel what
kind of strength he now has:

> Draw thy sword,
> That, if my speech offend a noble heart,
> Thy arm may do thee justice; here is mine.
> Behold, it is the privilege of mine honours,
> My oath, and my profession. I protest —
> Maugre thy strength, place, youth, and eminence,
> Despite thy victor sword and fire-new fortune,
> Thy valour and thy heart — thou art a traitor;
> False to thy gods, thy brother, and thy father;
> Conspirant 'gainst this high illustrious prince;
> And, from th'extremest upward of thy head
> To the descent and dust below thy foot,
> A most toad-spotted traitor. Say thou 'No',
> This sword, this arm, and my best spirits, are bent
> To prove upon thy heart, whereto I speak,
> Thou liest.   [V. iii. 127–41]

The weight and inexorable tread of the speech, too massy and
steady to be mere martial rhetoric, sees Edgar reaching his full
powers. When Kent used words like 'master' and 'patron' their
meaning was not encapsulable within the structure of mere Law.
So here with Edgar's word 'traitor'. Kent spoke the massive words
of civility in a way which connected easily with his seasoned
knowledge of all that was fortuitous in the Law, and hence all
that was inflated and pretentious in its rhetoric. The younger
Edgar now has something of the same poise and presence. There
is nothing prim, brittle or merely legalistic in 'the privilege of
mine honours,/My oath, and my profession' or in the evocation
of 'this high illustrious prince'. They are terms which reach back
not just to the structures of the Law but to the 'treasury of life'
itself.

Cordelia appears in only four scenes of the play — I.i, IV.iv
(her prayer to the earth's 'blest secrets'), IV.vii (the benediction
scene) and V.iii (a prisoner with Lear). The very brevity of her

role gives one the clue as to how to take her, as one whose 'individual character' will not convey a fraction of what her presence signifies. It is a matter of keeping one's sense of her firmly within the group of which she forms a part, and within the metaphysical movement created by that group in which she plays so vital a part. Within this movement she acts as a kind of agent for the completion or ensealment of that which, in the activities of the others, has been generated and brought into life. In the latter part of the play she rises up to fill the gap that awaits her with an inevitability which gives her this quality of 'completing'. Her words crown the deeds of Kent and Edgar, and the radiant daylight of her spirit completes the Apollonian dream to which Lear is just ascending as she comes upon the scene to give it form. She completes their doings, and gives plasticity and articulation to what they have created out of the play's central turmoil.

In her trusting deference to the judgment and experience of both Kent and the Doctor:

> Be govern'd by your knowledge, and proceed
> I' th' sway of your own will,   [IV. vii. 19—20]

there comes to completeness and articulation the spirit of deference which the others have manifested in deed. The opposite of the sisters' will and enterprise has taken plastic form. In her prayer to the 'blest secrets' and 'unpublish'd virtues' of the earth we again feel that form and plasticity are being given to things which we have seen in dramatic action — including the unpublished virtues of Kent and Edgar in disguise and the Old Man and Cornwall's servant in obscurity; and also the blest secret of the earth's movement towards delivery and spring as the winter of Acts III and IV blows itself out. In the delicate knowledge of the alchemy of life which this prayer portends our intimations of the play's emergence from darkness and winter find themselves 'arriving' as at an awaited clarity.

In the benediction scene this form-giving and completing continue. Her tender sense of the savage breach made in the King's 'reverence', and of the 'thin helm' of the 'poor perdu' who has endured the storm, takes on from Kent and Edgar's nurturing of the 'treasury of life' and gives articulate form to the opposite of the sisters' reductivisms and violations. It is the final establishment of the opposite of what was involved when haggishness and sadism rejoiced to dismantle the life of Gloucester and reduce him to 'corky arms' and 'vile jelly'. The same is true of her greeting to the awakening King:

How does my royal Lord? How fares your Majesty?

which not only brings Kent's word 'royal' sumptuously to completion but also 'mantles' the King in rich words of civility no longer merely connotive of legal status. And her forgiveness in this scene ('No cause, no cause') completes and crowns the movement through which Lear himself has gone to 'None does offend, none – I say none' and gives final articulation to the unembitteredness of Kent and Edgar who have cherished and rescued men who abused them.

So Cordelia is the awaited daylight. She comes at the end of a movement through the night and provides what Wallace Stevens might call 'words of the day', making the Supreme Fiction out of the raw materials of the 'real' as provided by the lives of the others.[7] But the Supreme Fiction is a mere falsehood or consolation for the raggedness of the contingent unless its elegant artifice is in intimate contact with the basic facts of the real. Cordelia *alone* would be a mere consolation (and has I think served as such for critics who have modulated *King Lear* into the terms of a less dynamic and energetic metaphysic than that of Shakespeare). But Cordelia as the *end point* in a general movement up from the most basic contact with the real, speaking her delicate and embroidered words *as a direct consequence of* the primal activities of King, Fool, Kent and Edgar on the heath – such a Cordelia is altogether more substantial, less sentimental and less gratuitous. She can give intimations of the Credences of Summer only in a certain context, and the context is that in which the full reality of winter has been endured not by herself but by the others upon whom she is dependent.

It is in this way that I think we should take her sublimity, and that of Lear upon whose ascent from the primal to the sublime she depends for her reality. Two key passages – the Gentleman's description of Cordelia as 'Sunshine and rain at once', and Lear's

'Come, let's away to prison' — will give us a sense of how the
metaphysical movement towards the birth of spring is brought to
completion, and of how that completion draws directly upon
primal 'reality' to get its convincing substance.

The Gentleman says of Cordelia:

> You have seen
> Sunshine and rain at once: her smiles and tears
> Were like a better way. Those happy smilets
> That play'd on her ripe lip seem'd not to know
> What guests were in her eyes, which parted thence
> As pearls from diamonds dropp'd . . .
>
> . . . There she shook
> The holy water from her heavenly eyes,
> And clamour moisten'd . . .   [IV. iii. 17—31 *passim*]

The description runs terrible risks of preciosity and sucrose
over-delicacy; but it survives these dangers because of the context
in which we have it and to which it makes strong reference in its
imagery. It is a beautifully delicate piece of Elizabethan
ornament; but, as with most of the finest of such daintinesses and
exquisitries, it derives its power from the fact that the elaborately
artificial figuring remains closely in touch with a primal natural
base — in this case the image of an April day. The co-presence of
rain and sun makes this very literally an image of spring ; and
then, because of that direct literal appropriateness to the
metaphysical context, its wroughtness, artifice and embroidery
come to life as the formal embellishments of natural forms. The
moment at which this embellishment can arise so easily from the
natural base is the moment when the Supreme Fiction of the
birth of spring is made — or the moment at which what is
Apollonian, without the hard artifice of the Doric, comes to meet
and take life from the Dionysiac heart of the play.

Lear's speech is tonally, metaphysically and structurally similar:

> No, no, no, no! Come, let's away to prison.
> We too alone will sing like birds i' th' cage;
> When thou dost ask me blessing, I'll kneel down
> And ask of thee forgiveness; so we'll live,

And pray, and sing, and tell old tales, and laugh
At gilded butterflies, and hear poor rogues
Talk of court news; and we'll talk with them too —
Who loses and who wins; who's in, who's out —
And take upon's the mystery of things
As if we were God's spies; and we'll wear out
In a wall'd prison packs and sects of great ones
That ebb and flow by th' moon   [V. iii. 17—31]

It also runs grave risks, and the Lear who speaks it has not escaped without censure from severely moralistic critics who find in this a sentimental escapism less admirable than Cordelia's determined resolution:

Shall we not see these daughters and these sisters?
                                              [V. iii. 7]

But it is a crass commitment to the 'real' (in Stevens' disparaging sense) that juxtaposes Cordelia's strength with the King's weakness in that way. The Utopian fantasy of his speech doubtless needs her clear-headed persistence at its side to react with it in our minds and keep it from preciosity, just as the elegant artifice of the Gentleman's description of her needed the full contextual presence of the play's tough metaphysic. But, given that tension, the fantasy is beautiful and delicate. The men on the heath have survived the winter, driven right back from the established securities of the Law to a primal level at which their deeper civility did not snap, and from which new and fresh words of civilization have risen. Lear's fantasy brings that movement to a blithe and airy epiphany wherein the most basic essentials of communal life — singing, laughter and talk — are the adequate and substantial base of his sublime imagining. The wintry side of the metaphysical cycle has been endured, and its ravaging of the old Law welcomed as a necessary fury. It is now a new and green time in which culture will be remade from the most basic forms of inter-personal contact.

So the whole festive-comic cycle has been recreated in the tragic world. The King himself has passed through every phase of the cycle and has drawn with him a group of characters, unique

to this play, whose varied tones range from the seasonedness of
Kent to the indestructible youthfulness of Edgar, from the
form-giving Cordelia to the formless hurly-burly of the Fool
whose mind vibrates faithfully to the chaotic percussions of the
contingent world. They 'place' the idea of Law as it never was
placed by any characters in the tragic plays discussed above, but
as it was traditionally placed by the characters of festive comedy
who knew (or learnt) how to keep their humanity in touch with
nature, their fictions in touch with the real.

7. *The gor'd state*

So the delineation of an emergent spring in the play's later phases
is unmistakable. The play's winter was of formidable fury. It
dismantled the edifices of the Law which, in Act One, as in all the
other plays we have so far examined, displayed themselves in
ignorant confidence. But out of that dismantling there came not
only a new respect for 'the thing itself' divested of the 'lendings'
of the 'sophisticated' but also new civilities whose delicate
excellence was celebrated in the Apollonian language of Cordelia
and Lear. From what began in scraps and fragments on the heath,
as the primal comforts of warmth and security were offered by
Kent to Lear and Lear to Fool, a beautifully unemphatic lyric of
the spring has grown. It has lifted itself towards an established
elegance in such beautifully paced scenes as that in which the
King is taken up and placed in a litter and that in which Lear and
Cordelia make their mutual benediction. And it has become
plastic in Cordelia's form-giving and the King's Utopian fantasy.

At the end of the play the spirit of that spring appears to be
reaching confident establishment as social fact, but Albany's
repeated efforts to solemnize that achievement at the level of a
new social order falter repeatedly in the face of the play's final
catastrophe. The new circle is cut by the deaths of three people:
Cordelia, whose death is a grotesque accident, Lear, who dies
partly hanging on to the illusion that Cordelia still lives and partly
cursing savagely in his horror at her death, and Kent, who dies of
emotional exhaustion – we have already heard of him 'tranc'd'
by his grief when 'the strings of life/Began to crack'. The animal

wailing of the King cuts across the Apollonian music which we have been hearing, and the agony which kills him stuns Albany's efforts at order-making into horror:

> All friends shall taste
> The wages of their virtue, and all foes
> The cup of their deservings. O, see, see!   [V. iii. 302–4]

Albany can finally only announce 'general woe' and call quietly for the 'gor'd state' to be sustained by Kent and Edgar, before half of even that wish is cancelled by Kent's withdrawal to his death.

One's difficulty in talking about this last scene is immense. Its assault upon the sensibility is of such power and such tonal complexity that a 'balanced' account of it is virtually an affront. Yet in insisting that it has complexity as well as power we are perhaps giving ourselves the relevant warning: no reading which reduces that complexity to singleness and offers the scene as tonally monochrome should be allowed much credence. With the complexity goes restraint, for this is clearly a scene which permits no orgy of consolation, no more than it permits an orgy of horror which might prompt and license easy intimations of the futility of all things. The scene has not finished its work upon us until the very last lines, which bring it and the play at large to their self-completion, and the tone of those lines is neither of horror nor of consolation. The play is closed and finished in those lines very flatly, with chastened and deferential acknowledgment:

> The oldest hath borne most: we that are young
> Shall never see so much nor live so long.   [V. iii. 325–6]

I find it hard to imagine how a Christian-consolatory play of redemption could end quite so fittingly with such lines; and even harder to imagine how an absurdist play, revelatory of the arbitrariness of all, could be content to lay itself to rest in so quietly unaffirmative a manner.

And yet I want for what I feel about this scene a good deal of the Christians' insistence that the play leaves one unsubdued by the terrors which it has confronted; and also something (though rather less) of the absurdists' counter-conviction that such

comforts as may be derived from it, by those who are thus
unsubdued, are not offered by the play as lightly as they have
often been taken. The play that Jan Kott has written about and
Peter Brook produced does exist. That vision is a part of what we
find in the complex ineloquence of the last scene, and their
insistence upon it is an understandable and salutary protest
against what is over-loquacious in redemptivist readings. No
lightly assumed metaphysical consolation should be allowed to
transpose Cordelia's death into terms other than those in which it
is given — a grotesque accident of timing sees her hanged in prison
by a hired man. But, equally, no determined ideology of blackness
should close one's eyes to what is also there — the undeflected
humanity of Edgar and Albany who have been victorious in the
humane resistance offered to tyranny. One should not try to
mitigate the blankness involved in Lear's howling, and in the
finality of his last statements:

> And my poor fool is hang'd! No, no, no life!
> Why should a dog, a horse, a rat have life,
> And thou no breath at all? Thou'lt come no more,
> Never, never, never, never, never.   [V. iii. 305—8]

But one should remember that this is not the sole product of his
life. There was equally a counter-force in him which led to
another apotheosis *as inevitable as this one* when he and Cordelia
articulated the Supreme Fiction of the spring, in whose aftermath
civilization will now gather itself together again.

In the end I have no patience with any reading of this scene
which does not implicitly acknowledge the interdependence of
such contraries, and which does not feel, in the superb restraint
and ineloquence of the scene's tone, the pressure of an awareness to which the loquacities of ideological pronouncement can
do no justice. Both Christianity and absurdism seem to me
ideological (and hence loquacious) in this sense. Both appropriate
the scene and the play to an ideology which I find markedly more
slight than the metaphysic from which it in fact springs. Both of
them hunger for one very partial kind of satisfaction, and have
over-keen eyes for that part of the play's life which might seem to
give it. The compulsory optimism of the one, and the compulsory

pessimism of the other are equally divisive and equally compulsory. And they therefore distort the uncompelled unity of a play which so fittingly ends with Edgar's quiet deference to an incomparably diverse life.

The main reason for these distortions is, I would insist, ideological. The Christian and absurdist reductions of tragedy have roots in the whole ideology of which they are a part. Their respective simplifications arise either from an habitual dwelling upon the comfort of the Resurrection, which can never quite engage with tragedy as a movement completed in this world; or from a determination to systematize or freeze tragic knowledge into an unchanging and unchallenging guarantee of the absurdist's rightness, who thereby furnishes himself with what Karl Jaspers aptly characterized as

the prop whereby the arrogant nihilist can elevate himself to the pathos of feeling himself a hero.[8]

The Christian's ideology must tend to make him feel at odds with the completeness of tragedy; the absurdist's ideology must make him avert what Jaspers calls its 'openness' or 'imperfection':

tragic knowledge mounts in intensity through contradictions which it leaves unresolved but which it does not freeze as necessarily insoluble. [*ibid.* p. 121]

These are severe judgments, but they have a necessary place in understanding how *King Lear* must escape the most widespread of its modern appropriations. But, short of such severe judgment, one should perhaps concede that Christians and absurdists alike may, to some degree, be trapped by the inflexibilities of their language. They may well feel more diversely about the play than their terms seem to me to imply. For conceptual and descriptive language operates, as Schopenhauer knew, high in the 'edifice of reflection', and far removed from the immediacy of experience. It is stiff in comparison with the fluidities of experience. Its decisiveness tends towards purities which are unreal.

Schopenhauer, as I say, knew this well, and his whole metaphysic is rooted in his sense of it. Nietzsche knew it also, as witness for example his scorn for the 'pathology' of the absolute which made him so helpful an interpreter of the world of Elsinore. I therefore find it unsurprising that *King Lear* – the tragic play with a festive-comic structure and the metaphysical summary of a whole tragic vision whose roots are in festive comedy – should yield to their conceptual language more readily than to most.

The end of the play makes me keep Schopenhauer's rich and full sense of 'resignation' in mind, though as soon as the word begins to smack of abnegation I reach for the Nietzschean corrective:

How differently Dionysos spoke to me! How far removed from all this resignationism!

And Nietzsche's own resolution of the paradoxes of tragedy into an idea of 'strong pessimism' seems to me to come nearer to the tone of this play than most descriptive language has done. It is an idea rich enough to include the quietude of Edgar's deference with which the play eventually comes to rest; but the centre of the idea, like the centre of the play, involves apprehension of that tragic paradox at levels of intensity and fury to which a *merely* quiet or resigned sense of contradiction does no justice. *Pure* quietude does not recognize the savagery of nature's destructiveness as it is caught in the Shakespearean metaphysic; nor does it recognize the sense of indestructible joyfulness which is so convincingly realized first in the fertility of Lear's imagination and then in the 'spring' or 'release' for the creation of which that fertility is the only guarantee.

Shakespeare realizes the tragic paradox in all its intensity by working with a model for understanding human life which has its basis in a metaphysic of the seasons, built in its turn on the popular dialectics of seasonal folk-lore, superstition and magic. His thought and language are impregnated throughout by the imagery and tonality of that metaphysic, and it gives both his 'winter' and his 'spring' incomparable richness. Nothing in the universe of the Romantic poets, for example, is as riotously fertile as Shakespeare's romanticism of spring; and, at the same time and by the same token, no Wordsworthian daffodil would ever have survived a Shakespearean frost. Wordsworthian nature is, as Rossiter said, a 'national park', wherein the mountains are rather low and not particularly forbidding;[9] and I find it to be an inevitable consequence of that that the Wordsworthian spring is a chaste and pretty affair full of metaphysical falsehood and false consolation.

Shakespeare's spring is inevitably violent. Old wood does not bear new leaves, and new leaves and shoots are blasted by frosts. He is a realist, as Wordsworth is not, about the *cost* of spring and the *price* of growth in human life. But his violent spring, because of that realism, is not only the more strong and more reliable but also the more beautiful. In a way *King Lear* is at bottom a great vision of the spring as seen by a Northern European man.

The songs
of Apollo and Dionysos

I have done ill,
Of which I do accuse myself so sorely
That I will joy no more . . .

I am alone the villain of the earth,
And feel I am so most. O Antony,
Thou mine of bounty . . .

[*A & C* IV. vi. 18–20; 30–2]

1. Shakespeare's lyricism

The death of Enobarbus is the death of a man who feels that in
forsaking Antony he has forsaken life itself. He has forsaken
bounty for barrenness, the fire of the sun for the pallor of the
moon, the heat of day for the damp and chill of night,
companionship for solitude. The betrayal is so complete as to
destroy him at once. The fullness of life that he has seen and
shared in Egypt has made him incapable of living and breathing in
the thin atmosphere of Rome. That atmosphere touches him like
a blight and the life of him simply stops. Life itself is 'a very rebel
to my will'. The sap of him has dried and hardened:

Throw my heart
Against the flint and hardness of my fault,
Which, being dried with grief, will break to powder,
And finish all foul thoughts. [*A & C* IV. ix. 15–18]

He leaves the world feeling himself 'infamous', a 'fugitive' – not only from Antony and Egypt but from all joy, daylight and delighted life.

The poignancy of the two scenes in which we see Enobarbus wither like a blighted plant (IV.vi. and IV.ix) depends upon our apprehension of the fiery lyric of life's capacity for joy which the play imparts throughout its duration — so that the quiet, muted hopelessness of Enobarbus' words has a dead-weight of loss or unqualified impoverishment in its tone, set off by the contrast with the lyric world. *Antony and Cleopatra* provides this apprehension of the lyrical with fulsome and voluptuous richness, its language impregnated with the festivity of the Dionysiac, its embodiment of life's most creative and fructifying forces being incomparably sure, sweeping and exuberant. It is an expansively lyrical play in which the romanticism of Shakespeare's metaphysic revels in its own life. It has been described as 'so little comforting to the romantic imagination',[1] and doubtless there are kinds of romanticism to which nothing in Shakespeare's very high-force world will be a comfort. But another, more characteristically Shakespearean romanticism, of a kind to which the last chapter has paid attention, receives the play's fullest and most generous endorsement; and receives in the play one of its two greatest lyric enactments in all Shakespeare's work.

The other great enactment of this lyric-romantic quality in Shakespeare's metaphysic is *Macbeth*. Perhaps that claim sounds even more warning notes than the description of *Antony and Cleopatra* outlined above; but I find that these two very dissimilar plays are vitally alike in one respect. Each contains an exuberantly alive romantic vision; and without response to that vision each will dwindle, in the hands of critic or producer, into flatness, primness, moralism or simple otioseness, deprived of the fire and sap of the vision out of which each of them is built. I shall not quite give these two plays a 'full and detailed critical reading'. I want only to get to what seems to me this lyrical quality of their vision to bring my dealings with Shakespeare's romantic metaphysic to a close. Much of what I say involves questions of broad tonality — an insistence as to the feel and colour of these two plays, and of their extraordinary poetic language. And it also involves some reaching back to the emergence of the romantic strain in Shakespeare's thinking in *Romeo and Juliet* and *A Midsummer Night's Dream*, the romantic plays of the mid 1590s which I have tended to associate together throughout this book.

It is of course obvious that *Macbeth* and *Antony and Cleopatra* are extremely different plays. In some ways it would be hard to imagine two plays which offered themselves less spontaneously for comparison; and if I bring them together now it is not in the hope of establishing a new Shakespearean 'group' whereby they will remain long in each other's company for critical perusal, like 'The History Plays', 'The Problem Plays' or 'The Last Plays'. But it is often useful to break up such traditional groups to get at some features of the individual texts which the virtual symbiosis imputed to them by criticism might tend to conceal; and in this vein I have indeed intimated some anxiety about what happens when the concept of the 'Problem Play' stops us from seeing *Measure for Measure* and *Troilus and Cressida* as the lucid and integrated imaginings that they are. Contrariwise, it may also be useful to bring two clearly different plays together for a moment so that when they part and go their separate ways again the experience of their fleeting contact might have given us some new perspective on their separate identities. I will not keep them together long, nor build up too many hopes for the stability of a union between the tight, ordered and economical *Macbeth* and the slow, lazy, voluptuous and unwinding *Antony and Cleopatra*.

The quality which is isolated by making this connexion is that uniquely Shakespearean lyric-romanticism. They are the most lyrical (and visionary) works of the tragic period, their vision and their poetry impregnated with a high-force and high-speed apprehension of the beauty, vitality and 'sap' of the contingent world which is the basis of their romantic life. As I have begun to suggest by means of some disparaging comments on Wordsworth at the close of the last chapter, I find this romanticism and the lyrical verse which carries it far more fierily alive than that of the Romantic poets themselves, and consequently far more capable of sustaining a capacious and viable metaphysic of human life. The 'something' which Wordsworth found 'deeply interfused' in the contingent world seems to me a rather blurred and vague category, idly gestured at for reasons of consolation, in comparison with the bewildering variety and detail of those racing undercurrents of life which Shakespeare's romanticism apprehends in the natural world. Keats' characteristic aggregations of nature's more luxurious aspects are cloying, stationary, ripe for gloating over or fondling, exotic products for the gratification of the sensuously affluent consumer, quite without the nimble charge of wild energy which is always there as the pulse of nature's richness in Shakespeare's lyric verse. Of the poets of the Romantic era, only Blake, kissing the joy as it flies, allows nature the speedy, lyric life of Shakespeare; and in consequence it is only Blake who can create out of his conception of nature images of human mental life which have anything of the psychological viability of such images in the work of Shakespeare.

Blake (one might as well make as much as possible out of this comparative excursus before returning) differs from Wordsworth and Keats in two ways which are useful in clarifying the vital differences between the various romanticisms I have in mind. Firstly Blake is humorous, dashingly and exuberantly so, where Keats and Wordsworth most markedly are not; and this humour, with its buoyancy, robustness and *vif*, is an essential part of the romantic life to which his poetry bears witness. And secondly Blake is a great poet of Eros, where Keats and Wordsworth again are markedly not; the only one of the Romantic poets (if he may be considered as such) in whom Eros is not sublimated either into religiosities or into aestheticizings. These two (related) factors, of humour and the erotic, differentiate Blake's vision from those of his near-contemporaries just as surely as they enable one to associate him with Shakespeare, whose lyricism also involves a rich responsiveness to humour and sexuality.

So it is this sort of lyricism which I find to be so potent in *Macbeth* and *Antony and Cleopatra*. In *Macbeth* it is potent throughout the darkness of the play wherein we can never forget the terrible deprivation of lyric life which the hero's 'deed' has brought about, so that we have a perpetual sense of the lyrical by watching its continuous violation or absence. And it is potent throughout *Antony and Cleopatra* in the laughing sunlight of life which Egypt strives constantly to create and of which Rome knows nothing. These two late plays bring to a climax of intensity and metaphysical validity the lyric strain in Shakespeare's writing which had its origins in *Romeo and Juliet* and *A Midsummer Night's Dream*. It is worth following it back to those origins to get its nature clear.

In reference to *Romeo and Juliet* I have called it the poetry of Queen Mab, and it is indeed in Mercutio's great speech that the essence of this lyric quality presents itself. But it pervades the whole play as it pervades *A Midsummer Night's Dream*. It involves the apprehension of fluidities of movement in the natural world which have their obvious mental counterpart (or manifestation) in high-energy states of the human mind — the intensities of dream, passion, witty exhilaration, incandescences of the spirit of the kind to which Theseus paid more tribute than he knew when he made his famous speech on the lunatic, the lover and the poet. I find the poetry of this spring- and youth-time lyric-romanticism 'breath-taking', and I have no sense of resorting vaguely to linguistic fire-works as I use the term. It takes one's breath away in that it moves with a rapidity of apprehension and articulation which, keeping up with the quickness of nature itself, seems perpetually almost too fast to follow; and yet its articulation is so sure and precise that airy nothing is indeed given a local habitation and a name, and one finds that one has arrived 'breathless' at the distant name and place to which the mind has so swiftly been transported. It is a poetry of exhilarated singing, magically swift, light and intense. Or a poetry in which chemical reactions between words take place at a speed which bids fair to imitate the explosive celerities of nature's own most volatile proceedings. We experience in such poetry the transports of an imagination which is recklessly quick and headlong, but also accurate and subtle; and its powers enable it to embody the most exhilarating aspects of that kinetic world which plays its great part in Shakespeare's general metaphysic.

Mercutio's speech on Queen Mab[2] not only *describes* these wanton powers which transport the mind; it *enacts* them, keeping up with their racing momentum with breathless haste. His 'gamesome' speech leaps and dances through extravagance after extravagance as it brings to life what is suggested when Queen

Mab is called 'the fairies' midwife' — the magical lightness of the inapprehensible, and the connexion of these powers with fertility and breeding. The description of her coach is an exultant fantasy of metamorphoses and transpositions succeeding one another with tumbling speed. But however fast the mind flies it never loses its accuracy or precision of reference: the contingent world is not dissolved to get rid of its impediments to the flying imagination, as it is for example in the Romantic poetry of Shelley. Rather it is the speed and intense energy of the contingent world itself which provides the basis for the imagining. The imagination, moving at this extraordinary pace and thus attuned to the world's quickness, plays among the objects of the world as the world itself 'plays' in its kinetic vitality:

> Sometime she driveth o'er a soldier's neck,
> And then dreams he of cutting foreign throats,
> Of breaches, ambuscadoes, Spanish blades,
> Of healths five fathom deep; and then anon
> Drums in his ear, at which he starts and wakes,
> And being thus frighted, swears a prayer or two
> And sleeps again.   [*R & J* I. iv. 82—8]

The lyric-romantic vitality of nature and mind of which this speech is the classic *locus* permeates the whole play. Friar Lawrence lives, amongst his herbs and phials, close to the dangerous, potent and mysteriously paradoxical energies of nature which animate the romanticism of the 'fair daylight' and the 'worshipped sun'. In youth, beauty and festivity such forces are carried, like 'well-appareled April' and 'fresh fennel buds', into the gaieties of social life; and they draw on the 'bewitched' spirits of lovers to incandescences of imagination in which the world presents to them its exotic beauty:

> It seems she hangs upon the cheek of night
> As a rich jewel in an Ethiop's ear,   [I. v. 43—4]

its wild splendour:

> It is too rash, too unadvis'd, too sudden;
> Too like the lightning, which doth cease to be
> Ere one can say 'It lightens'   [II. ii. 118—20]

and its most alluring and tumultuous elegances:

> O, speak again, bright angel, for thou art
> As glorious to this night, being o'er my head,
> As is a winged messenger of heaven
> Unto the white-upturned wond'ring eyes
> Of mortals that fall back to gaze on him,
> When he bestrides the lazy-pacing clouds
> And sails upon the bosom of the air.   [II. ii. 26−32]

The romantic lyricism in which the play abounds carries a jubilant vision of human potential of which the bawdy verbal gymnastics of Mercutio are also a part − making 'our wits run the wild-goose chase' − and in which there is also an inalienable tragic possibility, since the fiery temper of Mercutio and the 'unruly spleen' of Tybalt, 'King of Cats', cannot be separated from the 'affections and warm youthful blood' which the play as a whole generously and unequivocally lauds.

This praise of romantic possibility, dangers notwithstanding (the bawdy and the violence of youth do not relate to the lyricism as any kind of equivocal or moralistically 'placing' commentary), links the play to *A Midsummer Night's Dream* and thereby to the kinetic vision of festive comedy. In *A Midsummer Night's Dream* this same poetry of lyric-romantic fire serves to create a similarly generous and celebratory vision of human potential, and a similarly exhilarating one. The metamorphosing power of love, allied to the 'pert and nimble spirit of mirth', is an index of psychic vitalities corresponding to the vitalities of the natural world as they are embodied in the fairies and in the mischief of Puck. As in *Romeo and Juliet* such energies are paradoxical: Friar Lawrence's herbs contained both poison and medicine, the fairies' powers might unloose either fertility or a 'progeny of evils'. But again this paradoxical and hence dangerous quality of high-energy life should give rise to no 'hesitation' or moralistic circumscription of the play's romanticism. Romantic vitality is again a *sine qua non* of the life of nature and hence of the psychic life of man, and Shakespeare's imagery of the ecstatic is rich and convincing enough to be greeted without sceptical qualification:

Feed him with apricocks and dewberries,
With purple grapes, green figs, and mulberries;
The honey-bags steal from the humble-bees,
And for night-tapers crop their waxen thighs,
And light them at the fiery glow-worm's eyes,
To have my love to bed and to arise;
And pluck the wings from painted butterflies,
To fan the moonbeams from his sleeping eyes,

[III. i. 152–9]

or the voluptuous life of Eros within it:

in the spiced Indian air, by night,
Full often hath she gossip'd by my side,
And sat with me on Neptune's yellow sands,
Marking th' embarked traders on the flood;
When we have laugh'd to see the sails conceive,
And grow big-bellied with the wanton wind.

[II. i. 124–9]

This lyric language of ecstasy far exceeds in passional power, comic exuberance, mercurial speed and erotic richness, the romanticism of the Romantics. This has, I think, been well and widely recognized by recent critics and producers of Shakespearean comedy and of the early romantic tragedy of *Romeo and Juliet*. If I mention Peter Brook's justly famous production of *A Midsummer Night's Dream* or Franco Zeffirelli's excellent film of *Romeo and Juliet* I am reminding myself of how well the modern imagination has been able to grasp and realize the sumptuous and generous vitality of Shakespeare's romanticism as it appears in those two plays. But in production as in criticism the related romantic life of *Macbeth* and *Antony and Cleopatra* has been less squarely seen, less surely caught.

The whole vision of these two later plays depends at every point on the power and the subtlety of this romantic metaphysic. At the risk of simplification (the ensuing discussions of the two plays can modify though not withdraw what I say here) one may say that everything in *Macbeth* depends upon a romantic apprehension of the Apollonian, everything in *Antony and Cleopatra* on a romantic apprehension of the Dionysiac. Throughout *Macbeth* we feel the tragedy of the hero's terrible and irreversible loss of contact with the breeding and joy-giving powers of the natural world which, taken up reverently into social life, might give civilization the character of Apollonian dream. And in *Antony and Cleopatra* we see Egypt striving to make human life enter ever more completely into the equally breeding and joy-giving powers of the Dionysiac whence all energy springs. Macbeth cannot stop being aware of the breathless transporting powers of the lyric world from which his deed has alienated him, recording their presence with a language that picks up the sense of wanton flight which we have seen in the earlier plays:

> pity, like a naked new-born babe,
> Striding the blast, or heaven's cherubin hors'd
> Upon the sightless couriers of the air,
> Shall blow the horrid deed in every eye,
> That tears shall drown the wind.   [*Mac*.I.vii. 21–5]

Antony and Cleopatra, howsoever their courses may vacillate and waver, cannot cease returning again and again to that fiery centre of lyric life, recorded equally in the play's language of charmed and wanton flight, but for which the case of the spirit would be cold and the 'varying shore o' th' world' would stand 'darkling'. *Macbeth* is a play of night and winter wherein, however, the lost life of day and summer can never be completely shut out and forgotten. *Antony and Cleopatra* is a play of daylight and summer, clung to and striven after for their life-giving light and heat before 'black vesper's pageant' can enfold life in its cold and dark. And in *Macbeth*, as we have seen with Enobarbus in *Antony and Cleopatra*, a man's loss of contact with that lyric life means that he too will be 'alone the villain of the earth' and that he too will 'joy no more'.

These are simplifications, perhaps. But both plays seem to me to make the whole reality of this romantic vision come so fully into life as they are watched or read that it is worth running the risk of simplification in order to place immediate emphasis upon it. I have argued, of course, that all Shakespearean tragedies have this metaphysical aspect, and consequently that the idea of their 'general vision' is not a secondary critical abstraction analytically derived from, let alone imposed upon, their local life as plays: their local life as plays in the theatre is such as to bring their metaphysic to palpable life. But with these two late plays that is even more true, and its emphasis even more urgent. Both suffer even more than the others when criticism and production ignore their quite primary status as plays of vision and metaphysic. And when we put them together as such what we see is the lyric-romantic quality of Shakespeare's vision coursing freely through the Dionysiac *vif* of *Antony and Cleopatra* or creating the standpoint of the Apollonian dream from which the tragedy of Macbeth's sterile attempt to murder culture and nature is watched.

In one way the appellations 'Dionysiac' and 'Apollonian' suggest that these plays are polar opposites, and I shall indeed want to keep that sense of polar opposition in my idea of what is revealed when they are put together. They complement one another as opposites do. But they also relate in a manner that should suggest contiguity rather than opposition. Dionysos and Apollo, in Nietzsche's scheme, were opposites, but opposites that took life from one another from their contiguity in the experience of the tragic. These two plays show us something markedly similar in the vision of Shakespeare. For though I will call *Macbeth* Apollonian, and indicate thereby that its romantic life consists in its dream of humane ordonnance, I shall also want to keep the sense, clearly given by the play, that humane ordonnance of this kind is what it is because it seems constantly to touch and derive from the pulse of extra-human nature itself. And, *vice versa*, though I shall call the vitality of Egypt Dionysiac, and thus try to do justice to its fructifying chaos of fertility, I shall also want to keep the sense, again imparted by the play, that Egyptian life is not only a breeding chaos but also a culture, an image of life in which chaos constantly breeds or spawns the life of the humane. In *Macbeth*, in other words, the vision of human community sees it as constantly reaching down to the primal nature from which it springs; while in *Antony and Cleopatra* the vision of primal nature sees it as constantly creating community. Thus the opposites of Apollo and Dionysos reveal their contiguity and support a pair of radically unlike plays which nonetheless resemble one another in several vital aspects.

It is a very comprehensive romanticism which can give life to two such opposite but contiguous dramatizations of man's dealings with the lyrical high forces of his world; and one hastens to add that it is doubtless the fact that both aspects of the vision are realized with such clarity and force that makes either one of them as fine as it is — a poise beyond Blake, let alone the other Romantic poets. I find it entirely characteristic of Shakespeare that the spirit of these two climactic plays, from late in the tragic period, should not only be capacious and poised but also capaciously romantic. The romantic pulse of *Romeo and Juliet* and *A Midsummer Night's Dream* beats even more strongly here than there. It quickens the poetry of the two late plays into unparalleled speed and vividness and gives them a rich brilliance of linguistic colour. And it makes the vision which they jointly impart not only limpid and sublime (which it is) but also exhilarating and blithe.

2. Macbeth and the song of Apollo

At several points in my earlier discussions of Shakespeare's tragic view of human socialization I have had occasion to distinguish that view from nihilism. Shakespeare's continuous, sceptical under-view of socialization — its 'hoops' and 'rules', the partiality and accident of attachment, the illusion-creating of its preferred 'normality' — differs from the under-view of nihilism in ways which seem to me to be fundamental to the very business of tragedy. Shakespeare does not pounce on the truths of the traumatic with vengeful, or self-justifying, or consolatory relish; and when one of his characters does — like Hamlet or Timon — the tonality of the whole play within which he is set is such as to make us accept those truths with much humane qualification. The Shakespearean under-view depends for much of its life on a generous recognition of the stinging and cauterizing rightness of

Hamlet's wit or, to a lesser extent, of the anguish and outrage of Timon's moral repulsion. It depends too on a vigorous knowledge of the rightness of Thersites' acrid disbelief, Patroclus' 'scurril jests', Iago's deflationary intransigence. The voices of these 'outside' or extra-social men are deeply valued by Shakespearean drama for their creation of sceptical perspectives and their witness to qualities of highly individual vigour and perception which create liberty by setting the hoops and rules in disarray.

I don't want to go on to say that Shakespearean tragedy 'places' these voices: that suggests a welcome which is essentially dismissive, or a recognition which is merely condescending, while Shakespeare's dealings with them seem to me more vigorous and laudatory. His mind is more *dependent* on them for their radicalism of discovery and revelation than the superiority and loftiness of 'placing' would suggest. Nonetheless, none of them is allowed any simple status as 'truth-speaker'. There is a perspective to Shakespearean drama which sees not only radical intelligence but also a certain human loss — which the radically-seeing Jacques also shares — in the bitterly apposite under-viewing of the sceptic or detractor; so that the standpoint of the nihilistic or the absurd, though it reveals essential truths about the illusions of the socially normal, is a standpoint that pays for its acute relevance with a certain causticness of the spirit which is inimical to life, and capable of degenerating into the self-administered poison of a mind like that of Iago.

That is why Nietzsche's idea of the absurd and of its attendant nausea, as parts of a journey *through*, parts of a process *towards*, rather than as end-points of arrival in themselves, is so germane to the business of tragedy and its traumatic vision. And it is why the caveats about what is often taken for tragic knowledge, as classically expressed by Karl Jaspers, provide us with some vital distinctions between the openness and intensity of tragic perception and the ideological closure of pseudo-tragic nihilism.

That distinction is one of which Shakespearean drama makes us constantly aware. Shakespeare's poise and clarity in the matter is exemplary. God is permitted in these plays to stand up for bastards with more than usual aplomb; but that does not mean that the fine and flagrant jeering against 'a whole tribe of fops' and 'the excellent foppery of the world'[3] is allowed to stand either as the whole truth, or even as a truth to which an ungenerous mind will adhere with any over-warm enthusiasm.

The generous tragic poise which held that distinction so clearly throughout the plays of the tragic period now goes into the Apollonian dream of *Macbeth*. The Apollonian dream of humane ordonnance, which is the play's lyric back-drop to the hero's black and destructive solitariness, enacts the Supreme Fiction of civilization which is possible to the tragic but not to the nihilistic mind. It presents, as does the Supreme Fiction or Yeats' idea of Byantium (though with no propensity for believing that the soul must be 'out of nature' to experience the pull of 'the artifice of eternity'), the dream of flexuously alive ordonnance which establishes the plenitude of tragedy beyond the littleness of the absurd.[4] Staying for another moment with Yeats' terms (they are nearly enough apposite to be helpful), one might say that *Macbeth* opposes 'self-delighting reverie' to the 'grip of claw'; that it presents us with a hero who is the 'incendiary or bigot' who is ready

> To burn that stump on the Acropolis,
> Or break in bits the famous ivories
> Or traffic in the grasshoppers or bees.

Small wonder that we should get some helpful orientations from a poet who, like Shakespeare, gave all the bitter intelligence of his passionately sceptical mind to the mockery of 'the great', 'the wise' and 'the good', only then to give the tragic wheel one more triumphant turn with:

> Mock mockers after that
> That would not lift a hand maybe
> To help good, wise or great
> To bar that foul storm out, for we
> Traffic in mockery.

The most rigorously sceptical tragic writer stops short of trafficking in mockery. The lyrical, Apollonian dream of civilization in *Macbeth* is the product of a beautifully certain knowledge of where the truths of trauma give way to the truths of celebration.

It is thus that the celebration of civility in *Macbeth* gets its peculiar richness and poise. When I say that *Macbeth* is an Apollonian play I mean that it is not quite enough to say that what Macbeth violates is 'order'. Nietzsche's term certainly describes a spirit in which orderliness is of the essence, but, as we have seen, an orderliness which is flexible, light, capable of elaborating its most delicate artifice in open contact with the undominated energies of the wild. It is an orderliness which breathes sublimity, levity and delight — not command. It is free from Doric ossification or the tyranny bred by Socratic fear. It is vulnerable in a way that they are not — not pre-eminently vulnerable to traumatic disruption but vulnerable to the brute intrusion of violence against which it is unarmoured. *Macbeth* is sustained and animated by such a spirit.

What we normally mean by 'order', and what the more conservative critics have often meant as they applied the term to *Macbeth*, is something to which Sheakespearean drama is less sympathetic than has frequently been supposed. Shakespearean drama gives the voices of mockery and derision the freest play to develop their vitality; and the famous 'Degree' speech of Ulysses and the allied ideas of order espoused by Duke Vincentio receive the full caustic laughter (and anger) of the plays in which they appear. Falstaff offends against ideas of order of that kind, but that is no reason why he should be expected to fall to his prayers before a critic's disapprobation. So too does Cleopatra, but again she should not therefore provide occasion for critics to uplift her to the moral view and, like scald rhymers, ballad her out o' tune. But the sustaining Apollonian vision of *Macbeth* is much less morally little, much less mere Law, much less a mere system than what Ulysses and Vincentio proclaim and Falstaff and Cleopatra violate.

The Apollonian vision, by contrast with the idea of Law, embodies delicately lyrical conceptions of the community and continuity of human doings practised in open responsiveness to the sap of natural life. It is a vision of what is creative and delighting (as well as 'ordered') in the experience of social life. Its tones are of festal contentment, but a contentment which is animated and vivified rather than inert. It is pacific, but not passive. If we take out some of the key words from the play which support the conception we see that they are not only 'seated', 'sure and firm-set', 'royalty', 'gentle' and 'dignity'; they are also 'plenteous', 'wanton in fulness', 'nimbly', 'bounteous', 'wooingly'. Words such as these run harmoniously together in the Apollonian vision, combining there Shakespeare's superbly quickened conception of the lyric life of nature and his delicate respect, already recorded in the latter part of *King Lear*, for the Supreme Fiction of civilization.

This Apollonianism is there at the beginning of *Macbeth* before the hero's 'deed' ransacks and ravages it. It is there again at the end when the castle is 'gently rend'red' and the ransacker overcome. And it is there throughout the night and winter horror of the central part of the play, its images tormentingly ineradic-able from the mind of Macbeth himself, tormentingly present to him in the life of Banquo, agonizingly out of reach as he tries to force 'mirth', 'cheer' and 'pleasure' into his now derelict social life, and amazingly (to him) incapable of being wiped from the lives and minds of others no matter how thorough and far-reaching his violence. It is always against the background of the sweeping, lyric life of this Apollonianism that we see the tragic misery and dwarfing of the central figure who has cut himself off from sleep, pleasure and friendship, and from the fertility and vastness of 'multitudinous seas', 'the casing air' and the 'sure and firm-set earth'. He is not only 'cabined, cribbed, confined, bound in', but cabined, cribbed, confined and bound in while the bright and delightful spaciousness of the earth goes on 'nimbly and sweetly', 'wooingly', vexing him with the 'cherubin' and 'sightless couriers' that image its unstoppable life, and eventually outrunning his reserves of violent resistance with a 'moving grove' carried by 'unrough youths' in their 'first of manhood'. We take only a part of the experience of *Macbeth* if we respond simply to the terror of black incantation, deliberate violation and eventually hardened habituation of his poisoned mind. To take the play fully (its terror is not thereby averted) we must take also this exuberant sense of delighted life, projected in a spacious lyricism cut off from which the hero will 'dwindle, peak, and pine' like the sailor whose fate at the hands of the witches prefigures that of Macbeth. Then, like Enobarbus, he will 'joy no more'.

This Apollonianism — just to rehearse its main features

briefly — consists in a kind of stability both in the mind of man (the 'seated heart' and 'single state of man' which the witches throw into confusion) and in his outside world where culture touches nature without aggression ('th' estate o' th' world', 'humane statute' and 'the gentle weal' in harmonious proximity). It animates the idea of 'the dignity of the whole body' which the Waiting-Gentlewoman is horrified to see so ravaged in the sleep-walking Lady Macbeth, and the 'royalty of nature' which Macbeth cannot help seeing and shrinking from in Banquo. It is 'the vessel of my peace' in which Macbeth has poured poisons, the 'bosom franchis'd and allegiance clear' which Banquo firmly but not primly keeps, the 'measureless content' of Duncan who has 'borne his faculties so meek' and been 'so clear in his great office'.

It is such things in an individual mind; and in interpersonal relations it is the 'double trust' (as 'kinsman' and as 'host') which Macbeth betrays in killing Duncan; the rich pleasure taken in others which impregnates Duncan's language when he greets the victorious Banquo and Macbeth in I.iv; the 'joyful trouble' of the 'labour we delight in', in which Macduff believes and Macbeth affects to believe concerning the duties of service and hospitality; the 'ceremony' which is 'the sauce to the meat' so pitifully absent from the feasting at the court of Macbeth; the 'honour, love, obedience, troops of friends' which, in his desolation, he 'must not look to have'.

And then this richness of interpersonal life, promising to be 'full of growing' at the beginning before Macbeth blights it and 'planted newly with the time' at the end when he has been destroyed, links harmoniously with the 'procreant' life imaged in Banquo's speech about the martlets and with the general continuity of human culture seen as a rich store into which the murdered Duncan is received:

> *Ross.* Where is Duncan's body?
> *Macd.* Carried to Colmekill,
> The sacred storehouse of his predecessors
> And guardian of their bones. [II. iv. 32–5]

It all depends on exactly that connexion between primal

nature and the civilization which is more than Law which was
established in the fourth and fifth Acts of *King Lear* when
Cordelia gave plasticity to the spring and the daylight. Here as
there the delicate images of civilized life spring directly from the
images of nature; here as there the primal sap is felt to reach right
up to that which is most ornamented and exquisite in human
artifice. The imagery of rich jewels and tapestry ('his silver skin
laced with his golden blood', 'the sovereign flower', the
'kingdom's pearl') and the language of sacred ceremony (through
to 'the grace of Grace' at the end of the play) are both kept
animate, inspirited with life and thus quite without preciosity, by
the wonderfully sustained connexion between culture and nature
upon which the Apollonian dream of the play depends. Animated
thus, the dream of plasticity and the dream of vitality are one.
Within the elaborations of form joys may be 'wanton in fulness'.

We are, as I say, never far from a continuing sense of this
Apollonianism even when Macbeth's ravaging of it is at its most
violent potency. It is never from the standpoint of anything less
than that Apollonianism that we are asked to view his destructiveness and criminality and the misery of his consciousness of
himself; and the play asks us to keep alive in our imaginations the
whole vision of it as providing the terms in which we apprehend
every dramatic detail. This may be an effort of response to which
one's commitment to 'realism' could be an impediment. But it
should not be; for *Macbeth* is not an allegory or a merely
symbolic work in which an oppressive system of unrealism asks
to be taken *as a substitute for* the real. If it asks to be read
somewhat differently from a nineteenth-century novel, or performed in a way for which the theatre of naturalism would
suggest no prompting, it does not make such demands with any
casual or imperious disregard for the minute and local perception
of individual life. It is not 'about Scotland' as *Coriolanus* is about
Rome or *Othello* about Venice; but it does not, on the other
hand, sue for the validity of its Apollonian dream *in defiance of*
our waking knowledge of actual societies. Its vision is made and
held at a point of miraculous balance where the Supreme Fiction
is the unvarnished truth and where metaphysical generalization is
made palpable in the contingent world.

It seems to me extraordinary that *Macbeth* can be maintained at this point of balance for the whole of its duration. In *King Lear* the Apollonian vision was brief, if decisive; and indeed it would seem to be of the essence of the Apollonian, as of the Supreme Fiction, that the moment at which its vision is true or valid should be *a moment*. But in *Macbeth* the moment is sustained and held. The vision never blurs, never hardens, never resorts to the Doric frigidity of religious or pastoral fiction to keep itself alive (except, I think, in that passage in III.vi on the religious-magical healing powers of 'pious Edward' which is thin, gratuit-ous and separable from the body of the play at large). A contrast with the religious-pastoral fiction of the Last Plays, built out of what has by then become an altogether lesser metaphysic of nature and an altogether narrower and more relaxed conception of human community, should help make the point; or a contrast with the platonization and Spenserian conception of the divinity of the royal which is discarded in *Richard II*. It is not a mere platonic divinizing of the idea of royalty which sets King Duncan at the centre of this play's idea of civilization as Apollonian dream; and the depersonalizing Doric solemnities of the ending of *The Winter's Tale* are quite different from the live and festal Fiction which is the back-drop to *Macbeth*.

Both the pastoral and the religious visions of community are more vulgar, and therefore usually more moralistic, than what we get here. And they also enact the metaphysical lie of realism, imposing the fiction upon us (in Nietzsche's words) 'as crass reality'. The Apollonianism of *Macbeth* is different from the religious-pastoral Doric which sustains *The Faerie Queene* (and which, alas, gradually overmasters *The Winter's Tale*). It does not systematize its vision and thereby claim 'truth' for a mere ideology, as do pastoral and religion. It apprehends the moment of its validity with lyric exuberance and clarity; and then, astonishingly, makes the moment last for five Acts.

I think it is perhaps inevitable that this should happen only once in the late work of Shakespeare. Having as it does this air of fresh and almost incandescent discovery the extended moment of *Macbeth* is unrepeatable. The mind which has arrived at the Apollonian is already less Apollonian than the mind at the

moment of its arrival. The relaxedness and relative falsity of the
arrived mind is what we find in the romances of the Last Plays,
beginning to spin its inspirations into a frail web of opinion which
cannot have the imaginative life or validity of this climactic work.
Yeats will give us his help again. His late poem 'The Circus
Animals' Desertion'[5] recounts a process whereby the moment of
creativity 'brought forth a dream' for which the poet claims
validity: 'Heart-mysteries there'. But

> soon enough
> The dream itself had all my thought and love

and

> It was the dream itself enchanted me . . .

> Players and painted stage took all my love,
> And not those things that they were emblems of.

That seems to me exactly to capture the difference between the
greatness and robustness of *Macbeth* and the lesser frailties of the
Last Plays. *Macbeth* keeps the materials of its dream always in
dialectical contact with 'those things that they were emblems of'.
It thus keeps alive the inspirational fulness of the moment at
which the dream was 'brought forth', and from it creates the
perspective from which the barbarism made by Macbeth is seen.

That perspective is not one which promotes a moralistic sense
of superiority over the protagonist's dwindling into animality as
he tries to kill the Fiction of humane life. *The Faerie Queene*
does, of course, use its Doric idea of order as a moral platform,
sometimes savagely; and in *The Winter's Tale* Paulina has, one
fears, spent sixteen years on just such a platform before leading
her captive audience on to a solemn triumph. But the Fiction of
Macbeth is festal rather than solemn, and its view of the hero is
neither moralistic nor, certainly, savage. As was the case with
Angelo (who shares with Macbeth the agony of intense *consciousness* of his own spiritual dismemberment) we are taken too
urgently into the blighted psyche of this man to feel any
temptation towards the gestures of moralism and solemnity. We
are so close to the awful ease with which he becomes what he
becomes, to the utter desolation of his being that that entails, and

to the agony of his consciousness of it all, that we can only respond to his loss of the dream and its meanings with an acutely painful pity and an acute sense of the dangerous potency of what the witches embody.

There is so much life in him, so much spiritual and physical bravery, so much (as not in Brutus) imaginative intensity and animal vigour that when we see it all fall into the sere after one touch of the witches' poison the experience could scarcely be more awesome. Once he is 'rapt' with fascination for what they are and seem to offer; once he defines energy and ecstasy in their blackly flamboyant terms; once he gives over his lyric and passional life to the hideous counterfeit of imaginative intensity which they offer (a fatal transposition of passional power that we see archetypally in the Lady Macbeth of I.v – 'Come, you spirits/That tend on mortal thoughts, unsex me here . . .'): once these movements are made then at once he begins to wither and shrink. Still tormentingly capable of seeing, feeling, knowing and craving the joyousness of the Apollonian – 'wanton in fulness' – he knows too that the line has been cut, irredeemably. He has 'done the deed', and from there to the end nothing can stay his dwindling. His energy becomes the vulgar, substitute energy of the galvanized will in a state of panic, and it is not an energy which can keep him from the ever more insistent onset of torpor. The massive access of power that he sought from the witches, nerved by the lavish exhibition of such apparent power in his 'transported' wife, is by the end the noise of agony and distemperedness coming from a being who is now grotesquely small – to be pushed from his stool with ridiculous ease when his castle is 'gently rend'red' to the very young men of Malcolm's army.

It is awesome and pitiful, and it also has a painfully exacerbating sense of the grotesque or ludicrous in it. It all depends on the greatness of the play's Apollonian vision (hence the pitful grotesqueness of the man who has lost contact with it) as much as on its equally formidable sense of the destructive power of something in the universe and in the mind of man of which the witches are (in Yeats' sense) 'emblems'. That 'something' is a Dionysiac element in life, but a Dionysiac element with which no civility can have dealings. Like Nietzsche's 'barbarian Dionysos' (for the description of which he chose the same metaphor of the witches' cauldron) it is tumult, frenzy, but utterly without creative possibilities. It has some connexion (if the comparison, which is not entirely apposite, will help) with the fury of *The Bacchae* or *Medea*. It tears and lacerates beyond all hope of reconstruction. It mimics passional vitality with deceptive skill. And it appeals to that fierce 'will' element in man which we have already seen in Iago, Volumnia, Angelo, Goneril and Regan. But then it preys upon the will that it captures with a violence that leaves the mind 'full of scorpions', 'unmanned' and beyond all 'sweet oblivious antidote'. And then, perhaps even more terribly, it preys upon the mind for tormenting pleasure, tricking it with grotesqueries and inflated hopes that are comically empty and confronting it with a laughing nemesis when the unnoticed conditional clause in the contract suddenly looms large enough to make the apparently well-sealed bargain look foppish, ridiculous, a clownish underestimation of nature's power.

The vision of the Apollonian has the urgent delightfulness that it does, and the delicate naiveté that it does, because it is dreamed in the full and wakeful knowledge of this portentous opposite — as again pastoral is not. The figure of Banquo is one through whom the play carries to us a sharp sense of the precarious relationship between these juxtaposed imaginings. He, an Apollonian man, has intimations of the barbarian power. He too sees the witches and is, if not 'rapt', then at least shaken into uneasy cogitation:

A heavy summons lies like lead upon me,
And yet I would not sleep. Merciful powers
Restrain in me the cursed thoughts that nature
Gives way to in repose!   [II. i. 6—9]

These presences cut fearfully into a mind that had first greeted them with confidence as one impelled neither to 'beg your fear/Your favours nor your hate'. And, shocked with this presentiment, he needs to lean for support on a measured and open declaration of his humane values and hesitations:

>   So I lose none
> In seeking to augment it, but still keep
> My bosom franchis'd and allegiance clear,
> I shall be counsell'd.   [II. i. 26–9]

This is not, as I have said, mere primness. It stems from a deep awareness of destructive potential prompting formal self-avowal and self-remembering to avert the catastrophe of destruction. The Shakespeare who recorded this tentativeness and precariousness in Banquo (and again in the panic-stricken flight of Macduff, who is equally 'vulnerable') is reminding us thereby of his play's Apollonian conception of the humane. Spenser could never have recorded such precariousness except as a prompting to ever greater moral watchfulness and with an encouragement to increased stalwart resistance. But Banquo is not a mere stalwart of the Good or a robust potentate of Order and Rectitude. He is a delicately mature man, and hence precariously susceptible to disruption by the lavish fury of the witches' energy. That possibility – a permanent one – is the price paid for keeping humane ordonnance in contact with 'wanton' nature. But neither Shakespeare's nor Banquo's sense of that price makes either of them shudder back from its dangers into the armouredness of the Doric – which is why the Apollonian vision is an intrinsic part of a *tragic* world, and why our acclaim of it is a tragic acclaim.

3. *Antony and Cleopatra and the song of Dionysos*

The opposite but contiguous play, *Antony and Cleopatra*, opens with space, leisure and laughter:

> *Phi.* Nay, but this dotage of our general's
>   O'erflows the measure. Those his goodly eyes,
>   That o'er the files and musters of the war
>   Have glow'd like plated Mars, now bend, now turn,
>   The office and devotion of their view
>   Upon a tawny front. His captain's heart,
>   Which in the scuffles of great fights hath burst
>   The buckles on his breast, reneges all temper,
>   And is become the bellows and the fan
>   To cool a gipsy's lust.

Flourish. Enter ANTONY, CLEOPATRA, *her Ladies, the
Train, with Eunuchs fanning her.*

Look where they come!

Take but good note, and you shall see in him
The triple pillar of the world transform'd
Into a strumpet's fool. Behold and see.

Cleo. If it be love indeed, tell me how much.

Ant. There's beggary in the love that can be reckon'd.

Cleo. I'll set a bourn how far to be belov'd.

Ant. Then must thou needs find out new heaven, new earth.

[I. i. 1—17]

Poor Philo. No sooner has he been the play's first spokesman for
the official Roman view than the words and action of the play
move on out of his range of vision to suggest orders of lyric
intensity quite beyond Roman knowledge. If we follow his advice
to 'take but good note' we shall not find our responses being
much in line with his. His Roman words 'measure' and 'temper'
seem comically minute as the spacious range of Antony's words is
set against them. The impeding hardness of 'plated Mars' and 'the
buckles on his breast' is mocked by the sinewy and voluptuous
ease of movement which informs Antony and Cleopatra's
speeches. The 'scuffles' of Roman imperialism seem like petty
brawls in this atmosphere of leisured extravagance. And the
Roman, racial jeering contained in 'a tawny front' and 'a gipsy's
lust' is belied as a ludicrous insolence by the laughing and
delighted civility which, coquetry notwithstanding, lives in
Cleopatra's words. It is nothing like 'dotage' that we are seeing
and hearing but the modes of a life incomparably richer than
the precious Roman rhetoric of solemnizing grandiosity — 'office
and devotion' — can ever reach. The Roman version of Egypt is at
once set against the realities of Egyptian life; and at once that
version is seen not only to be far from the truth but — a vital
point — *comically* far from the truth. A few lines down and
Cleopatra will invite the continuance of that comic comparison,
mocking 'the scarce-bearded Caesar' and caricaturing the strutting
rhetoric of imperial command:

'Do this or this;
Take in that kingdom and enfranchise that;
Perform't, or else we damn thee'.   [I. i. 22—4]

These are the first notes of Dionysos' song, simultaneously lyrical and ribald, which will dominate the first half of the play and colour our view of Rome and Egypt throughout.

Of all the things commonly missing from criticism of *Antony and Cleopatra* a sense of this comedy is the most important. The creator of Rome in this play is the creator of Rome in *Coriolanus*; but he is also, and pre-eminently, the creator of the imperial grandiosities of the Greeks in *Troilus and Cressida*; or the creator of Hotspur, that 'mad fellow of the north' who talks in his sleep about parapets and culverins and who would have agreed with Caesar that a capacity for drinking horse-piss and stagnant water was a sufficient proof of manhood; or the creator of Falstaff with his ribald opinions about 'honour' and 'the rusty curb of old father antic the law'. The ribald, anti-imperial comedy of *Troilus and Cressida* and *Henry IV* has contributed a great deal to the portrait of Rome in *Antony and Cleopatra*; while on the other hand the comedy of lyric delight and love-play has given to the Egyptian part of the play a Bacchanalian romanticism which makes Egypt so impervious to the moralistic objections of Romans and critics alike.

In *Coriolanus* Rome was the society of anti-nature and, horribly, of anti-Eros. Its predatory attitude to Eros fuelled its cruelty and fanaticism. In *Antony and Cleopatra* Rome is similarly passionless, but the tone in which this is seen is now very different. This Rome has none of the frightening predatory language and blood-soaked violence of Cominius' praise of the warrior-hero. Neither Caesar nor Pompey, as the strong-men of the Roman world, has the terror of Coriolanus in him. Octavia, as the apogee of Roman womanhood, is a lightweight in comparison with the horrendous Volumnia; and, though formal and cold, she is almost garrulously fulsome in comparison with the scarcely audible Virgilia. Rome here, and particularly Rome in the first part of the play, has something Chaplinesque about it; or something of Rome as we might have been brought to see it by the Good Soldier Švejk; or something of the Rome of imperial inflatedness which Ezra Pound presents for the purposes of scurrilous comedy (and also for the critique of its 'anti-Eros' quality) in his *Homage to Sextus Propertius*.[6]

The Rome of the first half of *Antony and Cleopatra* is seen with airy and scurril comedy as absurd. Its great Titans, Caesar and Pompey, are petty and rather ludicrous men, peevish when they are defied, tetchy about rank and status, 'queasy' (as Agrippa happily puts it) at the 'insolence' of one who falls out of line — in Cleopatra's final opinion 'paltry' and 'absurd'. In the Rome of this part of the play we see little ('scarce-bearded') men living solemnly amid antic visions of themselves wherein they pace the world from edge to edge, frown at levity in the name of 'our graver business' and chase such farcical ambitions as that of Pompey who wants to own the sea. Its characteristic language is of a kind for which Pound's *Homage* will provide description — the language of the 'large-mouthed product' designed to 'expound the distentions of empire'. Pound has his Rome see its great imperial destiny in terms of laughable pettiness: 'Tibet shall be full of Roman policemen'. In Shakespeare's play imperial Caesar, in triumph, is no more than 'the universal landlord'.

We must be clear as to this tone, and have ears attuned to it, for though it seems to me extremely pervasive it has also been subtle enough to elude many critics and producers altogether. But subtlety is of its essence, for Shakespeare uses it not to provide the open torrent of spoof and parody of Pound's poem (or indeed to repeat the scurrilous acerbity of his own *Troilus and Cressida*) but, more gently, to ripple with disbelieving laughter and a quiet sense of knowingness beneath the orotundities and gaucheries of Roman rhetoric, politicking, propriety and self-opinion.

In I.i, as we have seen, the tone announces itself — its humour brought into play when Egypt is first made to sound so delightfully different from Philo's Roman severity on the subject, and then pointed to and enjoyed by the Cleopatra who mimics the order-giving Caesar. I.ii and I.iii then give much of their time to creating a mood of playfulness and levity, lived in Egypt in the bawdy-talk of the soothsayer and Cleopatra's women, inhabiting

Enobarbus' 'light answers' of a bawdy kind on Cleopatra's 'celerity in dying' etc., and inhabiting the coquetry and love-play which is interlaced with incandescent lyricism in Cleopatra's farewell to Antony. We note, in I.ii, that the 'Roman thought' which has struck Antony is said by Cleopatra not to have destroyed his 'passion' or his 'love' but his 'mirth'; and we note too that while we have been asked to begin to create the figure of Antony as the 'Herculean Roman' in our minds as part of our conception of him, we have also been asked to see

How this Herculean Roman does become
The carriage of his chafe   [I. iii. 84—5]

— a picture of a hero in a pique, whereby delighted levity comes to the rescue of what might have been overly grandiose.

Thus attuned we come to I.iv to find the dead weight of a solemn slab of Caesarism interposing its ludicrous presence in this lightened world. In Caesar's opening declaration we catch the authentic tone of weighty self-opinion which Cleopatra has already mimicked out of court:

You may see, Lepidus, and henceforth know,
It is not Caesar's natural vice to hate
Our great competitor.   [I. iv. 1—3]

And in the ensuing moralistics, which clearly carry the hatred he has just disavowed, the ripples of our amusement are set going at the expense of an ignorant, scarce-bearded man pouting with a sense of moral outrage:

(Antony) is not more manlike
Than Cleopatra, nor the queen of Ptolemy
More womanly than he   [I. iv. 5—7]

He is a slight man talking largely; and talking primly too (on the immaturity of which pleasure-seeking is a sign), and snobbishly (his distaste for Antony's keeping company with 'knaves that smell of sweat'), and parsonically (sermonizing to Lepidus on the man who is 'the abstract of all faults', from the observation of whom moral lessons can be learnt provided the observer is not 'too indulgent'). Throughout the scene Shakespeare's delicate humour, summoned to our minds already by the delighted levity which Egypt has presented, stalks Caesar subtly, making us quietly aware of every trace of stiffness, self-importance and inflatedness with which the universal landlord, chaste spokesman for old father antic the law, is replete.

The opening Act is so structured as to give Caesar little chance against the ripples of mirthful disbelief inspired by the airy lightness of tone in which life in Egypt is conducted. His appearance in this scene, to talk with a pout and a stamp of the imperial foot against Antony's 'lascivious wassails', has much mischief done to it by having to come after we have seen Antony, Cleopatra, Enobarbus, Charmian, Iras and the Soothsayer living a life which in no way prompts our enthusiasm for his judgments of it; and by having to come before the closing scene of the Act wherein Egyptian blood flows again not only in the language of passion

> Be'st thou sad or merry,
> The violence of either thee becomes,
> So does it no man else   [I. v. 59–61]

but also in the language of mirth or gamesomeness, as in Cleopatra's inability to take pleasure in aught an eunuch has or Charmian's baiting her with the memory of her 'salad days'.If we know how to hear the Act's subtly mirthful tone we shall know that we have seen the antics of Caesarism subjected to the *vif* of an easeful but probing scepticism which is given life and licence by the counter-comedy of Egypt where moments of incandescent lyricism rise repeatedly from a fertile chaos of humour, bawdy and animal vitality, all tangled together in a 'gamesome' vision of Dionysos' powers.

Built upon this basis, Act Two and the first six scenes of Act Three take the comedy of delicate derision and the comedy of festivity and play to exuberant heights. On the Roman side Pompey appears, full of self-importance, with:

> If the great gods be just, they shall assist
> The deeds of justest men   [II. i. 1–2]

and then spends his time in II.i gloating over his watery
dominions ('the sea is mine') and rearing the higher his opinion
of himself. In II.ii the fop Lepidus, beginning already to
look like a figure from Donne's satires, is pushed about by
Enobarbus' sharp tongue just as hopelessly as he was by Caesar's
moral lessons; and, in the negotiations that follow, Antony (now
struck by Roman thoughts) and Caesar (trying to pretend he
never spoke 'derogately' about the lascivious wassailer) experience a rough passage at the hands of Shakespeare's wanton
laughter, aided as it is by some fine stage-business:

> *Caes.* Sit.
> *Ant.* Sit, sir.
> *Caes.* Nay then. (*They sit.*) [II. ii. 30–2]

and by Enobarbus' capacity for an irreverent assessment of the
politicking of the 'noble partners' who are in the act of becoming
'brothers':

> Or, if you borrow one another's love for the instant, you may,
> when you hear no more words of Pompey, return it again. You
> shall have time to wrangle in when you have nothing else to
> do. [II. ii. 107–10]

Enobarbus, though told to be quiet and mend his manners,
clearly wins his playful skirmish, and celebrates his victory with
the famous description of Cleopatra in her barge, which has the
Roman Maecenas boggle-eyed with amazement yet still Roman
enough to miss the point entirely. 'Now Antony must leave her
utterly', he ventures. 'Never!', says Enorbarbus, with probability
enough. Then Maecenas:

> If beauty, wisdom, modesty, can settle
> The heart of Antony, Octavia is
> A blessed lottery to him. [II. ii. 245–7]

to the extraordinary unlikeliness of which there can be no reply,
so the scene ends without Enobarbus bothering to give one.

In II.iii the blessed lottery makes its sad contribution to the
proceedings as we first see the frigid formality of the Antony/
Octavia marriage; and then, after Egypt has interposed with

another sumptuously playful extravagance of unbridled emotion-
alism and mirth:

> *Cleo*. Give me some music — music, moody food
> Of us that trade in love.
> *All*. The music, ho!

> > *Enter* MARDIAN *the Eunuch*

> *Cleo*. Let it alone! Let's to billiards,   [II. v. 1—3]

the Act concludes with the delicious hilarity of the scene on
Pompey's galley.

The scene stirs one's memories of Gadshill, or of the great
set-pieces on the Greek and Trojan camps in *Troilus and Cressida*.
Lepidus is now clearly a character from Donne — the semi-
travelled fop who is quick to believe and pass on reports of the
marvels of foreign parts:

> Nay, certainly, I have heard the Ptolemies' pyramises are very
> goodly things. Without contradiction I have heard that.
>
> > [II. vii. 33—5]

And Enobarbus duly makes haste to derive as much amusement
as possible from the spectacle of a member of the great
triumvirate in his cups:

> *Eno*. There's a strong fellow, Menas.
> > (*Pointing to the servant who carries off Lepidus.*)
> *Men*. Why?
> *Eno*. 'A bears the third part of the world, man; see'st not?
> > [II. vii. 87—9]

But Caesar and Pompey scarcely fare better. The great Pompey
responds like a shoddy little gangster (but burdened with a sense
of propriety) to the proposal that his guests should have their
throats slit:

> > In me 'tis villainy:
> In thee't had been good service.   [II. vii. 73—4]

Caesar, feeling himself befouled by food and drink, 'antick'd'
by merriment, and opining solemnly that 'our graver business/

Frowns at this levity', is no more prepossessing. And when the Egyptian Bacchanals scatter the 'great fellows' and the revelry goes below stairs with Enobarbus and 'Hoo' and 'Hoo' we have watched a scene in which the spirit of the Lord of Misrule has done his traditional comic damage to the stiffnesses, repressions and formalisms of the law.

Egypt in this Act has been represented by the scene which began with Cleopatra calling for 'music, moody food' and went on with her wild rampage of haling the messenger up and down — both of which performances are too gustily alive with emotional turmoil, the creative chaos of Dionysos, for moral point-making to constitute an adequate response to them. And it has also been represented by the description of the barge. Here Dionysos is brought alive as a breeding chaos of self-replenishing energies creating kinds of luxury and magnificence which have nothing to do with mere 'ornament' or 'ostentation'. All is swarming with life; and once again it is all laughter-filled, gamesome.

Shakespeare found for this passage in Plutarch a description of luxury as lavish exhibition and show for which the moderate-minded historian had a tempered disdain. It was a part of the headily flamboyant spirit of over-played laxity which caught Antony in its trammels and made him fritter away his manhood in 'childish sports ... and idle pastimes'. All the emphasis of Plutarch's description, as translated by North, is on the lavish expense of 'gold and silver and of riches and other sumptuous ornaments' used by a calculating woman, mature in the ways of the world, to create a pageant of idle splendour:

(her barge) ... the poop whereof was of gold, the sails of purple, and the oars of silver, which kept stroke in rowing after the sound of the music of flutes, howboys, citherns, viols, and such other instruments as they played upon in the barge. And now for the person of herself: she was laid under a pavilion of cloth of gold of tissue, apparelled and attired like the goddess Venus commonly drawn in picture; and hard by her, on either hand of her, pretty fair boys apparelled as painters do set forth god Cupid, with little fans in their hands,

with the which they fanned wind upon her. Her ladies and
gentlewomen also, the fairest of them were apparelled like the
nymphs Nereides (which are the mermaids of the waters) and
like the Graces, some steering the helm, others tending the
tackle and ropes of the barge, out of the which there came a
wonderful passing sweet savour of perfumes, that perfumed
the wharf's side, pestered with innumerable multitudes of
people.[7]

Shakespeare's lyrical imagination transformed this pageant of
artifice into a picture of richness which seems like the florescence
of nature itself. Inanimate things become animated in this general
florescence of the world — the winds 'love-sick', the water
'amorous', the ropes of the barge swelling in (sexual) response to
animate touch, the banks of the river having 'sense'. And the
whole spectacle, in Shakespeare's version of it, is filled with a
self-fuelling and self-replenishing fire wherein 'fancy' and 'nature'
dance a playful dialectic of their respective powers. As part of
this every-burning energy the fans carried by Cleopatra's boys

>   did seem
> To glow the delicate cheeks which they did cool,
> And what they undid did.   [II. ii. 207—9]

As another manifestation of it Cleopatra, hopping through the
public street until she is breathless,

>   spoke, and panted,
> That she did make defect perfection,
> And, breathless, pow'r breathe forth.   [II. ii. 234—6]

And again:

>   she makes hungry
> Where most she satisfies; for vilest things
> Become themselves in her, that the holy priests
> Bless her when she is riggish.   [II. ii. 241—4]

This is the poetry of Shakespeare's lyric-romantic mind at its
finest. The innermost power of it is in that phrase 'become
themselves', or on the rhythm of 'undid did', 'defect perfection'
and 'breathless, pow'r breathe forth'. It is the poetry of the

metamorphoses and transformations of Queen Mab, building an extravagant lyric power out of a rapid and close apprehension of the processes of the organic. It is a poetry incomparably kinetic – or comparable only with the poetry of the world of light and space which Macbeth lost. Egypt's ability to generate such powers, with their attendant human qualities of sexual vitality and laughter, not only mocks the absurd pretension and juvenile insolence of Roman imperialism. It mocks all moralistics too, having in itself as it does the very essence of the Dionysiac which is seen by Shakespeare, here as in festive comedy, as a *sine qua non* of full psychic life.

So in the first Act the interposition of Rome in a predominantly Egyptian world makes Rome look petty and ludicrous. In the second Act, which has an opposite structure, the interposition of Egypt in a predominantly Roman world annihilates Romanness by its fire and colour and demands an absolute of recognition from the audience. In the Third Act the slow and swaying comedy of Dionysos' song continues, revelling through the contrast between the frigidity of Octavia/Antony and the gusty exaggerations of Cleopatra's enthusiasms; through Enobarbus and Agrippa's merriment at the sham courtesies of the politicians (to which language Lepidus then makes a characteristically ludicrous contribution); and through Enobarbus' later comments on the fall from the triumvirate of the 'poor third':

> Then, world, thou hast a pair of chaps – no more;
> And throw between them all the food thou hast,
> They'll grind the one the other.   [III. v. 13–15]

It all leads excellently to III.vi (before the change in the play's tone) where Rome's deflation by laughter is at its best again.

In this scene the ribaldry of Dionysos does its worst with Caesar before the catastrophe of the play becomes imminent in III.vii. It begins with another stamp of the imperial foot – 'Contemning Rome, he has done all this' – and another petulant exhibition of his snobbery – 'I' th' common show-place'. It sees Agrippa hitting that exact and unfortunate word 'queasy' to describe Rome's feelings about Antony's 'insolence'. It sees Caesar hoarding up bits of the world for himself (like Lepidus'

'Revenue'), and wanting to hoard up more (like 'Armenia'), while sending off messengers with cheap lies to excuse himself. Then, suddenly, it sees the arrival of Octavia: too suddenly for Caesar, who is thereby prevented from laying on 'an augmented greeting' to show 'the ostentation of our love' — though after forty lines or so he has gathered himself and is launched:

> Welcome to Rome;
> Nothing more dear to me. You are abus'd
> Beyond the mark of thought, and the high gods,
> To do you justice, make their ministers
> Of us and those that love you.   [III. vi. 85—9]

On that claim, made by the universal landlord, to some kind of ministerial status in a platonic, celestial empire, the scene's chicane at the expense of Caesarism has reached its climax. It is quickly finished off by Maecenas with his mouth very full of outrage:

> Only th' adulterous Antony, most large
> In his abominations, turns you off,
> And gives his potent regiment to a trull
> That noises it against us.   [III. vi. 93—6]

Rome has been dealt with by comedy. The catastrophic product of its imperial power will now begin to come forth.

We have reached what is almost exactly the mid-point in this tragedy and yet still the comedy of Dionysos dominates the play with its interlinked tones of scurrility and playful lyricism. Rather as in *Romeo and Juliet*, a 'tragedy of love' spends the bulk of its earlier energies in the creation of a dramatic life both festal and ribald. I labour the point about the play's comic vitality because if we do not feel both the festal laughter of Egyptian lyricism and the ribald laughter directed at Rome we shall read the play more solemnly than it requires and miss the very essence of the vision of the Dionysiac which it has to impart.

It is in one way similar to the case of *Macbeth*, which, without that quality of festal delight in its basic vision of the Apollonian, would have been a solemn, religious-pastoral pageant of Order. Without the delighted levity of the Dionysiac, *Antony and Cleopatra* would be a far lesser play than it is — serving either to advance a beglamoured myth of romantic love or (by under-mining such a myth with moral detraction) to advance a cautionary tale. But (again as with *Macbeth*) the play's vision is less 'organized' or 'fixed' into a system of opinion than either myth-making or myth-deflating. It captures alive its vision of the Dionysiac — as much a *sine qua non* of human vitality as was the Apollonian a *sine qua non* of humane ordonnance.

Humour is of the essence of this. The ribald comedy of disbelief in Rome is as much a part of Dionysiac life as is the lyricism of Egyptian passion. It carries the playful intelligence of the Dionysiac, its quick-witted vitality and humane freedom from code and law; and in the case of Egyptian passional life itself, interlaced with festive notes of topsy-turvy and misrule, the playfulness of the Dionysiac is again of supreme importance. It distinguishes the lyric of Egypt from the 'heroic' or 'transcen-dental' lyricism of many high romanticisms of love. This is not the love of Wagner's *Tristan and Isolde* or of Rubek and Irena in *When We Dead Awaken*. It has no other-wordly attachments and involves no flesh-despising or flesh-transcending. It lacks the fierce and self-isolating egotism of heroic passion and it lacks that hankering after darkness and dissolution which brings the language of mystery-religions into the romance of love. It does not thrive upon the sublimation of Eros into religious or aesthetic terms, bent as it is neither upon purity nor upon divinization.[8]

In comparison with the passion of *Tristan and Isolde*, the passional life of Egypt is full of the richness of the commonplace and the mundane. With the fibrous tangle of its roots deep in the slime of the Nile it is bent upon flowering in the light of the sun, not plunging into the darkness of religious mystery to find therein redemption from the false appearances of the daylight world. Being thus commonplace, rooted in the organic and content with the real, it is in essence laughter-filled. The uninhibitedness of laughter is essential to it, as is laughter's commonplace, social gaiety. The exuberance of laughter is, as in many great eroticisms, including those of Blake and Pound whom I have already brought forward for assistance, seen as an intrinsic part of the exuberance of sexuality. It is therefore as characteris-tic of Egyptian passion to be both *playful* and *erotic* as it is for Wagner's image of passion to be *heroic*, *sublimated* and *unsmiling*.

In that difference the greater humanity and greater *vif* of Shakespearean romanticism seem to me to lie.

So we come to the play's imminent catastrophe with such a vision fully realized before us, and the fulness of romantic life which the vision carries determines our response to the catastrophe. It determines our response to Rome's menace, which now takes over in our minds from our earlier sense of its derisoriness; and it also determines our response to the havoc and panic created by the Dionysiac quality of Egypt itself in response to threat. Both factors are important – Rome's destructive power and thrust and Egypt's own propensity for calamity.

Rome's destructive intrusion into the Egyptian world is terribly swift and quite decisive. In four scenes of scarcely 100 lines between them the organized power of Rome will 'cut the Ionian sea' and rout the forces of Antony and Egypt. Canidius says:

> This speed of Caesar's
> Carries beyond belief   [III. vii. 74-5]

and with that we get a chilling sense of the irresistible. For the rest of the play Caesar in Egypt is a colonialist ravager, bearing the armoured and calculating weight of an empire to the destruction of a flamboyantly alive culture. By III.xii he is installed and trading in the ugly 'realities'. Thyreus talks of his protective influence as 'his shroud', aptly thereby catching the tone of his regimen. At the beginning of Act Four more Realpolitik sees him pleased to use Antony's own soldiers to 'fetch him in' like a hunted animal. In IV.vi he is talking of 'universal peace' – an idea which is made hollow and unlovely by its placement in the midst of Enobarbus' desolation and his revelations as to Caesar's way with men who desert to him.

The low realism of Caesar's powers feels deadly and irresistible again in IV.xi:

> To the vales,
> And hold our best advantage.   [IV. xi. 3–4]

The public humiliation envisaged as their fate in Rome first by Antony and then by Cleopatra is a characteristic part of his procedures; and while some of his grief for Antony's death is clearly very genuine he goes on from expressing it, unruffled and undeflected, to plan the capture and use of Cleopatra. His vaunted gentleness and promised civility are lies: the reality of his political presence, again swift and efficient, is caught in the scene where Proculeius follows his talk of a 'princely hand' which is 'full of grace' by rushing the monument with easy success. Caesar is not savage, as Coriolanus is; but there can be no doubting the bleakness and lowness of his presence, the humanly impoverished nature of his authority, the mere efficiency of his marshalling of things.

It is important to note that record of a low power and its deadly weight which the latter part of the play gives us. The hysterical note in Antony's response to it and the wild panic of Cleopatra's gyrations cannot fairly be seen for what they are unless we see that they take place in the path of an oncoming and irresistible machine of conquest. It is perhaps a little like the panic-stricken flight of the princes and then of Macduff in *Macbeth*, or the controversial scene IV.iii in that play where Malcolm and Macduff reveal some apparently absurd squirmings of the spirit — until we realize that this is a picture of men who are more delicately alive and therefore more vulnerable than the machine of power with which they are living. That does not fully 'explain' the crazedness of Cleopatra's and Antony's behaviour in the latter part of the play, nor is it intended to. But it gives us some necessary context whereby a part of the truth can be seen.

But the other part of the matter, and the major part, concerns the nature of the Dionysiac itself, and it sends us, as we consider it, back through the long history of Shakespeare's dealings in tragedy and comedy alike with the hazards and dangers which live in the volatile and creative chaos of kinesis. Even in comedy the experience of the dream-wood of Puck and the fairies was fraught with hazard and it confronted the adventurer with the fear of the unknowable. The journey through Dionysiac tumult turns out to be liberating, joy-giving; but while the journey lasts that outcome is far from clear and inevitable. It is easy to suppose a bush a bear. And indeed it may well have *been* a bear — for we always come from these comedies of the kinetic with a sense that those who have traversed the wild and come out of it replenished have done so with a fair amount of luck. Particularly in the later comedies, preceding the plays of the tragic period and carrying as they do certain premonitions of tragedy, this sense of people who are simply *lucky* is strong. Olivia and Orsino are, as luck would have it, steered through currents too turbulent for Malvolio; and Beatrice and Benedick are felt to be 'lucky to get away with it' when they harvest all the quickness of passional life contained in their wit while the chaff of its isolating aggression is blown carelessly away.

The comedies always record this sense of fortunate chance in the way that the kinetic is endured. It is their witness to Shakespeare's 'high-force' world of a romanticism which is tough and realistic rather than complacent. To live in the tumult of Dionysos is to live creatively, but also to live exposed — without the stabilizing certainties of social evaluation and selection which support dwellers in an unmagical, workaday world. And in tragedy a realistic record of what that tumult feels like to one upon whom its forces are unleashed is given in the life of Lear, the 'poor perdu' on the heath. From contact with the wild flows energy, and the greatest imaginative forces of the psyche. But such contact can only be got from being perilously close to destruction and perilously exposed to torment.

In some sense it will therefore always involve the 'shirt of Nessus' which Antony wears when he is convinced that Cleopatra has betrayed him again. But it will also involve (with characteristic Shakespearean ambiguity) something far less 'elevated' than that — a kind of ludicrousness, exhibited by a mind subject to the mischief of Puck, the idiot bamboozlement of a mind tossed hither and thither without dignity, composure or ordonnance by the currents of racing mischief which are an intrinsic part of the high-force world finding their living emblems in Puck and Queen Mab. In comedy that mischief is hurly-burly, though it can occasionally hurt people as it hurts Malvolio. In tragedy it is the awful mischief that the world does to Lear, introducing that element of the grotesque into his tragic experience which was recorded when the thunder *laughed* at the folly of an old man venting his rage on the non-existent daughters of Poor Tom.

It is a sense of all this, generated by the laughing vision of a creative Dionysos, which we need for the latter part of *Antony and Cleopatra*. For there, under pressure from the dead hand of Rome, but also under the intrinsic pressure of the Dionysiac itself, Antony and Cleopatra go through a double process which is humiliating and exalting at the same time, grotesque and magnificent, an ebbing and decrescence of the spirit which is at the same time a spiritual triumph. There is no point in trying to sort out the pros and cons of it all to award moral points for and against. There is a certain moralizing tardiness of the imagination in the mind which wishes to conceive of one part existing without the other — the same moralizing tardiness which wants to feel that Lear is 'learning' and 'being redeemed' but which also wants to reserve the right to make a moral point or two about some of the things he says while the terrible process is going on. In *Antony and Cleopatra* the whole tangle of Dionysiac elements can only be taken as being of a piece, the whole chaos of it all taken as it is in the certain knowledge, imparted by this great romanticism, that without these grotesqueries there will be no creative life, without these indignities (painfully there when Antony botches his suicide, for example) there will be no possibility of Egyptian 'fire and air'. Again it is the case that if you banish Plump Jack you will banish all the world: banish the triple-turned whore and the strumpet's fool and you will simply make over the world to the bleak conveniences of Caesarism.

If we have heard the full power and range of Dionysos' song in the first half of the play, and understood both its high lyricism and its low humour, we should have no difficulty with the double progress of its major creators in the second half. Instead it will come with beautiful inevitability — the absurd bravado of Antony which Caesar summarily snubs, the hysterical and self-indulgent notes that now run through the vitality of his mind, the desperation of his efforts to recreate with his 'sad captains' the old life of supper, carousing and 'rattling tabourines', his humiliating failure to bring off the noble death he proposes; and the hideous whimsicality of Cleopatra's feigned death, the vacillating distractedness that runs through all her dealings with Caesar, the hysterical notes that she too sounds at moments in her grief and confusion: all of it will come through as the inevitable, essential, inalienable concomitant of that spirit which produces the contrary movement of the play's great lyric and triumphant end. Even Caesar catches a glimpse of the duality in the end — the 'strong toil of grace' catches exactly the unavoidably paradoxical nature of the forces involved. If it is for a moment within the mental compass even of the universal landlord, I find it hard to think that it should be beyond the powers of critics and producers.

That 'lyric and triumphant end' is, of course, what we get in the play's incomparable exhibition of the poetry of wanton, romantic exuberance and charmed flight which I have traced through from the plays of the mid-1590s. It reaches its apex in Cleopatra's speech of 'immortal longings' and 'fire and air', but it has been growing steadily to that peak ever since the 'sad captains' and the eclipse of the 'terrene moon' in III.xiii, where the decrescence of Egypt first began to produce the poignantly continuing autumnal fire which comes from a bounty with 'no winter in't'. Shrunk and dispersed almost to extinction, Egypt simply cannot help bringing forth from the strong toil of its grace that succession of wonderful images of exultation which share the last two Acts with the grotesque twists and turns of panic and humiliation. Out of the continually reiterated opposites of light and dark, sprightliness and collapse and (again) the dancing dialectic of nature and fancy whereby Cleopatra expresses what in Antony was 'past the size of dreaming' — out of these reiterated contraries comes the progression of this living and branching lyric.

I can find no more spirit of hesitation or qualification accompanying this song of Dionysos than I could find such a spirit accompanying the song of Apollo in *Macbeth*. Here as there the lyric is created in the full, wakeful knowledge of the power of the actual. But that does not mean that it is the function of the actual to make us receive the lyric in a qualified way; rather it makes our acclaim of it, again, a *tragic* acclaim. In *Macbeth* the humane fulness of the Apollonian involved a price, which served to remind us that the Apollonian dream was part of a tragic vision. The price was to be seen in that precariousness or vulnerability with which (as in Banquo) an unarmoured, humane ordonnance sustained itself in open and hence dangerous contact with a wild world containing witches. So too in *Antony and Cleopatra* the fulness of Dionysos involves a price, which again has to do with precariousness and vulnerability, and again makes it a part of an essentially tragic vision. The life of Egypt gets its exuberant and wanton energy from constant proximity to the tumult of the kinetic. It is thence that it draws into itself the tremendous resources of energy that place the quality of its life so far beyond the reach of Rome. But by virtue of that very proximity its life is lived in constant peril. It is constantly on a brink of self-destruction or self-dissolution; and it is people living on that brink whom we see create the song of Dionysos but also the panic and hysteria of their later life.

In *Macbeth*, as I said, Shakespeare's sense of this precariousness prompts him to no shuddering back from it into the securities of the Doric. So too in *Antony and Cleopatra* there is no shuddering back into the arms of Caesar. The critics who have had their 'reservations', let alone those who have followed T. S. Eliot in feeling that this play was a study in infatuation, seem to me to have been involved in just such a retreat from the furious but generous energies of Shakespeare's tragic metaphysic. That retreat might have been avoided had the connexions between tragedy and festive comedy been better understood; or had more people known as surely as Nietzsche did that 'one must still have chaos in oneself to be able to give birth to a dancing star'.

Notes

Chapter One

1. Nietzsche, *Thus Spake Zarathustra*, tr. W. Kaufmann in *The Portable Nietzsche*, London 1971, 129.
2. C. L. Barber, *Shakespeare's Festive Comedy*, Princeton, N.J. 1959.
3. *Love's Labour's Lost*, V. ii. 621.
4. David Hume, 'Of Tragedy', in *Four Dissertations*, London 1757.
5. Nietzsche, *The Birth of Tragedy*, tr. Francis Golffing, New York 1956, 12.
6. Nietzsche, *Ecce Homo*, tr. W. Kaufmann in *Basic Writings of Nietzsche*, New York 1968, 571.
7. This association, of peculiar interest to students of Shakespeare, is made in Nietzsche, *Schopenhauer as Educator*, tr. J. W. Hillesheim and M. R. Simpson, Chicago, Ill. 1965, 15.
8. Schopenhauer, *The World as Will and Representation*, tr. E. F. J. Payne, Gloucester, Mass. 1958 (2 vols., revised edn). The principal, and most famous, discussion of tragedy is at Vol. I, 242—55. But further important discussions and references are scattered throughout the work at e.g.: Vol. I, 212—13; 230—3; 319—23; 326—31; Vol. II, 349—60; 424—38; 573—88.
9. Nietzsche, *Shopenhauer as Educator*, ed. cit., 15.
10. Perhaps a simple diagram will make this clearer:

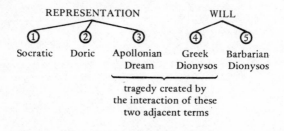

REPRESENTATION   WILL

① Socratic   ② Doric   ③ Apollonian Dream   ④ Greek Dionysos   ⑤ Barbarian Dionysos

tragedy created by
the interaction of these
two adjacent terms

11. Nietzsche, *The Birth of Tragedy*, *ed. cit.*, 5.
12. *Love's Labour's Lost*, IV. ii. 62—9.
13. Plutarch, *The Life of Marcus Brutus*, tr. North, in *Shakespeare's Plutarch*, ed. T. J. B. Spencer, Harmondsworth 1964, 116.
14. Nietzsche, *The Birth of Tragedy*, *ed. cit.*, 52.
15. *Ibid.*, 23.
16. *King Lear*, I. v. 43.

Chapter Two

1. F. R. Leavis, *The Common Pursuit*, London 1952, 136—59.
2. A. P. Rossiter, *Angel with Horns*, London 1961, 189—208.
3. I include Cassio as a member of the Venetian nobility. He is in fact a Florentine, but the play makes no dramatic use of this fact. His relationship to the core-culture of Venice is entirely orthodox.
4. Spenser, *The Faerie Queene*, Book VI (esp. Cantos 3, 6 and 12).
5. This is not to suggest that he has no connexions with the Vice — he clearly does. But the Vice figure was an amalgam, often a mystifying one, of many social and psychological types. Shakespeare penetrates the amalgamated symbol to understand its social constituents in highly differentiated detail.
6. J-P. Sartre, *Reflexions sur la Question Juive*, Paris 1946 (tr. Erik de Mauny as *Portrait of the Anti-Semite*, London 1948).

Chapter Three

1. T. S. Eliot, *Collected Poems 1909—62*, London 1963, 139.
2. Wolfgang Clemen (*The Development of Shakespeare's Imagery*, London 1951) has exemplified and helped perpetuate this kind of reading. The centre and origin of an 'image-cluster' tends to be taken as an index of Shakespeare's own views, without regard to which *characters* use the

images:

> It is Shakespeare's admiration for great and heroic men
> that leads him to characterize them by means of images of
> boldness and force. . . . We find brave and noble animals
> as symbols of the heroic nature of Coriolanus. (p. 156)

3. I am indebted here to Eric Partridge, *Shakespeare's Bawdy*,
   London 1969 (revised edn). His glossary is by no means
   complete; but it is nonetheless a very useful work in a field
   still open to critical and scholarly study.
4. IV. v. 53–147. Note the formal self-avowal and declaration
   of status by Marcius; then the ecstatic response of Aufidius,
   full of the imagery of erotic transfer; and finally the taking
   of hands to introduce the betrothed partner to Aufidius'
   household and state.
5. *King Lear*, IV. ii. 85.

Chapter Four

1. William Carlos Williams, *In the American Grain*, London
   1966, 65. (See also, on the spirit of puritanism, pp. 63–8;
   81–129 passim.)
2. The most extraordinary (and widely influential) version of
   this case is F. R. Leavis, 'Measure for Measure', in *The
   Common Pursuit*, *ed. cit.*, 160–72.
3. It has often been noted that many of the Duke's opinions
   here 'come from Montaigne'. But they come through the
   distorting barrenness of the Duke's own mind. All Montaigne's
   generosity has gone. His scepticism, used zestfully to
   demystify, is here taken over to vilify and degrade.
4. *Johnson on Shakespeare*, ed. W. Raleigh, Oxford 1908, 78.
5. Montaigne, *Essays*, tr. Florio, London 1910 (Everyman edn),
   Vol. III, 92.

Chapter Five

1. Rossiter, *op cit.*, 301. The essay on *Troilus and Cressida* is at
   pp. 129–51.

2. *Romeo and Juliet*, I. iv. 113; *All's Well that Ends Well*, II. i. 57–8; I. ii. 29–30.

Chapter Six

1. Nietzsche, *Beyond Good and Evil*, in *Basic Writings of Nietzsche*, ed. cit., 316.
2. The four studies are in T. S. Eliot, *Selected Essays* (London 1919), George Santayana, *Obiter Scripta* (London 1936), G. Wilson Knight, *The Wheel of Fire* (London 1930) and L. C. Knights, *Explorations* (London 1946).
3. Knights subsequently revised and tempered his views considerably in *An Approach to Hamlet*, London 1960.
4. T. S. Eliot, *Four Quartets*, in *Collected Poems 1909–62*, ed. cit., 192.

Chapter Seven

1. W. B. Yeats, *Collected Poems*, London 1950, 333.
2. Wallace Stevens, *Collected Poems*, London 1955, 400.
3. John Danby, *Shakespeare's Doctrine of Nature*, London 1961, 20. Danby's study is a fine and major work, the best interpretation of the play I have read; but the Cordelia-centred modulation of the play's metaphysic still produces serious distortions. Kent is merely an 'average man', Lear is guilty of 'escapism'. Somewhere this has got to stop.
4. *Antony and Cleopatra*, IV. vi. 32; IV. ix. 8.
5. W. B. Yeats, *Collected Poems*, ed. cit., 338–9 ('Lapis Lazuli').
6. *Hamlet*, III. i. 143 *et seq.*; III. iv. 82 *et seq.*
7. It may be that Stevens' terms are unfamiliar or idiosyncratic enough to be unhelpful. In 'The Idea of Order at Key West' (*Collected Poems*, ed. cit., 128–30) the formulation 'words of the . . .' describes the moment when a creative response to the external world so exactly accords with the nature of that world as to 'complete' it, without distortion. The imagination has then created not merely a 'fiction' but 'The Supreme Fiction'. In Stevens' world there are two kinds of mind

which are notably incapable of the imaginative poise and power of The Supreme Fiction. One kind tends to create false fictions, in defiance of the real, like the solaces of religion. The other kind, eschewing fiction altogether, lives in the dullness and vulgarity of the real. Stevens' dialectic of nature and mind is, like Shakespeare's (to which it is clearly indebted), impregnated throughout with the imagery of the seasonal cycle.

8. Karl Jaspers, *Tragedy is not Enough*, tr. H. A. T. Reiche, Boston, Mass 1952, 118.

9. Rossiter, *op cit.*, 302.

Chapter Eight

1. L. C. Knights, *Some Shakespearean Themes*, London 1959, p. 76.

2. *Romeo and Juliet*, I. iv. 53–103.

3. *King Lear*, I. ii. 14, 116.

4. Yeats is a highly suggestive but dangerous guide. His work is often very closely and intensely in touch with the dialectics of tragedy. Yet he also writes a kind of 'para-tragic' verse which is not free from manner or gesture. I quote below from two great poems whose enactment of tragic experience seems to me entirely genuine and without gesture: 'Meditations in Time of Civil War' and 'Nineteen Hundred and Nineteen' (*Collected Poems*, *ed. cit.*, 225–37) The phrases quoted above (from 'Sailing to Byzantium', *ed. cit.*, 217–18) are perilously close to his para-tragic mode; but perhaps they survive it well enough to offer some comparison with the fully achieved tragic Apollonianism of *Macbeth*.

5. W. B. Yeats, *Collected Poems, ed. cit.*, 391–2.

6. Ezra Pound, *Collected Shorter Poems*, London 1952, 225–47. I quote below from this edition.

7. Plutarch, *ed. cit.*, 201.

8. This is much indebted to Denis de Rougemont's excellent study of the idea of divinizing love as carried by the Tristan myth (*Passion and Society*, tr. Montgomery Belgion, London 1956, revised edn).

Index